GUERRILLAS IN UNIFORM

Eric Morris

GUERRILLAS IN UNIFORM

Churchill's Private Armies in the Middle East and the
War Against Japan 1940–1945

Hutchinson
London Sydney Auckland Johannesburg

First published in 1989 by Hutchinson, an imprint of Century Hutchinson
Ltd, Brookmount House, 62–65 Chandos Place, London WC2N 4NW

Century Hutchinson Australia (Pty) Ltd.
89–91 Albion Street, Surry Hills, NSW 2010

Century Hutchinson New Zealand Ltd.
PO Box 40–086, 32–34 View Road, Glenfield, Auckland 10

Century Hutchinson South Africa (Pty) Ltd.
PO Box 337, Bergvlei 2012, South Africa

British Library Cataloguing in Publication Data
Morris, Eric, *1940–*
    Guerrillas in uniform: Churchill's private
    armies in the Middle East and the war
    against Japan, 1940–1945
    1. World War 2. Military operations by
    British special forces
    I. Title
    940.54′86′41
    ISBN 0–09–173523–8

Printed and bound in Great Britain by
Butler and Tanner Ltd, Frome, Somerset

To My Mother

Acknowledgements

I owe so much to very many people who helped in writing this account. First to the veterans, the men in the Special Forces. It has not been possible to include all their stories in this account, but to all those who shared their experiences with me, my grateful thanks.

Three ladies coped with the transcription of tapes, interviews and documents: Louise Figgins, Dorothy Fox and Jean Hayes all did a magnificent job. My colleague and friend Alan Hoe has been particularly helpful in many aspects of the Special Air Service Regiment. Paul Sidey has shown patience, forbearance and a deft touch in editing the manuscript.

Last and by no means least, thanks to my wife, Pamela, for all her support and encouragement, and for typing the manuscript.

Contents

List of Illustrations

All photographs courtesy of the Imperial War Museum

List of Maps

Introduction

This is an account of British special forces raised in the Second World War. *Churchill's Private Armies* traced their origin in a beleaguered Britain and operations in Occupied Europe to 1942 and the St Nazaire Raid. Thereafter roles changed, and they were absorbed into the expansive Combined Operations empire as amphibious shock troops.

Guerrillas in Uniform tells the tale of special forces in the Middle and Far Eastern theatres. The need for a different kind of force, raised to meet a particular need, was recognized belatedly by the high command, when their field army had been ousted and had surrendered the initiative to the enemy. The Special Air Service, Popski's Private Army or Wingate's Chindits were true guerrillas, sent to raid and destroy, to occupy and distract the enemy until such time as the conventional armies were able to return to the fray. Once the latter had achieved an ascendancy, the need for special forces diminished to the extent that they became 'surplus to requirements'.

All special forces have a tempestuous relationship with the conventional army. From the outset there are complex, seemingly intractable problems which are associated with raising a special unit. By and large armies do not like self-declared elites because they make everybody else second best. Yet special units need a certain type of soldier, men with a wide range of professional skills, personally brave, possessed of an adventurous spirit. To succeed when the odds are heavily in favour of the opponent requires the fighting best. However, no regiment or battalion worth its salt is prepared to see its finest officers and men enticed into another formation.

In the heavily tribal British army with its proud heritage and regimental traditions, even the dictats of the most senior generals can be thwarted by elders of the tribes. So it was too often the case that those tasked to raise a special force had to make do with the most unpromising material, undesirables in an infantry battalion 'persuaded' to volunteer, or other people's hand-me-downs who frequented the base reinforcement pools. It is to their everlasting credit that these men were, in the hands of men such as David Stirling, Popski and Orde Wingate, transformed into some of the finest fighting material. Their success only reflects on the failure of the conventional army in its training methods.

It was a long and arduous process to mould the new recruits, which made inroads into precious resources and also demands for preferential treatment, leaving a trail of resentment and frustration from others in the queue. All too often by the time the new special force was ready for action the need for its use had disappeared. The war had moved on apace. In these circumstances there was ample opportunity for those in the higher echelons of the professional military establishment to lobby against special forces and plot their demise.

The guerrilla units, once created, were desperately afraid of being left on the shelf. This made them vulnerable to a form of moral blackmail which meant they took on tasks and missions which they were singularly ill-equipped to handle. This was frequently the case with the Middle East Commandos, roundly abused and misused by generals who could not, or wilfully chose not to understand their tactical role. On a more grand scale, the same problem applied to the Chindits in Burma. They began life as a political pawn and eventually were sacrificed on the high altar of Anglo American harmony to placate a geriatric general called Stilwell, who possessed an abundance of evil intent and little military talent by way of compensation. For the sake of this man's vanity, Chindit columns were militarily abused, although this was nothing compared to the treatment he meted out to their equivalent among his own countrymen, Merrill's Marauders.

There were other forms of excess. In a surfeit of enthusiasm and poor judgement units of special forces were raised in response to perceived needs based on the most flimsy of evidence. In the Middle Eastern theatre of operations it is extremely difficult to support the creation either of Popski's Private Army or the Special Interrogation Group.

Wingate's Chindits were an example of a shocking extravagance in the use of resources, as were the claims made by their leader on their capabilities and promise of achievement. The Chindits provoke debate and controversy in military circles to this day as do competing verdicts on the sanity of their leader.

In contrast, the Western Desert spawned two special forces who became the true elites. The Long Range Desert Groups were true aristocrats whose record spoke for itself. The Special Air Service, though comparative latecomers, showed what could be achieved when such a force was used with intelligence and deft skill. It was a tragedy for the SAS that its leader should have been captured as the campaign drew to a close, and a pity that the LRDG never managed to emulate its own success once it left North African shores. Such comparative failures simply encouraged their opponents to move for disbandment the moment war was over.

Yet none of these blemishes ought to cloud the fact that special forces were composed of very brave and honourable men. For the most part volunteers, they endured incredible physical hardship and suffering and demonstrated great valour in the face of enormous odds. These guerrillas in uniform also demonstrated a level of leadership at the junior or tactical level that was singularly lacking in the conventional field army and it was often the case that they were more respected by their opponents than admired by comrades in arms.

Eric Morris
Barry, November 1988

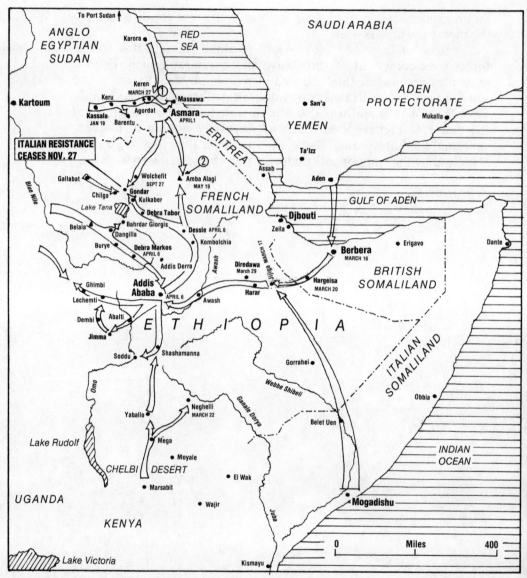

The Campaign in East Africa

PART ONE

EARLY DAYS: THE MIDDLE EAST COMMANDO

*'Never in the history of human endeavour have so few
been buggered about by so many.'*

Troopdeck graffiti
The assault ship
HMS *Glengyle*

CHAPTER ONE

In the Footsteps of Lawrence?

In July 1940 Britain stood alone and isolated. The European allies had succumbed to the German war machine and now lay broken and occupied. Confronted by the threat of imminent invasion, Prime Minister Churchill took drastic action which included the raising of a number of irregular but elite fighting units which were to be called Commandos.

Edicts despatched from Whitehall authorizing the creation of special forces applied not only to the Home Commands but also to General Sir Archibald Wavell, the Commander-in-Chief Middle East.

Italy had entered the war and, although Hitler had not asked them to join, their presence materially altered the balance of power. The fall of France and the evacuation from Dunkirk and the French ports meant that there were precious few troops available to reinforce the small fraction of the British Army that guarded Egypt and the Sudan against the imminent threat of invasion from Italian armies in Libya and East Africa.

The situation was all the worse because Italy's entry into the war had made the sea route through the Mediterranean too precarious to use regularly, and reinforcements had to come by the roundabout Cape route – down the west coast of the African continent, and up the east coast into the Red Sea. Even a fast troop convoy could take two months to complete the voyage.

Numerically the Italian armies were overwhelmingly superior to the British forces opposing them. General Wavell, as Commander-in-Chief Middle East, had fewer than 50,000 troops against more than half a million of the enemy. On the southern front the Italians in Eritrea and Abyssinia numbered 200,000 men, while the British garrisons in Kenya and the Sudan had fewer than 15,000 between them. In North Africa 36,000 British and Imperial forces held the line of the Egyptian frontier against a quarter of a million Italians under Marshal Graziani.

The Italians has other assets too. Their Navy might not have been able to guarantee Il Duce's boast that the Mediterranean was 'mare nostrum', but it was a modern, fast and well-balanced fleet. The Royal Navy had battleships which had fired in anger at Jutland and elderly cruisers commissioned before the air threat was taken seriously. That of course was the other advantage for the Italians: whether their forces were on land or at sea, they could enjoy the protection of an extensive land-based air umbrella, while the Royal Air Force and Fleet Air Arm had limited and obsolescent resources with which to meet their commitments.

Provided their armed forces were strong and of good quality, then Italy enjoyed an enviable strategic position in the Mediterranean. Before the war, the received wisdom from the experts portrayed Italy as a solid, well-organized, disciplined country, and it was treated as such by others. It was a country perceived as ready for war at the drop of a helmet, under the leadership of a Napoleon called Benito Mussolini. First Lenin, later Churchill and Hitler believed Mussolini to be one of the outstanding characters of the twentieth century, and perhaps all history.

In reality Italy was demoralized and flabby, deluded by its own propaganda. The jackbooted, goose-stepping military with their fancy uniforms and eau de cologne were good at striking postures but little else. This was to prove a paper army armed with ancient guns. The infallible leader was in truth an incompetent, self-taught elementary schoolteacher who had been catapulted to a position which was way above his talents. Mussolini was a gifted rabble-rouser, but divorced from reality.

However, on paper the Italians appeared formidable, and clearly enjoyed a strategic advantage over the British. By the same token, the Italians had a long line of communications to defend across North Africa, and isolated garrisons dotted about the islands of the Aegean. They were vulnerable to attacks from the sea.

It was a strategic picture tailor-made for Commando-style raiders. The first Commando raised as a result of the edict from Whitehall was probably the best. No. 50 (Middle East) Commando was made up of volunteers who came from the ranks of the pre-war Regular Army and were commanded by Lieut-Colonel George Young, a respected and resourceful officer.

The Commando also included 70 Spaniards, refugees from their own Civil War. It would be good to report that they were all dedicated anti-fascists determined to fight alongside those who would make a common cause in a great crusade. But they were not. The Spanish troop comprised casualties of that terrible war – bemused and confused men of no particular persuasion who had chosen the wrong side and ended up in France as did so many when Franco triumphed. The French recruited them and despatched them to the Army of the Lebanon, out of sight and out of mischief. When the Army declared for Fascist Vichy, these professional refugees took off again, across the border into British Palestine.

Some reports and commentators have extolled their dedication and their prowess as night fighters; others have dismissed them as a rabble. The truth lay somewhere in between these extremes. Their champion was Major R. L. McGibbon, himself something of an oddball. McGibbon was a French-speaking Canadian who was serving with the 2nd Battalion Royal Leicesters, a regular unit then part of the Middle East Garrison but destined later to become Chindits. McGibbon was fluent in Arabic, and could converse in Spanish. Recruited to command these Spaniards, he became their champion and mentor and was reputed to be the only man who could control them.

The second Commando came by way of the Royal Scots Greys, and was something of a gift which the Commander-in-Chief found it difficult to refuse. 'Kid' Cator M.C. was a First World War veteran, gentleman farmer and Reserve officer who had joined his old regiment at the outbreak of war. The Royal Scots Greys were stationed in Palestine and destined to become the last British cavalry regiment to surrender its horses for the armoured fighting vehicle. Cator was the oldest subaltern in the Greys until detached (and given the acting rank of Major) to raise a company of Pioneers from the Palestinians. The volunteers, half Jews and half Arabs, were at first carefully segregated into separate platoons, and in January 1940 Cator took them to France to serve as a labour unit with the rear echelon.

Under Cator's command, the Palestinians distinguished themselves in combat during the chaos of retreat and were evacuated to England via Cherbourg.

Cator had connections. His estates were close to Sandringham in Norfolk, and he lost no time in lobbying his Royal neighbours for the Palestinian Pioneers to be made into a proper fighting unit. It was not that difficult, especially in the panic of that summer in 1940. With the threat of imminent invasion any coherent unit was a bonus. The Palestinians were quickly mobilized and deployed as part of the defending forces along the South Coast.

Admiral Sir Roger Keyes, an elderly crony of the Prime Minister who had been returned to the Active List to head the directorate in charge of special forces, offered 'Kid' Cator the command of one of the new Commando units, but would not accept the Palestinians. However, Cator refused to be separated from his men, and instead was able to use his Royal patronage to have the unit returned to the Middle East. There General Wavell found it difficult to ignore a Royal request and eventually allowed Cator to choose a further 300 Palestinians to form No. 51 (Middle East) Commando.

The third unit to be raised was No. 52 (Middle East) Commando. This was a volunteer force, but of indifferent quality and led by mediocre officers. By this stage Commanding Officers were disenchanted with the request to yield yet another crop of volunteers and had no intention of losing their best material to a special force in which they had neither faith nor sympathy. The result was that No. 52 received all their least desirable and unwanted elements.

Headquarters Middle East established a training base and depot for their Commandos at Geneita near the Great Bitter Lakes in Lower Egypt. The new units were designated as 'Raiders' and this was carried through into the rank structure: thus Private Smith became Raider Smith. With the Home Forces in Britain, the Commandos were originally intended to operate independently of existing military and naval organizations. They were trained to be resourceful and self-reliant. In the United Kingdom the standard varied, since the tone and quality was set by the individual COs. Even so, the standards of military efficiency and discipline were by and large quite good.

In the Middle East there was neither direction nor control, pace and quality again being set by the individual Commanding Officers. Young made no concessions to any Special Force ethos and instead concentrated on training No. 50 Commando in the skills of conventional infantry tactics. Subsequent events were to vindicate such an unimaginative approach. Cator, now an acting Lieut-Colonel, had to fight the prejudice that existed in the theatre against a Palestinian bearing arms, whether he be Jew or Arab. In No. 52 Commando, the Commanding Officer set a more informal tone where saluting officers was a matter for the individual raider's discretion. Discipline throughout was lax, which could only be a recipe for trouble in a unit which comprised so many cast-offs from other regiments.

The Middle East theatre did however contribute a more enduring feature of the Commandos. The Commando knife originated in the Police Museum in Cairo; it was a wicked weapon with a seven-inch blade and a handle incorporating a knuckleduster. Called the 'fanny' by the raiders, it was used more frequently in brawls and bar-room battles in the 'off limits' areas of Cairo and Port Suez than against the enemy.

In a Headquarters where there was neither support nor favour for the concept of the Commando, none of this was an auspicious beginning. At best the General Staff in Cairo regarded the Commandos as a temporary expedient, which view prevailed in attitudes shown towards the most effective of all the Special Forces.

In 1942 an English newspaper described the Long Range Desert Group as the 'bravest, toughest and brainiest unit in Britain's Army'. Such hyperbole aside, there is little doubt that the LRDG were the aristocrats among the Special Forces and private armies that proliferated in the Middle East.

The LRDG saw the Desert Campaign through from start to finish. Though other Special Units were to steal the headlines with the derring-do of their exploits, none can match the LRDG's record of achievement. The more swashbuckling raiders such as the Special Air Service or the oddball 'Popski's Private Army', all turned to the LRDG in the first instance; it was from these professionals that they learned the essential elements of their trade – desert travel and navigation, and above all survival in such a hostile environment.

The LRDG can also trace their lineage back to the First World War when the Italians were Britain's allies. Yet if Mussolini had not been so brash as to declare war when he did, then the Long Range Desert Group might never have come into existence.

In 1915 the Germans and the Turks bribed the Senussi Arabs with guns, money and a few advisers, persuading them to rise in rebellion against their Italian masters. These marauders threatened to unite into larger bands and raid across the border into Egypt.

It might have been a better idea for Cairo to 'up the ante' on the bribes and offer the Arabs more than the Germans did to stay at home. It certainly would have been more economical than the conventional military wisdom of deploying large numbers of troops to chase and keep them out of Egypt.

The eyes and ears of the expeditionary force against the Senussi were the Light Car Patrols. The regular horse cavalry patrolled and policed the coastal region, while the Yeomanry mounted in Fords looked after the interior. Their armoured cars had a Model T chassis, oversized (for their day) $3\frac{1}{2}$-inch tyres and a single Vickers machine gun. The Patrols pioneered new routes deep into the desert; they developed the sun compass to assist in navigation and invented a condenser for the radiators.

This was an unglamorous role, locked into the sweltering metal interiors of their desert iron-clads, but it was successful if unsung. The praise and the glory went to that other desert raider, the flamboyant Lawrence and his private army in Arabia.

In the years of peace that followed the war, one man in particular

7

continued to pioneer desert travel. Major Ralph Bagnold was a rather retiring Royal Signals officer. Regarded by many as an eccentric, he nevertheless mounted ambitious expeditions which quartered the desert between the Mediterranean and Northern Sudan. He received every encouragement from the Royal Geographical Society, but neither support nor backing from military officialdom. The result was that such desert forays had to be financed by the members themselves. In these forerunners to the package tour, men and women paid £20 sterling for every thousand miles of desert travel.

By the early thirties Bagnold's parties had reached the Gilf el Kebir and Oweinat, where Egypt, Sudan and Cyrenaica meet – 680 miles from Cairo and over 300 miles from Kharga oasis, the nearest point for supplies. They penetrated deep into the Egyptian Sand Sea and altogether covered thousands of miles in the same type of Ford cars as had been used by the intrepid Yeomanry. They pioneered routes across sand dunes and desert rock which had hitherto been considered impassable to motor vehicles. In the peacetime Army, when service overseas allowed officers to indulge in such eccentricities, Bagnold improved on the sun compass and perfected sand channels and mats to give his vehicles mobility across the most treacherous of ground.

Bagnold's exploits inspired others to try their hands at desert travel. Vladimir Peniakoff – Russian emigré, Belgian citizen, French Army war veteran and B.A. Cambridge University (failed) – enjoyed a comfortable life working in a sugar refinery at Hanwandiah outside Cairo. He had heard about Bagnold's exploits and was determined to try this experience for himself. Peniakoff was bored with the cocktail circuit of Cairo's cosmopolitan society, bored with his work and his marriage, and in need of fresh stimulus to feed his restless soul.

Ralph Bagnold had by this time completed his tour of duty and returned to England and a course at the Army Staff College at Camberley.

Peniakoff owned a two-seater Ford of ancient heritage. This old car, known affectionately as 'the pisspot', was easily converted by a backstreet metal shop into a pick-up truck and fitted with balloon tyres. He bought some rudimentary navigational aids, studied the charts and at weekends took off on his own into the desert.

At the outbreak of war in Europe Bagnold was back in the Middle East. Like so many regular officers of his seniority he had been rapidly promoted to meet the needs of an expanding citizen army and had to take his soldiering seriously. Now a red-tabbed brigadier, he was en route to a staff appointment in East Africa when his ship was damaged in a collision and forced to put into Alexandria for some temporary repairs. Bagnold travelled up to Cairo, where he paid a courtesy call on General Wavell who had only recently arrived there.

Wavell had need of every officer he could find with experience of the desert, for even in those early days it seemed but a matter of time before Italy entered the war. It was not difficult to persuade Bagnold, especially when the alternative was an appointment in an East African backwater. Strings were pulled and Brigadier Bagnold transferred to the General Staff at Headquarters Middle East Land Forces as the resident expert on desert warfare; and there he languished.

Bagnold prepared detailed proposals for Wavell's consideration on the creation of a new desert patrol group, but the 'phoney war' was not a period for innovation and the schemes were rejected.

However, all of this changed suddenly in June 1940 when Italy declared war. Wavell ordered that a desert patrol group be established without delay and Bagnold was tasked to raise the unit.

There were other Special Forces knocking on the door of the Commander-in-Chief, in search of recognition and patronage.

The ironies of international relations become all too apparent when those Arabs who had warred against Britain and her Italian allies in the First World War, were now considered by many to provide a fertile source for recruits to a new guerrilla force.

The new formation was called the Libyan Arab Force and originally it was intended to be raised and organized into irregular groups of guerrillas. Under the command of specially selected British officers, the guerrilla bands were to skirmish on the flanks of the main army in the desert and penetrate into enemy territory on reconnaissance missions.

The Libyan Arab Force was recruited from the Senussi Arabs, Libyan Arabs and Arabs who came from the Jebel Akdar, the 'green mountain range' that runs parallel with the Mediterranean coast 170 miles from Derna to Benghazi. They had fought against the Italian occupation long after the Germans and the Turks had departed the scene, but the arrival of General Rodolfo Graziani brought an abrupt change in their fortunes. The general had a reputation for severity and cruelty, as well as outstanding administrative ability; in the later 1920s his stick-and-carrot approach culminated in a series of planned massacres against which the Arabs had no defence. After twenty years of guerrilla warfare their formal resistance ended in the capture of Kuffra, an oasis deep in the desert, a shrine as well as their last bastion and stronghold.

Many Arabs fled as refugees and eked out a nomadic existence on the fringes of the Western Desert. Others joined the cosmopolitan riff-raff of the big cities such as Alexandria and Cairo. They had lost their wealth, identity and way of life; but all still acknowledged allegiance to their spiritual leader, Sayed Idris El Senussi – himself an honoured refugee and pensioner of the British in Egypt.*

The exiles had brothers and families who lived under the Italian occupation, and could thus be sure of a warm welcome and sanctuary. The potential in terms of harnessing their hatreds and raising the banner of rebellion was felt by many to be one way of tying down large numbers of Italians and thereby reducing the enemy strength.

Colonel Bromilow, a senior Staff Officer at headquarters, promoted the idea of an Arab guerrilla force. An experienced cavalry officer of the old school, he nevertheless had the wit and imagination to appreci-ate the value of directing such bitter feelings against the Italians. Wavell sanctioned the raising of the Libyan Arab Force and gave Bromilow command and approval to recruit the officers and senior NCOs necessary to train and lead the new battalions.

Commanding Officers once again ran for cover as Bromilow's requirements were promulgated throughout the regiments in Egypt and Palestine. On this occasion, however, only a small proportion came from the ranks of the conventional forces, for Bromilow needed Arabic speakers and men who knew the desert ways of the nomadic peoples. From the outset he was desperately short of British officers of the right calibre and invariably had to take what was on offer.

Vladimir Peniakoff had been a neutral alien in the war to date, but the German invasion of his country in May 1940 made him an Allied alien and thus eligible for service in the British Army. Though middle aged, he applied for and was eventually granted a commission in the General List as a second-lieutenant. No doubt it was envisaged that Peniakoff would simply push a pen in some staff appointment, but he had other ideas. He applied for a posting to the Libyan Arab Force and shortly afterwards was interviewed and accepted by Colonel Bromilow.

By this time the Libyan Arab Force had been in existence for months and already numbered more than 3,000 Arab volunteers. National enthusiasm combined with the attraction of regular food and pay in producing a good response.

Little headway was made, however, in preparing the Arabs as guerrillas. Powerful voices in Middle East HQ simply mistrusted the fighting capabilities of the Libyans and advocated their deployment on guard duties in Egypt, which would in turn relieve more British soldiers for front-line service.

Bromilow argued long and persuasively against such a decision, but

---

*After the war, Idris El Senussi became the first king of a new Libyan state under British and later American protection and patronage, until deposed by an officer's rebellion led by Colonel Gaddafi.

he was a regular soldier with a career to consider. Promotion suddenly came his way with a command appointment in the Iraqi Army, where he had served before and knew well – far better than his Libyans. Those who succeeded him had little or no experience of Arab troops and were not inspired to fight any battles on their behalf. Some of the officers who had been seconded to the Libyan Arab Force became increasingly disillusioned, regarding their commanders as men who treated the force as a convenient stepping-stone to something more lucrative and congenial. The better junior officers, disgusted by such callous neglect, drifted away in search of more active military duties and the Arab battalions quickly went into decline.

The political departments in Middle East HQ also had a role in mind, and combined with the military sceptics to ensure that the Arab Libyan Force fitted in with their scheme of things.

In December 1940, General O'Connor attacked the Italians with his two weak divisions and drove all before him. The Libyan Arab Force had neither been called upon nor needed in the role for which it had been raised, and war against the Italians appeared to be all too easy in any case.

Occupied Enemy Territory Administration (OETA) needed a police force to keep order in Cyrenaica following O'Connor's victory. They got what they wanted and the Libyan Arab Force was redesignated as a paramilitary gendarmerie.

CHAPTER TWO

First Forays

Within a month of General Wavell's edict, the Long Range Desert Group* was operational. It was a remarkable achievement. In that short time Brigadier Bagnold had traced, contacted and then secured the secondments of those who had been with him in the early days. Kennedy Shaw came from Jerusalem, where he was frittering his time away in the Colonial Service censoring Palestine newspapers. Clayton flew up from Tanganyika; he was the most distinguished veteran of desert travel, having previously spent eighteen hard years as a key member of the Egyptian Desert Survey.

Guy Prendergast, destined to command the LRDG after Bagnold, was rushed out from London. Bagnold also secured the services of Captain Mitford, a Tank Corps officer in Cairo. Mitford was one of that select band of Englishmen who had actually journeyed deep into Italian Cyrenaica and travelled the road from Jalo to Kuffra.

These were the key members of the Group, the first squadron commanders, administrators and instructors. For his soldiers, Bagnold turned to the New Zealand Expeditionary Force, the first elements of which – under their legendary commander, Bernard Freyberg V.C. – had just arrived in the Middle East.

Freyberg had been recalled from an early retirement to become commander of the New Zealand division. He had been raised in the country and his loyalty to the men under his command and the

---

*For the first four months of its existence the unit was called the Long Range Group, until the name was changed to LRDG.

government in Wellington proved firm and lasting, much to the chagrin of his British contemporaries.

Bagnold's request immediately encountered a political obstacle, since the New Zealand government was most reluctant to place its own men under British Command. Considering the way in which the generals had squandered their manpower in the First World War, one can hardly blame them. On the other hand, the numbers required were small and the concept of a desert reconnaissance force was for the benefit of all.

Freyberg agreed to a compromise. The New Zealanders would be allowed to serve for a three-month secondment to the Long Range Desert Group, after which time they were to be returned to their parent unit.

The first volunteers were recruited from the New Zealand Divisional Cavalry. From the outset, their Patrol (it was a further condition that they were to have their own unit) set a high standard which all subsequent Patrols had to emulate, some more successfully than others. They were mostly farmers, more mature and older men than troopers from the Yeomanry who were to join later, independently minded and used to 'making do'. They had a natural eye for the ground, like all those brought up in the countryside, and the knack of knowing how to survive when the elements turned hostile.

The New Zealanders had other useful talents. They could drive – a skill unusual in the British Army at the time – and proved adept at keeping machinery running through improvisation and the odd bit of inspired cannibalism. The patrols could expect to be out for three weeks and more and therefore were totally dependent upon their vehicles.

Bagnold had selected American trucks, since there was nothing at all suitable in the British Army. The Chevrolet Company of Detroit had been shipping their 30-cwt utility truck into Egypt for some years; with its high-horse-powered engine and rugged durability it had proved popular with oil companies and even the Egyptian Army.

The Chevrolet needed conversion, however, and the Company's engineers in Alexandria were especially cooperative. The initial order was for 30 trucks, which after the years of austerity and depression must have represented a significant coup for the Company. The Royal Army Ordnance Corps fitters provided the muscle. Trucks were stripped of their doors, windscreens and canopies, and converted into large open pick-ups. Specially made bulbous tyres, strengthened suspension and a radiator condenser gave the vehicle a desert mobility that was unique in its day. Gun-mounts, fabricated fittings for radios, sand channels, water containers and rations etc, completed the refit.

The condenser usually came in the form of a steel tank bolted either to the front step of the truck or to the running-board behind the wheel arch. Sealed and part filled with water, it was connected by a tube to the top of the radiator, which was itself sealed, and the overflow blocked off. When the radiator boiled – which it did frequently during daytime travel in the desert – the steam would be 'condensed' in the water of the condenser tank; when the radiator cooled, the vacuum thus formed would suck water back until the original balance and level was restored. Provided the seals were tight, which was rarely the case, there would in theory be no need to top up the radiator during the patrol. Even with seals that leaked a little, mobility was much improved and radiators could be topped up at the end of the day.

When a Chevrolet left Abhassia Barracks – the home of the LRDG in Cairo – for patrol, it had an all-up weight in excess of two tons. Each vehicle carried a crew of four or five men and all their rations and needs for a three-week patrol of up to 1,200 miles. This did not take into account stores replenished from specially sited and pre-positioned dumps.

Weapons were another matter. Brigadier Bagnold had been given a high priority, but even so he could only choose from what was available in armouries which had not yet recovered from the years of neglect. Thus the patrol vehicles were armed with a mixture of the tried and trusted Vickers .303 heavy machine gun, venerable Lewis guns and the Boys anti-tank rifle. One vehicle in each group carried a 37mm Bofors anti-aircraft gun bolted to the floorboards. The problem was that until they had the benefit of a few operations behind them, nobody could make a judgement about the right weapons mix for a patrol of trucks.

Abhassia Barracks became a hive of activity. Kennedy Shaw devised the rations scales, based to a large degree upon experience gained in pre-war days. This was a remarkable achievement since he got it right first time; it was a well-balanced ration designed to meet the needs of desert warfare. This ration scale served the needs of other Special Forces who later followed on in North Africa.

By early August the first draft of 100 New Zealanders was undergoing intensive training. At the same time, plans were being drawn up to extend the recruiting drive into other units and nationalities. Yeomanry, Rhodesians and the two battalions of Foot Guards serving in Egypt (3rd Battalion Coldstream and 2nd Battalion Scots Guards) were all considered potentially rich sources for the right kind of recruits to augment and replace the New Zealanders.

Bagnold and his desert cronies, who had been ridiculed in the past, set the tone and the pace which enabled the Long Range Desert Group to become a true *corps d'élite* within the British Army. In the three years of war that lay ahead, the fortunes of the Desert Army were to fluctuate with alarming frequency, winning costly battles and suffering massive defeats. Perhaps Winston Churchill's assessment was accurate when he said at the end that the Army never won a victory in the desert. The LRDG, in contrast, never varied from the high standards which it established at the outset.

Unlike other private armies, it was never a death or glory outfit. Neither did it cultivate a swashbuckling image, yet at no time was it short of the high-grade volunteers necessary to sustain its strength. Every man who joined lost rank, pay and status, but there was always a waiting list.

The distractions of such special service were obvious. Operating behind enemy lines for long periods was a hazardous business made all the more stressful by the desert's terrain and climate. Conditions on occasions could be primitive in the extreme, where simply to survive was an achievement and all considerations of tactical movement were foolhardy.

But there were compensations. Men will always be attracted by the appeal of an élite where selection is a rigorous business and the mere factor of success marks one out as different and somewhat special.

Besides the camaraderie of the small group, the LRDG and other like units did offer a means of escape from those petty tediums and irritants of everyday life in the British Army. Drills, guards, fatigues and inspections were almost totally absent in the LRDG, and those in authority had to prove their worth. There were no dim, braggardly NCOs; officers led by example and thereby earned the trust and confidence of those under their command. Service in the LRDG also offered the best food in the Middle East and a job which was always interesting and on occasions exciting. Best of all, for the ordinary soldier it meant service in a unit where there was a minimum of being 'mucked about'.

The Long Range Desert Group became an exclusive club in which the best remained members for years, while the unfit, idle, curious and unsuitable very quickly left.

The pity was that the LRDG outlived its usefulness with the end of the North African War, and thereafter lived off a declining reputation while performing a role for which it was not particularly suited.

All of this, however, was in the future. As trucks became available, instructors took small groups out into the desert to experience the conditions for themselves. There were no maps which were of any value, so navigation became a precision skill of compass and astro-fix observations.

It was Kennedy Shaw's task to train the navigators, especially in the use of the sun compass. He described it thus:

The sun compass consists of a horizontal circle, divided into 360 degrees with a central needle casting a shadow across the graduations. By rotating the circle, which is fixed to the dashboard of the truck, throughout the day to correspond to the sun's movement through the sky, the shadow is made to indicate the true bearing on which the truck is travelling.*

The sun compass was clamped to the dashboard in such a position that it could be read by the driver quite easily, and he could follow the direction indicated. The beauty of it was that it allowed an accurate direction to be maintained despite the magnetism of the metal chassis. On a journey of 500 miles a two-degree error would miss the objective by 17 miles, and for a patrol behind enemy lines, or one searching for a supply dump and much needed replenishment, that could spell disaster.

The English High Schools in Cairo and Alexandria found their logarithm tables requisitioned. Theodolites were borrowed from the Egyptian Government's Survey Department, or bought in the second-hand stores in the squalid back streets of the big cities. A notice was even pinned on the board of the Gezira Sporting Club, asking for the members to lend their binoculars for the duration.

Captain K. H. Lazaras was a professional survey officer seconded to the LRDG. He set out in the desert with a patrol of three trucks in an effort to equip the unit with its own detailed source of maps and drawings.

Radio operators were trained to an equally high level; the sets with which they were equipped were powerful enough to transmit over distances of 1,000 miles and more. Though the radios were well mounted and secured in the redoubtable Chevrolet, these operators were a vital part of the team and it was their task to ensure that when the time came to signal coded data to Headquarters, they and their sets were on top line.

Despite the progress that Bagnold was making in forming the unit, Wavell was impatient. Within a very few months he and his successors would be extremely well served by the 'Ultra' code breakers in England and their special liaison unit which was already en route to the Middle East; but for the time being there was little information available upon which to assess enemy intentions.

After almost a year of uneasy calm in the Mediterranean, British reaction to Mussolini's declaration of war had been one of relief. Hitherto everything which had been done in the Middle East had been constrained by the need not to provoke the Italians, though the enemy had observed no such inhibitions.

---

*W. B. Kennedy Shaw, *Long Range Desert Group* (Collins, London, 1948).

Right through to the beginning of June 1940, reserves and reinforcements for the Duke of Aosta – Mussolini's viceroy in the East African empire – had been permitted to flow through the Suez Canal. This was a crazy situation, particularly in the three months leading to the declaration of war when the passage of Italian troopships and transports through the Canal had been an almost daily occurrence.

Rome had been absolutely scrupulous on one point, however: the Canal 'fees' had been paid promptly and without question. Even so, the irony could not have been lost on those who were preparing for war against a potential foe using a vital facility to swing the balance of power very much in its favour.

Now that war had been declared, what would Mussolini's strategy be? There was a garrison at Kuffra and it was known that another force occupied a landing ground near Jebel' Uweinat, a 6,000-foot massif which straddled the juncture of Libya with the Sudan and Egypt.

British intelligence could only surmise the outcome should their forward bases be reinforced. To the south in Chad the French garrison was split in its allegiance, and a show of strength might easily be sufficient to oust the Gaullists and secure the province for Vichy.

From the Jebel' Uweinat, an enemy could raid east to interdict Wavell's line of communications which linked Cairo with Khartoum. An obvious target on that route was Wadi Matfa, dockyards and a railway junction that was weakly garrisoned and in no position to prevent a spoiling raid. If the raid also linked up with naval operations such as a blockade by Italian submarines and warships from the East African bases, in the Red Sea narrows, then the vital supply lines to southern Africa could be neatly severed and the British isolated.

In the midst of their own preparations, Bagnold despatched Clayton – his most experienced officer – to find some of these answers. In early August he set out on the first of two missions. Using Chevrolets borrowed from the Survey Department, together with their Sudanese crews, Clayton reconnoitred deep into enemy territory and close to Kuffra. He found nothing to suggest the Italians were about to take the initiative. In truth, he found not a single Italian on the main track that led from Jalo to Kuffra.

Returning only to report and replenish, the intrepid Clayton set out for a second time to look at the area around Jebel' Uweinat. On this occasion he decided that he would need to get fairly close to his objective – closer than the vehicles could manage undetected. Therefore one of the Chevrolets was stripped of its stores and weapons, and a camel loaded instead.

Clayton completed his solo reconnaissance. Both he and the camel returned safely to the waiting trucks and the journey home to Cairo. There were no Italians to be seen.

Wavell was delighted with both the efforts and the achievements of these operations, for they were epic journeys in their own right which largely passed unnoticed in the preparations for war.

During Clayton's absence, the New Zealand recruits hurriedly completed their training. The final phase involved travelling the track that led beyond the highway and westwards into the desert to the still relatively safe areas around the Egyptian frontier. They prepared dumps along the track where petrol, water and other supplies were stored so that patrols could cross the forbidden territories fully replenished.

By the end of August, Bagnold was able to report that the Long Range Desert Group was ready for operations.

CHAPTER THREE

'A Tactician's Paradise and a Quartermaster's Hell'

The Western Desert region is in fact one of limestone, with very little real desert, and stretches for 1,400 miles between the terminal points of Tripoli in the west and Alexandria in the east. The German General von Ravenstein described it as 'a tactician's paradise and a quartermaster's hell', for there was only one natural defence line between El Agheila and El Alamein, and except for the coast road the entire region was devoid of communications.

Thus the further a force advanced the weaker it became. This was because its lines of communication became longer and more vulnerable to rupture – either from the enemy or self-inflicted – while the opponent even in retreat became stronger. Over the next couple of years this coastal strip was to change hands frequently in what became known as the 'Benghazi stakes'. It was a race. The aim or objective was always to outpace the enemy, whether fleeing from his wrath or seeking to break through his own rearguard and cause mayhem amongst his rear-echelon vehicles and troops. For the British it was a time of cavalry-type encounters, with pennants fluttering from aerials atop Yeomanry and Hussar tanks and armoured cars. It was also a time of increasingly disgruntled and disillusioned infantry who were all too frequently left to their own devices until they came to loathe their own armour.

Special Forces, such as the Long Range Desert Group and the many others that were to follow, had to master these conditions before they could use the desert to their advantage. And this was the easy part. Initially both sides believed that their southern or interior flanks rested on what was known as the inner desert. This was a vast, completely uninhabited area which comprised seas of sand, barren hills and trackless scrub – a wilderness which extended over 800 miles to the Tibesti mountains where a few primitive nomads pastured their flocks.

In September the LRDG left Cairo on their first operation. Clayton intended to lead a patrol and penetrate beyond Libya to the French post at Tekro in Chad province, then to investigate the possibilities of linking up with forces loyal to de Gaulle. Another patrol, meanwhile, would attempt to interdict the Italian route to Kuffra to confirm Clayton's original findings. A third party drew the short straw, their task being to establish forward supply points and mark out an emergency air-strip albeit behind the enemy's front lines. The operation was also intended to be a training exercise in which the men would learn how to come to terms with the formidable obstacles presented by desert warfare.

The first obstacle lay immediately across the border. It took the party two days of desperate effort to cross the 150 miles of the Great Sand Sea. Kennedy Shaw vividly describes this vision of hell.*

> There is nothing like these sand seas anywhere else in the world. Take an area the size of Ireland and cover it with sand. Go on pouring sand on it till it is two or three hundred feet deep. Then with a giant's rake score the sand into ridges and valleys running north-north west, and south-south east, and with ridges at the highest five hundred feet from trough to crest.
>
> Late in the evening when the sands cool quickly and the dunes throw long shadows the Sand Sea is one of the most lovely things in the world; no words can properly describe the beauty of those sweeping curves of sand. At a summer midday when the sun beats down all the shapes to one flat glare of sand and the sand drift blows off the dune crests like the snow plume off Everest, it is as good an imitation of Hell as one could devise.

Big Cairn marked the western boundary of the Great Sand Sea. There, deep into Italian territory, Clayton regrouped and rested the three patrols. They had trail-blazed a route across ground hitherto considered impassable and in the process taken the first great steps towards making this inner desert their own acknowledged preserve.

The raiders split up. One group – the least fortunate – was to return across the Sand Sea to bring supplies forward to Big Cairn. The Great Sand Sea would always remain an obstacle, but never on quite that

---

* W. B. Kennedy-Shaw, *Long Range Desert Group* (Collins, London, 1948).

scale. The uncertain summits of the sand dunes would always catch out those who failed to approach them with caution, for the reverse slope might be a drop steep enough to tip the vehicle end over end, or it might be a gentle gradient into a patch of soft sand in which a truck buried itself down to its differential before the crew had time to react.

Clayton set off for Chad and the Free French, while Mitford led the remaining patrol in search of the Italians at Kuffra.

On 20 September Mitford intercepted and captured the 'Kuffra Mail'. This grandiose title was given to a couple of six-ton Fiat diesel trucks owned by Truici and Mosti, civilian contractors, who had the franchise to supply the isolated garrisons that led south from Jalo to Kuffra.

It was on an anonymous feature called Landing Ground No 7* that the two Italian truck-drivers and their Arab assistants had the fright of their lives. Mitford's patrol came upon them unawares and made off with the loot, which besides the prisoners and the vehicles included the official mail, despatches and 2,500 gallons of petrol.

The raid produced the intended effect. Immediately the loss had been realized the Italians provided an army escort and air cover for all subsequent convoys. To cause an enemy to divert forces from their main tasks is the perfect result for a guerrilla operation, and for LRDG to achieve this on their first operation was especially pleasing.

Mitford rendezvouzed east of Kuffra with Clayton – who had had a most promising meeting with the Free French in Chad – dumped the trucks belonging to Truici and Mosti and returned to Cairo in triumph.

It is 650 miles in a straight line from Cairo to Kuffra, and the reputation of the LRDG in its interception of the 'Kuffra Mail' spread amongst the British Forces in Egypt. Although the tale became exaggerated in its telling, it was a reputation which they never lost.

On 28 October 1940 the Italians made their play. The long awaited offensive fell not in the Middle East but in the Balkans, which immediately excited the interest of the British Prime Minister. When the Italian Air Force bombed Athens, Churchill directed that the Royal Air Force should bomb cities in Northern Italy by way of retaliation. At the same time he ordered that plans be prepared to render every assistance to the Greeks despite the shortage of British troops in the theatre, and to prevent Crete falling into enemy hands.

Meanwhile, Bagnold followed up Clayton's visit; he flew to Fort

---

*Unmanned emergency air-strips built by the Italians and stocked with supplies and fuel.

Lamy, the French Headquarters in Chad and there discussed plans for a joint operation. The French were anxious to capture Kuffra, which would in turn allow them to develop it as a forward base from which they could strike into Libya. The Fezzan region with its oases and garrison towns promised rich pickings for raiding parties.

On Monday 9 December, as has already been mentioned, the two British divisions of the Western Desert Force launched an offensive against the Italian Tenth Army in its fortified position south of Sidi Barrasi. Under the brilliant leadership of General O'Connor, the 4th Indian and 7th Armoured Divisions routed the enemy and within a very few days had won a resounding victory. The Italians fell back in disarray on Bardia.

Wavell, remote in his HQ and unaware of the significance of O'Connor's success, withdrew the Indian Division to the Sudan. There followed a delay of three weeks – and one which was to prove fateful – before the 6th Australian Division could be rushed to the front from Palestine.

On Boxing Day, Clayton left Cairo with the full contingent of Long Range Desert Group. G Patrol, which had been formed with the volunteers from the Guards battalions and led by Captain Michael Chrichton-Stuart, joined with T Patrol, the well-tried and tested New Zealanders. Seventy-six men and 24 vehicles drove out of Abhassia Barracks for an operation which was destined to last 45 days and cover 4,500 miles. The objective was to capture Kuffra, but first the party was to rendezvous with a Free French contingent. The two groups were then to combine for an attack on the Italian garrison and air-strip at Murzak deep in the Fezzan and 1,000 miles from Cairo. The raiders were subsequently to retire south into Chad to regroup before striking north once more for Kuffra.

Bardia fell on 4 January, the same day that Clayton and the LRDG linked up with the Free French. The latter were led by Colonel d'Ornano, a tall, hawk-featured monocled figure who, clad in turban and burnous, looked as if he came straight from a film studio in Hollywood. There is no record of how many Frenchmen Clayton had been led to believe would join the enterprise, but he must have hoped for more than the nine men who travelled with their colonel.

Capitaine Massu, the second-in-command, was to become famous in later, troubled years as a leader of 'Les Para' in French Indo-China and Algeria. There was also an Alsatian Lieutenant, two French sergeants and five Arab tribesmen – all spoiling for a fight.

They had their wish at Murzak but the attack was a messy inconclusive affair. The Italians put up a spirited resistance and, although the air-strip was destroyed, the raiders lacked the firepower to reduce the fort. In attempting to rush the enemy, Colonel d'Ornano took a burst of machine-gun fire full in the throat and died instantly, and there were several casualties amongst the New Zealanders.

Clayton broke off the action and led the raiders even further south to rendezvous with the French Camel Corps. At Tummo, on the border of Libya with French West Africa, a group from Sarazac's Group Nomade de Tibesti were waiting to escort LRDG down to Faya.

Bagnold flew down to join this party and to meet Colonel d'Ornano's successor – an officer who used the name Leclerc as an alias. The Vicomte de Haute Cloque was a modern d'Artagnan who had already been captured and escaped from the Germans on two occasions during that short period known as the Battle of France. When de Gaulle had toured French Equatorial Africa in October, he left this most trusted officer to organize the resistance and link with the British to the north.

Clayton led the New Zealanders and set out as the advance party for the raid on Kuffra. Many had been appalled at the lack of security shown by the French during the stay, and the toast of 'Vers Kouffra!' had frequently sounded during lavish and very public evenings in the officers' mess.

The LRDG had every reason to be concerned. Spotter aircraft shadowed their journey through Sarra and Bishara, two oases which had been abandoned to the desert after the Italians had blown in the wells. On 31 January 1941, in a narrow defile at Jebel Sherif some 60 miles from Kuffra, the LRDG trucks were neatly ambushed. Their Italian equivalent, the Auto-Saharen riding in powerful Lancia diesel armoured cars, opened up with their 20mm Breda cannon and called down fighter aircraft in support. Two trucks were destroyed, including the lead vehicle in which Clayton was travelling; he and the two crew members were wounded and captured.

Lieutenant Ballantyne assumed command, regrouped and withdrew his force. Four other members of the party* were missing as they fell back on Sarra, where the Guards patrol was waiting in reserve along with Leclerc and his Free French Column.

Leclerc agreed that no good could come of further operations against Kuffra at the present; the enemy were thoroughly alerted

---

*The four – Trooper Moore who was a New Zealander, Guardsmen Easton and Winchester, and an RAOC fitter named Tighe – evaded the Italians and set out on what was to become the first of the epic desert marches which punctuate the North African Campaigns. Ten days later they were spotted by the Free French, but rescue came too late for Guardsman Easton who died the same evening.

and any attack could only result in heavy casualties. One vehicle and its crew stayed with the French to instruct them in desert navigation, while the remainder swung south by way of the Sudan and home.

In many respects this epic journey is typical of the operations experienced by the Special Forces. The scale of the endeavour, the individual courage and heroism can be seen as a tremendous achievement. While we are in awe of such men, we must at the same time stand back and ask what did their sacrifice achieve?

New routes were pioneered across the trackless wastes and much was learned about the desert. Bagnold's men did achieve their training objective. Nevertheless the conclusion remains that the operation was divorced from O'Connor's attacks to the north, and his failure to secure a more complete victory was the fault of the higher command in Cairo and in London.

The Free French waited for the dust to settle, then having assembled a large force Leclerc scattered the Auto-Saharen and attacked Kuffra in classic style. By this time the Italians had been totally defeated in the mainland battles, Tobruk and Benghazi had fallen and there was no hope of relief or rescue for those isolated in Kuffra.

On 1 March 1941, after twenty-two days of siege, the Italians at Kuffra capitulated.

Nobody could have known what a haven Kuffra was to become for Special Forces in the years to come. Five hundred miles from the coast and isolated in the desert wastes, tiny Kuffra lies in a depression. Having flowed 1,000 miles north from the equatorial rain-belt, sweet water wells up and irrigates shady palm groves and gardens of millet. There was also salt water at Kuffra. Two salt lakes of the deepest blue water were favoured spots to bathe tired limbs after a long patrol; they were so salty that it was impossible to sink. The Italians had built a fort on the highest ground and this dominated the oasis. They had also built a school and a little hospital, and there was a small market where Arabs came to trade.

The French retained a token garrison more for political than military reasons, but the LRDG made Kuffra into their main base for operations. Two patrols were later detached under Western Desert Force Command and based at Siwa, another oasis about 200 miles south of Sollum on the coast.

All these preparations went ahead to establish the bases, though with what purpose in mind is still unclear.

Churchill had ordered Wavell to halt his advance after the fall of Benghazi and leave only a minimum force to hold Cyrenaica. A new expeditionary force was to be despatched to Greece and every effort made to overcome Italian resistance in East Africa. In so far as the

Prime Minister and the War Cabinet were concerned, the Desert Campaign in North Africa was over and the Italians a beaten, spent force.

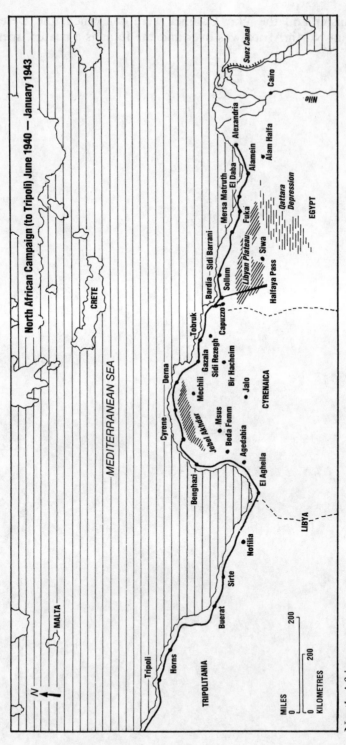

North African Campaign (to Tripoli) June 1940 — January 1943

MEDITERRANEAN SEA

CRETE

MALTA

N

Tripoli
Homs
Buerat
Sirte
Nofilia
TRIPOLITANIA

El Agheila
LIBYA

Agedabia
Beda Fomm
Msus
Jebel Akhdar
Mechili
Benghazi
Cyrene
Derma
Tobruk

CYRENAICA
Jalo
Bir Hacheim
Sidi Rezegh
Gazala
Capuzzo
Bardia — Sidi Barrani
Sollum
Halfaya Pass
Siwa
Libyan Plateau
Fuka
Mersa Matruth
El Daba
Alamein
Alam Halfa
Qattara Depression
EGYPT
Alexandria
Cairo
Nile
Suez Canal

MILES
0   200

KILOMETRES
0   200

North Africa

CHAPTER FOUR

East African Interludes 'An Improvisation after the British Fashion of War'

Italy's empire in East Africa comprised Eritrea, the oldest and most prestigious colony, Italian Somaliland, and Ethiopia which in 1936 had been conquered by Mussolini. The Italian garrisons were strong in number and well supplied. They were commanded by the 41-year-old Duke of Aosta, viceroy of Ethiopia, an Anglophile veteran of the Great War and a professional soldier possessed of mediocre skills.

Strategically the Italians were isolated. Unless General Wavell suffered a major reverse in the Western desert and the Royal Navy were unable to control the Western Mediterranean and the Cape route, there could be hope of neither rescue or reinforcement.

Maybe nothing much would have happened, for a while at least, had the Italians opted for a quiet war. Wavell had his hands full in the Western Desert, and once Mussolini had attacked in the Balkans he was under fresh pressure to prepare a contingency plan to reinforce Greece.

However, the Italians struck first – but in the wrong direction. In August 1940, 26 battalions with armour and air support invaded British Somaliland. Had Aosta and Graziani launched a joint offensive – half a million men, to invade Egypt from the west and south – it might have been a different story.

Five British and Imperial battalions fought a delaying action until they could be safely evacuated by sea to Aden. On 15 August the

Italians entered Berbera, the seat of colonial government, amidst great scenes of jubilation in Rome.

The subsequent British campaign to reclaim East Africa was planned and implemented in stages. Wavell described it as 'an improvisation after the British fashion of war'.

The Italians were defeated in a pincer movement. In the south, Lieutenant-General Sir Andrew Cunningham advanced into Italian Somaliland from Kenya with a force of three small divisions. There were West Africans, British-officered regiments from Nigeria and the Gold Coast, brigades of the King's African Rifles from Kenya and Uganda, and the 1st South African Infantry Division. These were the anvil to the hammer that came from the north. Lieutenant-General Sir William Platt, GOC Sudan, had the 4th and 5th Indian Divisions, together with some battalions of Sudanese troops.

Two of the Middle East Commandos were despatched to General Platt's command as Special Forces to be used at his discretion. In Eritrea the Italian lines of communication were long and horribly exposed, an inviting target for a raiding group.

No. 52 Commando arrived in November 1940 and was attached to Brigadier Mayne's 9th Infantry Brigade which was advancing on Gallabat.

When the fortress eventually fell, the Italian defeat marked the first victory by British forces in this theatre of war. It was a tiny affair, so tiny that it passed unnoticed, but even this battle had its moments of high drama when a battalion of the Essex Regiment deserted the field. A South African pilot was flying a reconnaissance mission at the time and his radio messages served as a commentary on the events below.

Arthur Braine, who was with the Indian Divisional Signals, monitored the message:

'I can't make out what is going on because the Italians are fleeing in one direction and the Essex are going off in the bleeding other direction.'

The story is told that the Essex fled after they had captured the fort. A stray shell landed and an elderly major, veteran of the Great War, yelled 'Gas' and they all ran.

The Commandos did not perform much better. This was in part because Brigadier Mayne and his Staff had never come across such a unit before and had no idea how they should be used. The men spent most of their short time providing a tactical reconnaissance service to the forward battalions, or mounting aggressive fighting patrols.

Disgruntled, disenchanted and with their ranks depleted by the ravages of dysentery and malaria, they were withdrawn from the theatre and returned to Egypt.

Lieutenant-Colonel Cator and his Palestinians of No. 51 Com-

mando managed to stay with the Campaign from beginning to end.
This tough, mixed national unit had some twenty officers – English,
Canadian, Rhodesian and South Africans – who commanded their
Palestinian Arabs and hardened Jewish expatriates. About three-
quarters of the 600-strong Commando were French, Germans,
Italians, Poles, Russians and Spaniards, most of whom were Jews
recruited in Palestine. For those who believe that the Middle East
today is in a hopeless mess because Jews and Arabs can never work
together, it is perhaps worth pointing out that the 51st Jews and Arabs
were integrated into platoons and even sections. They lived, fought
and died side by side. Even so the force had its critics. an Indian
account of 51 Commando* described them as 'the sweepings of Palestine, Jews and Arabs who were thieves and murderers'.

After months of enforced idleness and misuse in Egypt, the Commando was despatched to East Africa, where they were attached to
General Beresford-Pierce's 4th Indian Division. Cator's task was to
deploy his unit, by troop and section, into the mountains as probing
patrols laying ambushes and conducting detached reconnaissance.

Their first major engagement was the battle for Keren, a town which
stands over 4,000 feet above sea level and is protected by a ring of
mountains. It was a natural fortress defended by 23,000 Italians,
including some of their very best regiments.

The 4th Indian Division was kept at bay for seven weeks. The
Commandos were instrumental in launching flanking attacks against
this formidable defence and in drawing off large numbers of the enemy.
They were sent in against Mount Samanna, an important feature in
the ring of hills that protected Keren. Here the Commandos held the
lower slopes, only to be thrown back by a strong enemy counter-
attack.

Cator led his men on a return encounter the following evening. On
this occasion they were successful, although the Italians subjected
them to a withering artillery bombardment. 'Kid' Cator was badly
wounded in the leg and had to be evacuated. His place was taken by
the second-in-command, Major S. D. Miller of the Tenth Hussars,
who was to lead the Commandos throughout the remainder of the
Campaign.

The Italians lost 3,000 men before they abandoned Keren and fell
back southwards into Ethiopia, where they made their next stand in
the mountain stronghold of Amba Alagi. Meanwhile the Indians
broke through to Asmara and the Red Sea Coast. By this time,

---

*M. A. R. Skinner, *Sworn to Die*, p. 193 (Lancer International, New Delhi,
1948).

General Platt's troops had routed six Italian divisions and taken 40,000 prisoners.

The battle for Amba Alagi proved a bitter and fiercely contested affair. It was an infanteer's war with little opportunity for dash or manoeuvre, where subtlety extended no further than hard pounding with artillery and an advance supported with tanks at walking pace. The Palestinian Commando played their part courageously as mountain specialists engaging the defenders on numerous occasions in hand-to-hand combat with their fanny knives.

This was not the war for which Cator had trained them, and all those long hours spent on boat-drills seemed to have been for nothing. By this stage, however, the Commando had carved a place for themselves as a tough light infantry force living through a series of long marches and short sharp engagements. Wellington's Green-Jacketed infantry in the Peninsula would have been equally at home in such a role.

By now Cunningham had advanced more than 1,000 miles, conquering Italian Somaliland and linking up with an amphibious force which had landed close to Berbera and liberated British Somaliland. The joint force then marched deep into Abyssinia and on 6 April, having defeated more than 70,000 of the enemy, entered the capital Addis Ababa.

Cunningham joined forces with Platt and together they attacked the Italians at Amba Alagi some 250 miles north of the capital. After a week of bitter fighting the Duke of Aosta surrendered on 17 May.

The rainy season set in with a vengeance, and there was little that could be done by way of active campaigning. The Commando was pulled back to Adi Ugri, where they spent the next couple of months resting and refitting. It was called upon from time to time – one of its more intriguing assignments being to provide a close escort to the Commander of another private army which had been unleashed into the province of Gojjam, where the Italians were making another stand.

In the years since the Second World War, controversy has grown around the activities of Orde Wingate in Ethiopia. It is hard at times to distinguish fact from fiction in a legend which claims that the country was liberated by the efforts of the Ethiopian Patriot Forces, who answered the call of their Emperor and were led in fierce battle by a man whom many liken to a second Lawrence of Judea.

It is no more than legend and largely myth.

It was as a captain in Palestine in 1938 that Wingate had first demonstrated, under Wavell's watchful eye, his brilliance as a guerrilla leader. Bands of marauding Arabs, subsidized by the Germans and the Italians, were repeatedly cutting the Haifa-Mosul oil pipeline and terrorizing the local Jewish population.

With grudging British permission, Wingate organized an anti-ter-
rorist unit, night-fighting squads of only a few hundred men. This
force, half British and half Jewish, proved more than a match for the
local terrorists who were beaten at their own game.

The Jews came from the Hagannah, the supposedly clandestine
security force for the Yishav or Jewish community in Palestine.
Dressed in blue shirts and Australian bush hats, the night fighters
under Wingate's command helped to drive the Arab guerrillas out of
Galilee and far from the petroleum pipeline.

The parallel between Lawrence and Wingate was not too exaggerated; they were even distantly related. Wingate was a charismatic
figure with an unusual empathy for strange races, and a fundamentalist
belief in the Bible and the avenging sword.

Orde Wingate saw the Jewish people's struggle to return to Palestine
as a just and righteous cause. Like so many romantics, he hardly
spared a thought for the Arabs who for centuries had settled that
land, and dedicated himself to making the Hagannah an effective
fighting instrument. It was during this period that Wingate gave Yigal
Allon, Moshe Dyan and other future Israeli army commanders their
first formal instruction in warfare, particularly in counter-guerrilla
tactics.

Had it not been for the Second World War, Wingate would never
have risen to military prominence. Though a professional soldier in a
peacetime army which had its eccentrics, his outrageous behaviour
would almost certainly have condemned him, at best, to middle rank.
He had brains, imagination and tenacity, but his bullying ways with
those who disagreed with him and his public contempt for superiors
would have marked him down.

By the time Wingate departed Palestine, he had left an indelible
imprint as the single most important influence on the military thinking
of the Hagannah. But in professional terms he had paid a high price.
In May 1939 his personal file records:

> Orde Charles Wingate D.S.O. is a good soldier, but so far as
> Palestine is concerned he is a security risk. He cannot be trusted.
> He puts the interests of the Jews before those of his own country.
> He should not be allowed in Palestine again.

In November 1940 Wavell summoned Wingate from obscurity to
Khartoum, where he was invited to lead and direct the Abyssinian
resistance. There were parts of the conquered kingdom which, thanks
to the benign policies of the Duke of Aosta, had flourished under
Italian occupation. The British were often to find little sympathy and
even hostility to their campaign. Nevertheless, there was a chance that

31

a tribal revolt could be fomented, especially in the west of the country which had remained loyal to the Emperor Haile Selassie.

Wingate's first task was to make contact with the head of Mission 101, a special task force which liaised, after a fashion, with the guerrilla underground in Gojjam. Colonel David Sandford was another bizarre figure from a quaint colonial past. This 60-year-old Scot had retired from the Army and settled into a comfortable life in Addis Ababa, where he had cultivated vegetables and sold them to the British and European Legations before being appointed Haile Selassie's purchasing agent.

After the Italian conquest he had slipped across the frontier from Sudan with letters from the Emperor. It was a 300-mile trek to make contact with the Degachi, guerrilla leaders who were still keen to fight the Italians.

In November 1940 Wingate risked life and limb to take an ancient biplane to Sanford's home-made air-strip. There he met with the Degachi, whom he impressed with his oratory and his promise to support their revolt.

Wingate raised a force of 1,800 Sudanese and Ethiopian Askaris, a sprinkling of British officers and some stalwart NCOs, together with 1,500 camels, pack-mules, some mountain guns and trench mortars. He called his command 'Gideon Force' after the biblical Gideon whose exploits are related in the Book of Judges:

> With 300 men Gideon marched against the hosts of Midian which lay along in the valley like grasshoppers in multitudes. With the Lord's help Gideon routed the Midianites and sent messages throughout all of Mount Ephraim calling on the people to come down against the Midianites and take waters into Jordan.

Gideon Force took to the field in January 1941 where Wingate, with the Emperor alongside, fought a quite brilliant campaign against an opponent who vastly outnumbered him, albeit in a province which was quite remote from the main operations. The defeat of the Italians in Gojjam was a mixture of bravado and bluff; Wingate and his men had to endure great hardship and danger in a miserable and inhospitable country.

Their ranks were swelled by hundreds of Ethiopians attracted by his success, but these destitute souls simply overstretched the logistics without increasing firepower. At one stage the column was so weak with hunger that Wingate despatched some men to buy food from the nearest Italian garrison. Gideon Force ate their fill and then captured the fort.

On another occasion Wingate was standing in the orderly room of a fort which had just been captured, when the telephone rang. One man in Gideon Force spoke Italian fluently – Edmund Stevens, foreign correspondent for the *Christian Science Monitor*.

Wingate grabbed Stevens and pushed him towards the phone.

It was a neighbouring outpost asking for news.

'Tell them 10,000 British troops are closing on them,' he ordered.

Stevens promptly did as he was told and embellished the news in spectacular Italian fashion. Playing the part of a desperate officer on the point of defeat, with no hope of escape, he advised the caller to spread the word and evacuate as quickly as possible.

The Italians promptly abandoned a whole string of forts which guarded crossing points along the Blue Nile.

On 5 May 1941 Wingate made a formal entry into Addis Ababa, a month after Cunningham's 1st South African Division had liberated the city. He rode on a white charger at the side of Haile Selassie in a ceremony which marked the conclusion of a remarkable little campaign. In four months Gideon Force and the Patriots had cleared the Gojjam. Legend has it that 40,000 Italians were killed or captured, though fact would place the figure nearer to 10,000. In strategic terms it contributed little to the outcome of the East African Campaign for, with the defeat of their main forces by troops under Platt and Cunningham, the fate of the Italians in the Gojjam was sealed in any case.

At Gondar, the last major position to hold out, although isolated and surrounded the Italians still put up a fierce resistance.

Gondar fell in November 1941 to a determined, set-piece assault. The Palestinian Commando played an important part in launching night assaults, but this was to prove their last battle. The unit returned to Egypt and was then sent on leave to Palestine before being disbanded. Operation *Crusader* was in full swing. The Eighth Army's counter-offensive had sent Rommel's Panzers reeling back and the siege of Tobruk was raised.

It is hard to understand the decision to scrap a tried and battle-tested unit at a time when military experience was at a premium, but HQ Middle East was on a high and the services of this tough and now veteran Palestinian unit were no longer required.

CHAPTER FIVE

Stepping Stones to Rhodes

The Greek island of Crete was crucial to the strategy of the Mediterranean Fleet, even before Greece became a belligerent. Its main asset was seen as Suda Bay, a fine natural harbour which was deep enough for heavy cruisers and provided an excellent base from which the surface fleet could protect Malta-bound convoys from the Italians. The Royal Navy looked all the while to the big surface action and failed to appreciate that the Greeks had also built airfields on the island, the main one being at Maleme.

There were some bitter lessons to be learned before the Royal Navy in the Mediterranean became air minded.

Initially the Greeks were neutral and refused to allow the Allies to use their facilities, so the French naval squadron in the Levant was tasked with 'safeguarding the integrity' of Crete.

The fall of France and the Italian declaration of war in the same tragic month changed the strategic picture completely. After the bombardments at Casablanca and Oran, the French Navy declared for Vichy and thus enhanced the potential of the Italian Fleet. The Royal Navy needed Crete, and in particular Suda Bay, more than ever. When the Italians invaded the Balkans, the Greek army in Albania stopped them in their tracks. For reasons which will be examined in the next chapter, the Greek government was wary of a Britain bearing gifts and loathe to accept military assistance other than air support and a small garrison for Crete.

Despite all the demands placed upon his overstretched resources, Wavell was ordered to find a brigade for the defence of Crete.

No. 50 (Middle East) Commando had so far experienced a frustrating war. It had been stood by on a number of occasions for amphibious operations in support of O'Connor's triumphant advance, only to have them cancelled at the last moment.

Nothing can be worse for a raiding force than to have its operation cancelled at the very last minute. This was to happen time after time to the Special Forces in every theatre of war, and probably did more to undermine morale and blunt their fighting edge than the heaviest battle casualties.

Men of 50 Commando barely had time to give voice to their anger and frustration before they were ordered to join with 14 Infantry Brigade as the new garrison for Crete. Staff officers decreed that as Crete was Greek and therefore a part of Europe, the garrison should be equipped accordingly. Battledress was issued, which for many in the Commandos was a new experience. These were the long service veterans, some of whom had been overseas and in tropical uniforms since before 1937 when the new battledress was introduced.

The 14th Infantry Brigade travelled in style to Crete. The soldiers sailed in the company of the battleships *Warspite* and *Valiant*, the carrier *Illustrious* and the heavy cruiser *York*, whose sister ship *Exeter* had already won fame in the Battle of the River Plate.

The Commando settled into the western part of the island where, with all the acquired skills of long service, they soon made themselves at home with the local population. The Italians received another bloody nose from the Greeks, and for the garrison on Crete the war seemed as far away as ever.

Christmas came and passed; then in the New Year of 1941 the War Cabinet decided to adopt a more aggressive policy in the Aegean.

Colonel Laycock left England with the three Commandos codenamed Z Force for an attack on Rhodes; Admiral Cunningham was ordered to use those Special Forces available to prepare the way for the main operation with reconnaissance missions and raids among the Aegean Islands.

Two of the three Commandos were in East Africa, so No. 50 (Middle East) Commando was shaken out of its lethargy and ordered to prepare itself for raiding. Their fighting edge had been first honed and then blunted by cancelled operations, and the unit had stagnated through the winter in the dull tedium of garrison duty with its chores, guards and fatigues. Lieutenant-Colonel Symons in command had sought ways and means to introduce some variety into their existence, but a garrison outpost in time of war is short of resources and opportunity. The result was that orders were greeted with no great enthusiasm; when a unit comprised of long service regulars is 'browned off', then the officers have trouble indeed.

Kasos, a tiny picture-postcard island, was the nearest of the Italian

Dodecanese group to Crete, and very close to Scarpanto; the latter was important because it had an air base. The plan was for the Commandos to seize and occupy Kasos. Afterwards the island would be properly garrisoned, fortified and equipped with artillery to fire on Scarpanto and its airfield. How all this activity could take place without alerting any enemy artillery response on Scarpanto does not seem to have been a consideration. The Kasos straits, the stretch of water between the two islands, was hostile – a popular route for Italian torpedo boats and submarines on passage from their bases into the Eastern Mediterranean.

The first requirement was for the Commandos to conduct a reconnaissance of Kasos and its beaches, since nothing was known about the island or the strength and deployment of its garrison.

A reconnaissance group sailed in HMS *Derby*, a venerable sloop with a sedate turn of speed. Improvisation was very much the name of the game. A couple of extra whalers were loaded on board, but there were no scrambling nets available.

The whalers were damaged when they were manhandled over the side, and both started to leak, so the operation was aborted. There did not appear to be any great sense of urgency and it was a month before HMS *Derby* sailed a second time. The sloop arrived off the island when the tides were wrong and there was nothing they could do but scuttle back to Crete.

Beach reconnaissance was a specialized affair which required proper equipment and trained frogmen. Such a unit was en route for the Middle East with Z Force, so it seemed more prudent to dispense with reconnaissance until the proper means were to hand.

The Kasos operation had been compromised, so Naval Intelligence now directed the attention of the Commandos to Castelorizzo, an island nestling very close to the Turkish mainland which today forms part of the Greek Magiste group. The Navy fancied Castelorizzo for its sheltered coves and a deep natural harbour; it appeared an ideal location for MTBs to lie in wait for enemy ships en route from the Aegean to the Mediterranean. Castelorizzo was also a useful stepping stone to Rhodes; it was much closer to Rhodes than to the nearest British troops on Cyprus: but it was a tiny island which the Italians could easily isolate and destroy. Its selection was another strange decision.

Secrecy was of paramount importance. On the night of 24 February 1941 the Commando embarked on board the destroyers *Hereward* and *Decoy*. The elderly gunboat *Ladybird* joined them to provide close inshore fire support.

Once the ships were at sea, the sealed orders detailing Operation *Abstention* were opened and the Commandos learned for the first time what their target was to be. It was a hare-brained scheme dreamed up by officers who had no conception of military geography and even less idea how best to use Special Forces.

In order to reach their objective, the task force had to sail through waters which were regularly used by Italy's submarines and light naval forces, and constantly patrolled by aircraft from Scarpanto and Rhodes including the first squadrons of the Junker 87 Stukas, advance party of a Luftwaffe deployment into the Eastern Mediterranean.

It was for this reason that Commander MacGregor in *Decoy* sailed west from Suda rather than east through the Kasos Strait. He was anxious to give the enemy patrols a wide berth, but this used up precious fuel.

Meanwhile the Commandos studied their orders and planned for the operation. In normal circumstances Lieutenant-Colonel Symons and his officers would have welcomed the time at sea as an opportunity to prepare more thoroughly for what lay ahead.

Not on this occasion: although the plan was clear enough. The Commandos were to land and secure the island, which they were then to hold for no longer than twenty-four hours. They would be relieved by a battalion of infantry sent from Cyprus to provide the new garrison. There was only a plan. Intelligence on the island amounted to a single Italian merchant marine chart and some pre-war picture postcards. Enemy strength, deployment and positions were totally unknown and not even Naval Intelligence was brazen enough to hazard a guess.

The submarine HMS *Parthian* had been sent ahead to act as a navigational beacon off Castelorizzo. The rendezvous was made, the destroyers anchored just 200 yards offshore. The first flight of whalers were away at 0300 hours on the morning of 25 February; they were late, and Commander MacGregor had no desire to be caught in these waters come the dawn.

The navigator in the lead whaler confused the bearings and, instead of landing on a beach, led the first wave into Paleocastro, the main harbour. By some stroke of great good fortune they were not spotted, and the boats returned to the destroyers – or at least some of them did. The Senior Naval Officer was all for abandoning the operation and clearing off, but a couple of the whalers were missing. There was a heated argument between Lieutenant-Colonel Symons, who was not about to abandon his men, and MacGregor who could not expose his destroyers to enemy air attack, which would surely happen if they were not under way very shortly.

The whalers eventually reappeared, but minus their soldiers; clearly a landing had actually taken place. The Navy was shamed into not abandoning those already ashore, and the landing was reinforced by the main party.

The first group ashore had ambushed an Italian patrol, which promptly scuttled back into their fort at Paleocastro locking the gate behind them. The Commandos joined forces and laid siege to the fort, which fell about ten o'clock that morning when *Ladybird* sailed into the harbour and opened up with her single six-pounder gun.

The enemy on Rhodes reacted strongly. Both the Luftwaffe and the Regia Aeronautica subjected the island to constant bombing and strafing attacks. Luckless *Ladybird* was singled out and, badly damaged by a succession of near misses, she departed the scene and limped off to Cyprus.

There were some casualties, but the Commandos survived the ordeal by bombing and, come nightfall, settled down to wait for their relief, which according to the timetable laid down in the plan was due before dawn.

It was probably for this reason – or maybe because they were asleep – that the Commando guard picquet failed at the dead of night to challenge the warships which sailed into the harbour. An Italian destroyer opened fire on the fort and in the confusion landed a small party of marines, who with great dash rescued their own people from prison. It was a perfectly executed operation and the marines were away before the Commandos had time to recover from their surprise.

Throughout the next day the now thoroughly shaken Commandos were subjected to constant air attack, the first British troops in the Middle East to suffer from the dreaded Stuka. For these professional soldiers who had years of peacetime service behind them it was an unnerving experience.

The relief force had been delayed.

The Commandos on Castelorizzo were expecting a battalion of infantry. In the event B Company from the 1st Battalion The Sherwood Foresters left Famagusta in the Armed Boarding Vessel *Rosaura* on the morning of 25 February to rendezvous with the 3rd Cruiser Squadron. The latter, under Rear Admiral E. de F. Renouf, was to provide escort to Castelorizzo.

It was a stormy passage and many soldiers were seasick. When the task force came in sight of Castelorizzo, HMS *Hereward* failed to make contact with the Commando ashore. Uncertain of the situation, the Admiral decided to postpone the landing for twenty-four hours. However, the destroyers were now short of fuel, so the whole force set sail for Alexandria, since there were no refuelling facilities at Famagusta. The soldiers were transferred from the *Rosaura* to *Hereward* and *Decoy* for the return journey to Castelorizzo.

Nobody had seen fit to communicate the change in plans to the

Commandos. It was not until the night of 27/28 February that the task force arrived.

After subjecting the British garrison to constant air attack, the Italians determined to recapture the island. While the defences were smothered in air strikes, two destroyers and a couple of gunboats sailed into the main harbour. A landing party was quickly put ashore and soon established a beachhead. The Commandos fought back, but with nothing heavier than a Bren light machine gun there was not very much they could do.

The Commandos abandoned Paleocastro and dug in along the beach and the high ground behind the town. Though low on ammunition and supplies, they clung on until nightfall.

It was now the Italians' turn to be outgunned, but the task force only had a company of infantry. The accompanying cruisers each had a contingent of Royal Marines, well trained as a landing party. At this juncture of the war, however, the Navy were beginning to appreciate the deficiencies in their anti-aircraft defences, and a Marine landing force would have taken time to organize, leaving the cruisers still offshore at daylight. Admiral Renouf decided to cut their losses and abandon the island.

Even the evacuation did not go smoothly and some of the Commandos who had been fighting in isolated pockets of resistance were abandoned in the naval haste to be clear by daylight. Sixty commandos were left behind despite the protests of Symons and his officers. Some of the soldiers attempted to swim the three miles to the Turkish mainland, but only a few survived to be later repatriated to the British authorities.

When Winston Churchill heard news of the disaster he was furious, and telegraphed Anthony Eden who was in Athens:

> How was it that enemy could be reinforced by sea observing we had supposed we had local command of the sea? What was the Naval and Military force which relieved and reinforced? Where did they come from; how did they get there?

Operation *Abstention* had been badly conceived and the Commandos were poorly served by the Royal Navy, who were all for a cover-up. Cunningham advised the Prime Minister that there should be no official communiqué and the word put around that it had been a highly successful raid.

Churchill refused to sanction such a whitewash. The disaster at Castelorizzo boded ill for the more ambitious operations being planned against Rhodes. At the time Laycock and Z Force was less than a week from the Suez Canal, on the final leg of the voyage around Africa.

In early March Churchill minuted Admiral Sir Dudley Pound, the First Sea Lord: 'What disciplinary or other measures are going to be taken upon this deplorable piece of mismanagement occurring after we have had already eighteen months experience of war?'

A Board of Inquiry was quickly convened, though it met in secret and its findings have never been published. Publicly and in characteristic fashion, Admiral Cunningham shouldered all the blame, for clearly the Navy had been at fault. Admiral Renouf was relieved of his command, although the Navy would insist that he was already a sick man.

Innuendo and gossip marked down 50 (Middle East) Commando as an inferior force found wanting in their first action, which was an unfair slur on a Commando which had performed well under difficult circumstances. Nevertheless, they returned to their barracks at Geneita under a cloud.

CHAPTER SIX

Layforce

The assault ships *Glenroy* and *Glengyle* docked on 7 March 1941 and the Commandos disembarked. It had been a voyage of ten weeks from the Clyde to Suez.

The Commandos were part of Z Force, which comprised some of Britain's new warrior élite. The 1,500 officers and men were all volunteers for hazardous service and trained to the peak of efficiency. They formed Numbers 7, 8 and 11 Commandos, and A Troop from Number 3 Commando. There was in addition another section especially trained as frogmen and canoeists; the latter, led by Captain Courtney, were intended for SOE-type operations.

The Commandos, some of whom were recruited from the Guards and Cavalry regiments, included more than a sprinkling of officers of noble lineage, around whom hovered the hangers-on – men with no precise role or military function to perform. The later included the Prime Minister's son, Randolph, who had some military liaison role but really collected tittle-tattle for his father, intrigued in the Mess and was largely held in derision by the others. There was also the younger son of Admiral Lord Beatty who, judging from his bizarre behaviour, should have been committed rather than allowed to don the King's uniform and be sent to a theatre of war.

Admiral Sir Walter Cowan, K.C.B., D.S.O. came along for the ride and to collect gossip for his friend and mentor Roger Keyes. Now seventy-four years of age, Cowan had commanded a river gunboat on the Nile during the Sudan campaign under Kitchener, whom he served under again during the Boer War. In 1902 he took over a flotilla of destroyers from Roger Keyes and they had been chums ever since.

Keyes thought that his first-hand knowledge of the Mediterranean would be invaluable to Laycock.

Churchill called the Commandos his 'Young Leopards' and had despatched them to the Middle East not as general reinforcements, but with a specific operation in mind – the capture of Italian-held Rhodes.

Whitehall believed that such a victory, besides causing alarm and despondency among the Italians, would bottle their fleet into the Aegean, and perhaps through its sheer audacity entice the Turks off the fence and into the war on Britain's side.

While the Commandos settled into the barracks at Geneita, their commander Colonel Robert Laycock hurried away to Headquarters Land Forces to receive his orders and be briefed on the general situation.

First came the good news. The units under his command were increased in number. Numbers 50 and 52 (Middle East) Commandos were to be amalgamated under Lieut-Colonel Young and to serve under Laycock. Young was able to select the best men from the two units, which for the most part were the regular elements of No. 50 Commando.

Then came the bad news. Z Force was redesignated *Layforce* and placed in the Middle East Strategic Reserve. In effect it became a light infantry brigade of the 6th Infantry division under the command of Major-General Evetts.

The strategic picture had changed drastically during the time that Laycock had been en route to the Middle East, and for the worse. The operation against Rhodes was cancelled. The fiasco at Castelorizzo had not helped, but it was the appearance of the Germans both in Bulgaria and in Tripolitania which was giving the cause for concern.

'Ultra' revealed to Wavell the arrival of General Rommel in Tripoli and the advance elements of the 5th Division. He knew too that the 15th Panzer Division was to follow. General O'Connor had been taken ill after the success of his first desert offensive, and was in hospital in Cairo. The units in the Western Desert beyond Benghazi were a scratch force, comprising a depleted tank brigade drawn from the inexperienced 2nd Armoured Division and a brigade of Australian Infantry. It was a calculated risk, but such forces were probably sufficient to counter a weak and demoralized Italian Army which had had most of the fight knocked out of its regiments, though German Panzers were something different. The 'Western Desert Force' was at present commanded by Lieut-General Philip Neame, who had been recommended by O'Connor. His Victoria Cross indicated a man of action and physical courage, but he possessed neither tactical flair nor imagination.

Wavell took a chance. He did not expect Rommel to attack until May at the earliest and it would – so his advisers assured him – take Rommel that long to assemble and acclimatize his Wehrmacht divisions, and to build up supply points along that long line of communications which stretched from Tripoli to the forward battle area.

Nobody thought to make any allowances for an enemy commander who would disobey the orders of his superior.

The Italians in East Africa were beaten and it now required time to mop up and secure their surrender, which would soon release more troops for action elsewhere. Wavell felt confident that the situation was in hand on the two fronts in Africa, and that he could now concentrate on the Balkans.

In the days before the war, and as early as April 1939, the British government had signed an agreement with Greece guaranteeing to come to her aid if her independence was threatened.

Ever since Mussolini had attacked in Albania in October 1939, the British had been anxious to send forces into Greece. Churchill's romantic notions were excited by the thought of rescuing the 'cradle of civilization' from the Fascist barbarians, Wavell also needed little persuasion. He did not regard the battles against the Italians in either East Africa or the Western Desert as being of any great consequence. What mattered was a second front against the main enemy, Germany, and the Balkans seemed at that time to afford the best opportunity.

The British offered and the Greeks accepted an Expeditionary Force. The first elements were the 1st Armoured Brigade group, the 6th Australian and 2nd New Zealand Divisions. A second group comprising the Polish Independent Brigade Group and the 7th Australian Division – both of whom were completing their training in Palestine – would join at a later date.

The assault ships *Glenroy* and *Glengyle* had barely sufficient time to complete unloading Laycock's Commandos before ANZACS began swarming aboard for the voyage to Greece.

Wavell was hopelessly over-committed and he had no intention of frittering away precious resources on raiding operations. Though still code-named *Layforce* the Commandos were 'de-specialized' and renamed as conventional infantry along the following lines:

> No. 7 Commando (Lieut-Col Colvin) became A Battalion
> No. 8 Commando (Lieut-Col Daly) became B Battalion
> No. 11 Commando (Lieut-Col Pidder) became C Battalion
> No. 50/52 ME Commando (Lieut-Col Young) became D Battalion

Their fall from the pedestal of Special Forces was far worse than it appeared at first sight, for the Commandos had become less than a conventional infantry battalion. The latter had firepower in terms of support weapons, mobility in its transport, and a B Echelon for supplies. The Commandos, organized as a light scale raiding force, had none of these.

The reorganization produced an immediate crisis of morale. When the British Commandos had originally formed in June, the troops had volunteered for six months detached special duty on the promise of active service. The time limit had now long since passed and special duty had disappeared. None of the troops had volunteered to leave their parent units in the United Kingdom to form a lettered battalion in the Middle East.

Laycock managed to quell the worst of the unrest with the expectation of special operations in the near future, once more trained soldiers had become available in the Middle East. Even he could not have expected action and the demand for a raid quite so quickly.

At the end of March, with the Wehrmacht's 5th Light Division diluted by Italian armour and lorried infantry to form battle groups, Rommel launched a surprise offensive. Neither Neame nor his troops proved a match for the Germans and the Allies fell back in disarray and confusion.

As Rommel's forces swept on, and Tobruk was besieged, it became clear that the British intended to retreat even from Palestine to establish their line of defence further north. The national command of the Hagannah decided in 1941 to establish nine companies of commando troops – Plugot Mahatz, known as Palmach – which would be a national reserve prepared for immediate action. These commandos were earmarked to protect the Jewish community by waging guerrilla war against the Arabs and the Germans.

Yitzhak Sadeh, a senior member of the Hagannah, was appointed first Commander of the Palmach. He personally chose his company commanders, who included Allon and Dyan, and they in turn began to hand-pick their recruits.

In desperation, Middle East HQ sanctioned a Commando raid. A battalion boarded HMS *Glengyle* and, with a destroyer escort, sailed west from Alexandria. The intention was to raid along the shore at Bardia, hit vital supply dumps and cause sufficient mayhem to force Rommel into diverting troops from the front to protect his vulnerable rear areas and supply points.

Glengyle made the landfall and on the night of 19/20 April the Commandos stormed ashore. The assault boats landed the raiders on the wrong beaches and thereafter the operation went from bad to worse. The specially identified targets existed only as figments of the imagination of the intelligence experts; they certainly were not to be found in the environs of Bardia, which was also devoid of enemy forces.

The Commandos blew up an old tyre dump and a bridge before re-embarking, but in their haste a troop of 67 men was left behind. Next morning they tamely surrendered to an Italian patrol which had been sent to investigate 'a disturbance' in Bardia.

Meanwhile the Germans had struck in the Balkans, and with a vengeance. Hitler was anxious to secure his southern flank, now made unstable by Mussolini, before unleashing his divisions on Russia. On Palm Sunday, 6 April, the Luftwaffe bombed Belgrade and Athens.

In Albania the Greeks surrendered to the SS Division Leibstandarte Adolf Hitler. Another army surrendered in Thrace. The British Expeditionary Forces had still not learned the answer to blitzkrieg, and as the rear-guard fell back through the pass at Thermopylae, Wavell sanctioned its evacuation.

The Navy played its part once more and dumped the Army on Crete.

With the Germans rampant on two widely separated fronts, Wavell was desperate for troops. In Egypt the 6th Infantry Division was dismembered for units to plug the gaps in the Balkans and the Desert, and in the process *Layforce* was scattered. A and D Battalions were kept as a fire brigade in strategic reserve and under Laycock's personal direction, while B Battalion was detached to the desert headquarters in Mersa Matruh, and C Battalion left for Cyprus where it was to reinforce the garrison.

On 29 May 1941 the Germans followed up their conquest of Greece with Operation *Merkur*, the invasion of Crete. The attack was spear-headed by Hitler's élite parachute division, Fallschirmjaeger, under General Student.

Within days Laycock was ordered by Wavell to take the two Com-mando battalions from the strategic reserve to Crete. Despite all the odds in their favour, the garrison had been outwitted and outfought by Student's Fallschirmjaeger and was in full retreat.

It was not a role for which the Commandos had ever been intended, but that of rear-guard was one which made the greatest demands on military skills and discipline.

They held the Germans at bay for five days. The Commandos joined a force of Royal Marines, New Zealand Maoris and some bloody-minded Australians who had had enough of being pushed back. Together they stood rear-guard over the evacuation of 16,500 men until it was their turn to make a dash for the last destroyer.

German casualties were staggering. One in every four of the Fallschirmjaeger were dead, and a third of the fighting men were casualties. Hitler was appalled at the losses suffered by such an élite, and would not sanction their use as an airborne force again.

It fell to Lieut-Colonel Young, a Commando battalion leader, to negotiate the surrender of the troops at Sphakin – 12,000 in all. His battalion, which had fought particularly well in the rear-guard action, was comprised largely of regular soldiers from the peacetime army. Their success was due to their professionalism and to Young's insistence on conventional infantry – rather than Special Forces – training, for the battalion.

There were those who refused to surrender. Some survived to tell the tale like the group of stragglers, including Commandos, who sailed an abandoned landing craft across the Mediterranean to freedom. They made a sail out of army blankets tied together with bootlaces, and after six days reached safety. Others slipped into the mountainous interior to join up with the guerrilla bands and continue the war. Precise numbers are unknown, but an assorted force of Greeks, British and ANZACS made it into the hills. Most were rounded up within a few weeks, but a substantial group fought on for years.

Was Crete worth all the sacrifice? At the time it appeared to be a strategic position of considerable value. The irony is that with its capture it ceased to have any importance, and made no further contribution of note to the Mediterranean War.

Perhaps its value lay in the spirited defence and the losses inflicted on Germany's élite airborne units. Had they survived intact, then the Germans would have given serious consideration to the capture of Malta.

CHAPTER SEVEN

Battle of the Litani River

At the outbreak of war the Army of the Levant was one of the most powerful elements in the French military establishment. After the Armistice it numbered about 30,000 men, a quarter of its original strength.

In London the Free French convinced Churchill that forces in the Levant would, in response to a reasonable show of strength, change sides. The Prime Minister was impressed, for the Levant (modern-day Lebanon and Syria) had been a cause for increasing concern in the War Cabinet. It did present an open flank and, if the Germans chose to force the issue, a new base of operations. With Crete gone and possibly Cyprus next, German air bases in Cyrenaica and in Syria would complete the ring around the British in Egypt and Palestine and render a major presence untenable.

There was already ample evidence to show that the Germans, operating from Syria, had sought to subvert and undermine the British position in Iraq.

Wavell, though alert to the threat, was not at all convinced by the Free French assessment of the situation in the French colony. In his opinion the French Army there comprised hard-core professionals solidly committed to Vichy. Their officers regarded de Gaulle and his supporters as a traitorous, dissident faction whose continued resistance to the official government simply blocked all prospects for France to sign an honourable and tolerable peace treaty with Berlin. The French commander in Damascus was Général Henri Dentz, described by Wavell's intelligence people as a tough soldier who buttressed his pro-Vichy patriotism with a stringent, personal Anglophobia.

Churchill was unimpressed by Wavell's response. For some time the Prime Minister had had doubts about his Commander-in-Chief; there had been too many defeats in the Middle East, and Wavell was also held to blame for failure in Greece and defeat in the Western Desert. Nevertheless the views of Wavell's intelligence staff were presented to the Free French in London, who promptly backed away from their original position. De Gaulle was prepared to admit that there could well be resistance in the Levant. However, this became less of a consideration now that the Prime Minister had directed his thoughts to the strategic significance of the region and its importance to the integrity of the British presence in Egypt and Palestine.

On 20 May, even as the Germans launched their attack on Crete, news reached London that the Luftwaffe had landed in Syria. Vichy 'neutrality' had been compromised. Churchill ordered Wavell to prepare an expeditionary force for Syria, and to take the field at the earliest possible moment. Initially the intention was to provoke a political coup and declare the province free and independent.* A declaration for the Free French could have a significant impact on Turkey and Spain, not to mention Vichy France itself. Accordingly a Free French force under General Catroux was to 'effect entry' while the British role was limited to logistics and air support.

The problem was that the Free French did not have the trained manpower available and, even if they had, were not willing to become embroiled in a civil war with brother members of the officer corps. None of this detracted from the strategic significance of the region, and so Churchill ordered Wavell to prepare a full military expedition.

Major General 'Jumbo' Wilson GOC (General Officer Commanding) Palestine and Transjordan, was given the task of preparing for the attack. Wavell ordered him to capture Beirut and Damascus.

At two o'clock on the morning of 8 June 1941, elements of the 7th Australian Division, a Brigade of the 4th Indian Division (which had been rushed back from Eritrea) and two regiments of the 1st Cavalry Division, including the Royal Scots Greys (who were still riding their horses into battle), together with a weak, token contingent of Free French, crossed into French territory.

This is a campaign where the place names and the battles fought are tragically familiar to us today as we witness Lebanon being torn apart nightly on our television screens.

One British column, a screening force, probed north into the Bekaa

---

* Legally the status of the French in the Levant was similar to that of Britain in Palestine – it was a mandated territory held through the League of Nations. Lebanon was a French creation and device.

Valley along the road to Damascus. The main force attacked up the coast by way of Tyre and Sidon towards Beirut. The Israelis were to follow the same route in their blitzkrieg of June 1982 and indeed to encounter many similar problems. Militarily, however, the solutions they employed were markedly different and infinitely more successful.

A major obstacle was the Litani River, which runs east-west along the narrow gorge just to the north of Tyre. In June 1982 the Israelis made bold use of their special forces in a series of amphibious loops to turn the coastal flank and in seven days take their armoured spearhead to the outer suburbs of Beirut.

In June 1941 the British Army called on C Battalion of *Layforce* as their amphibious answer, the one Special Force capable of overcoming the obstacles created by military geography in the region.

It is here, at the conceptual stage, that any comparison between the campaigns ends.

This Commando had spent its time in the Middle East as garrison troops in Cyprus. The battalion had come in for no more that its fair share of fatigues, drills and chores as is the way of any garrison force, but these had been enough to blunt their fighting edge. Morale was poor under Lieut-Colonel Pidder, their feared and much hated Commanding Officer.

There had already been a scandal when a Commando subaltern, Paddy Mayne – a well-known Irish Rugby Union International player – was placed under close arrest for punching Pidder. Mayne was a big man, and more than the CO's dignity was hurt in the fray.

The Commandos were brought from Cyprus to Port Said, where they joined the assault ship HMS *Glengyle*, only just released from evacuation duties between Greece and Crete. Pidder was ordered to land on the beaches to the north of the Litani's estuary. The Commando's task was to seize a beachhead and a bridge inland which spanned the gorge at Kafa Bada; they were to hold that ground until relieved by the forward elements of the 25th Australian Infantry Brigade.

The landing was scheduled for the night of 7/8 June to coincide with the main advance of the Expeditionary Force into French territory. Intelligence sources reported the position around the vital bridge across the Litani to be weakly held by a small French garrison.

There was a bright full moon and a cloudless Mediterranean sky. It was more day than night as *Glengyle* with her escorting destroyers *Ibex* and *Hotspur* closed on the estuary of the Litani.

The task force was quickly spotted and engaged by a coast artillery battery and the operation compromised from the outset.

Pidder might have lost the element of surprise, but he was determined to press ahead with the landing. There were 27 officers and 456 soldiers in the Commando and, as they began to board the assault craft, a small motor-boat buzzed off the beach for a closer reconnaissance. The currents were treacherous off this part of the coast and the *Glengyle*'s Captain had wisely brought along an officer who was familiar with the area. Lieutenant F. H. Colenut, RNVR, had been a policeman in Palestine before the war and was a keen amateur yachtsman. He had a detailed knowledge of these waters.

Colenut returned from his reconnaissance to report that there was considerable surf running and it was too dangerous for the operation to proceed. Pidder remonstrated with the Captain of *Glengyle*, arguing that the possible swamping of a couple of landing craft would be a small price to pay in return for getting his Commandos ashore and on to their objective before the French could react properly. The *Glengyle*'s Captain was not prepared to put the operation at risk, especially if it meant flying in the face of local advice. The force stood out to sea and then returned to Port Said; they would try again the following night.

The enforced 24-hour delay had not compromised the timetable for the battle on land. From the outset the Vichy French had defended fiercely; they were well supplied, dug in and led by competent officers. A successful counter attack by Vichy tanks at Kuneitra had caught everybody by surprise. Within the first hours of the operation it became apparent that nobody was going far very quickly, and the Australians were a long way short of the Litani River.

The second evening the Commandos returned as planned. Fresh intelligence had reported that the defenders had blown up the bridge at Kafa Bada and retreated behind the Litani; Pidder redeployed his command in light of this new information. The objective now was to secure a bridgehead on the northern bank of the Litani in sufficient depth to allow engineers to bridge the river unmolested by enemy fire. The Commando would then land in three detachments on the north side of the estuary, strike inland and take the French defences from their right flank and rear.

The landing came just before dawn, when for some unaccountable reason the French appeared unprepared for the assault. The Commandos came ashore with the setting moon behind them and a rising sun ahead. On the left flank Captain George More led his group to attack the artillery battery covering the Litani River. Colonel Pidder led the main group in the centre, his objective being to capture the French headquarters in a redoubt, a little 'Beau Geste' style fort, and its adjacent barracks.

Major Geoffrey Keyes, the Commando second-in-command, was to come in on the right flank with a reserve ready to lend support to either of the two attacking groups. The only problem was that the

Navy had not been told of the change of plan, and Keyes left the navigation to the RNVR officer in charge. His Commando stepped ashore on the south side of the Litani's estuary. Even Keyes did not realize the mistake until he moved inland, only to spot the masts of some fishing craft on his left when they should have been on his right.

The French garrison was much stronger than the Commandos had been led to believe. Comprising elements of the 22nd Tirailleurs, a colonial infantry regiment recruited in Africa with good French officers and NCOs, they were soon putting up a stout resistance.

More led his detachment at a rush and their impetus carried them into the battery before the gunners could respond. Surrendered enemy outnumbered More's Commandos and in the midst of disarming the enemy and consolidating the position, the French counter-attacked with armoured cars.

The fighting was heavy and confused.

At Kafa Bada, Pidder found that the bridge had not been destroyed. Having led his men forward in a charge to capture the redoubt and secure the bridge before the French could blow it up, he sent back a runner to find Keyes and bring up reinforcements.

Pidder led his group at a headlong charge and into a hail of well-directed fire. The Colonel was the first to fall, shot through the head, and soon all the officers were killed or wounded. The Sergeant-Major quickly assumed command and led the survivors into a deserted barracks where they prepared to hold their ground until relief arrived.

Keyes led his detachment northwards to the river bank and the sounds of gunfire, where they linked up with the scouting patrol of Australians; the latter had found a couple of small boats which Keyes commandeered as ferries. While the Australians kept up a covering fire, Keyes managed to get himself, another officer and 14 men across; the intention was to rush the bridge from both banks of the river. Once Keyes was across the Australians made a run for the bridge, and were within fifteen yards when the French blew it up in their faces.

The Commandos were now isolated on the far bank of the Litani and engaged by an enemy force far superior in numbers and firepower. Keyes reached the barracks and assumed command of the main party from the stalwart Sergeant-Major.

Captain More's group had become fragmented and isolated. The French gathered their forces and, in a series of carefully coordinated attacks, drove More further back. The battle raged throughout the day. Towards evening some of More's Commandos were able to swim across the Litani to reach the Australian lines, but the remainder were pushed back to the beach and there, with ammunition all but exhausted and no hope of relief, More surrendered.

The Australians quickly organized their own forces to effect a rescue of the Commandos. Once night had fallen, sappers started to build a temporary bridge across the river, while Keyes kept the redoubt under fire to distract the French.

By morning the sappers had completed their task and the Australians crossed over to the far bank to join up with Keyes and the survivors. The French commandant realized that further resistance was futile, freed his prisoners and then formally surrendered his garrison to a bemused Captain More.

The Litani River had been a costly action for the Commandos. A quarter of their number, 123 men, had been killed or wounded and they had little to show for such a sacrifice. The speed with which the Australians had bridged the Litani raises the question as to whether the landing operation was necessary in the first place.

Keyes assumed command and took the Commando back to Cyprus.

The offensive against the Vichy French was to drag on into a thoroughly nasty and bad-tempered campaign. There were frequent violations of both the Red Cross and the White Flag, while the Vichy French treated Allied prisoners abominably. Additional Allied troops had to be sent in to join the battle, and these included a unit of Palestinian Palmach. One of their officers was Captain Moshe Dyan, who lost an eye during the campaign.

CHAPTER EIGHT

Post Mortems

In May 1941 the future looked bleak for Commandos in the Middle East. After two months *Layforce* had suffered 800 casualties and all the 'battalions' were in need of reinforcements. The trouble was that there were few men to be spared in the Middle East, where High Command was in no mood to allow Laycock to sift through those who were available to find those of the right calibre.

Wavell had decided that the Commandos should be disbanded and the reasoning was sound enough. The Mediterranean, or at least the important areas, now belonged to the Luftwaffe, and the Royal Navy sailed into those dangerous waters at its peril. The Navy had suffered heavily too and had no ships to spare for Commando raids.

There were many others who favoured an immediate and total disbanding of the force. Brigadier Dudley Clarke, the officer who created the concept of the Commandos and gave them their name, served on Wavell's staff, in charge of deception plans. Less than six months earlier he had resigned his appointment at the War Office, where he was in charge of raiding.* Whatever his personal views, Dudley Clarke had no intention of entering the firing line for a second time, and made no attempt to defend the Commandos.

The disaster at Castelorizzo still caused vibrations in the theatre and provided extra ammunition to those who opposed the Commando concept. Many of the Commando officers could see the writing on the wall and began to look for alternative employment.

---

*Eric Morris, *Churchill's Private Armies: British Special Forces in Europe 1939–42*, Vol I, p. 142 (Century Hutchinson, London, 1986).

Randolph Churchill, on the staff of Z Force, had joined the General Staff of Middle East Headquarters in the Department of Information and Propaganda. In June he received a letter from his father:

> I sent you out an enquiry about the 60 men [i.e. those who had surrendered at Castelorizzo] because I heard a great deal of criticism here about those special troops surrendering in droves, and so on, and whatever other people may think, I am quite clear that these men ought to have fought till at least 30% were killed or wounded. Large general capitulations are of a different character, but small parties are expected to put up a fight and not walk out of a cave with their hands up like a lot of ridiculous loons.*

The Prime Minister raised here an interesting point of military ethics. The Commandos left behind on Castelorizzo had been abandoned to their fate by an admiral who had at his disposal more than sufficient forces to take that miserable little piece of Italian real estate. There was nowhere for them to hide and further resistance was futile. Military honour, according to the Prime Minister, would have meant that a third of them should be casualties before surrender became the decent option.

Other members of *Layforce* were looking to the failure in a more positive fashion. A Scots Guards' lieutenant called David Stirling, of 8 Commando, was convinced of the need to conduct a different kind of raid. He believed the answer lay in smaller forces than the Commandos, who needed valuable assets like the assault ships before they could function properly. Stirling advocated using trained parachutists as raiders who could then be lifted out by the Long Range Desert Group.

Fifty parachutes en route to India 'fell off the back of a ship' which had docked in Alexandria and Laycock gave Stirling permission to put his theory into practice. Stirling recruited three more men from the Commando and persuaded the Royal Air Force to put an ancient Valentia transport at their disposal. It had no proper facilities, so Stirling rigged up the static lines for the parachutes by anchoring them to the seats inside the plane. The official parachute training school was still in its infancy and based at Ringwood outside Manchester; there were no parachute instructors in the Middle East.

The Valentia is not designed for parachuting and the risks are obviously much greater if the static lines are rigged incorrectly. The inevitable happened on a dummy run when Stirling's 'chute snagged the tail plane and rents were torn in the canopy. The Scotsman was 6

---

*Martin Gilbert, *Finest Hour*, (Heinemann, London, 1983).

feet 5 inches tall and at 16 stone exceeded what most regarded as the safety limit for parachuting in those early days. He hit the ground at a terrible speed and jarred his back so severely that he was paralysed. It was to take two painful months in hospital before Stirling would be up on his feet again.

In mid-June Wavell ordered that *Layforce* should be disbanded. For men at the depot the order had immediate effect and those with regiments serving in the Middle East left to join them. Others were sent off as reinforcement drafts.

No 51 Commando was still fighting in the East Africa Campaign and never come under *Layforce*. Two other 'battalions' were on active service; there was the remains of C Battalion which had returned to Cyprus under Geoffrey Keyes, and there was B Battalion in Mersa Matruh.

One group of Commandos who had survived Crete elected not to return to their parent units. Instead they went under Captain Jocelyn Nicholls – their senior officer after Crete – to form Mission 204, a new force being established to assist the Chinese in guerrilla warfare.

It is a moot point whether Wavell had the authority to disband the Commandos, for they had originally been raised in England. He must have known that it would win him no popularity awards at home, since the Commandos had been inspired by Churchill. Laycock objected, and Wavell allowed him to travel home to plead his case. Historians cite this as an example of Wavell's fair-mindedness and sense of honour; alternatively, he may not have had the time or inclination to lock horns with the War Office. Laycock could go home and London could sort out the future.

Wavell had more important issues with which to contend, not least a crumbling theatre of operations in the Mediterranean and Rommel rampant in the Western Desert and laying siege to Tobruk. In the face of these crises there might not have been any long-term future for the Commandos, but in the short term the Commander-in-Chief still had need of their services as a fire brigade in the strategic reserve.

Earlier in the year, Winston Churchill had gone against Cabinet advice and the received wisdom of the military establishment to denude the Home Defences of every spare tank and fighter aircraft. The Tiger Convoy, five fast transports, sailed from England and carried these – the Prime Minister's 'Tiger Cubs' – through the Mediterranean and direct to Alexandria. It was a brave decision on the part of the Prime Minister. Even though the threat of invasion had receded with the autumn, Coventry had just been virtually destroyed by the Luftwaffe. Britain to all intents and purposes was still an island under siege.

In early May, four of the transports arrived in Alexandria with 300 new tanks and 50 Hurricanes. Churchill lost no time in pressing Wavell for immediate action in destroying Rommel and relieving Tobruk.

It was warfare in the classic sense. Tobruk was a fortress which lay astride the enemy's main lines of communication between the front and the supply bases to the rear. On two occasions Rommel attempted to storm the fortress. His failure revealed for the first time the tactical shortcomings in blitzkrieg. Under the vigorous direction of the Australian Commander, General Leslie Morshead, the mixed remnants of British and Indian formations – together with the Australians Rommel had ousted from Benghazi – renovated the old Italian defences and dug in for a long siege.

The British High Command, from the Prime Minister down, took a long time to appreciate the true strength of the German Army. They simply looked at figures and numbers and in the process failed to take account of qualitative factors. The strength of the Wehrmacht lay in its Panzer divisions, and what the Allies could not grasp was that the independent all-arms battle groups which comprised such a division made it so much better, more powerful and more mobile than the equivalent British Armoured Division.

British tactics in armoured warfare were tragically inferior to those of the enemy. In 1941 British armour roamed the battlefield in concentrated tank brigades, like massed heavy cavalry, looking for the Panzers. They lived for the decisive encounter, the clash of arms between hussars and dragoon guards. The Germans, however, had no such regimental hang-ups, neither did they believe it was the task of their Panzers to do battle with British tanks. In the Panzer Corps, and especially in a side-show like North Africa where resources had to be husbanded, it was the job of artillery to take on the enemy tanks, leaving their own armour free to smash the enemy infantry and clear the battlefield.

Wavell prepared a new offensive to relieve Tobruk. While the newly equipped armoured brigades advanced westwards, the plan was for the garrison in Tobruk to divert German strength away from the main battle front by raiding the lines of communication.

A detachment of five officers, including Lord Jellicoe – at the time a lowly second-lieutenant – and 75 men from B Battalion of *Layforce*, which had hitherto been waiting for the call at the Desert HQ in Mersa Matruh, were dispatched to Tobruk.

Upon arrival officers were taken to meet Captain Haselden. The latter was an Arab speaker and another Lawrence-like figure from G(R) Branch of the Middle East Land Forces, given to wandering behind the enemy lines on intelligence missions dressed in Arab costume.

Haselden had arranged for some Arab guides to lead small groups of Commandos through the enemy defences across the desert and on to the airfields at Gazala. The plan was for the Commandos to sabotage aircraft and installations in a series of short sharp raids which coincided with Wavell's offensive.

The Arab guides were not much help. They claimed that the enemy had thrown a 'ring of steel' around the perimeter of Tobruk and there was no way through the positions. The operation was cancelled and Haselden slipped quietly away into the desert; we will meet Haselden again. The Commando prepared to join a larger raiding force which was to make a sortie out of Tobruk as Wavell's offensive to relieve the garrison, codenamed Operation *Battleaxe*, drew near, obliging Rommel to reduce the besiegers so as to stem the new threat.

The offensive began on 15 June and three days later, his armour squandered, Wavell called off the operation. The beleaguered garrison in Tobruk was locked up more tightly than ever.

General Morshead was determined to maintain an aggressive defence. He instigated a policy of fighting patrols and raiding parties, so as to dominate the no-man's land and sustain morale. He retained the Commandos, who over time became expert trench raiders.

Such operations obviously had a tactical influence, but were also within the skills of any reasonably trained infantry battalion.

CHAPTER NINE

Nemesis

The Prime Minister could not forgive Wavell's failure to stop Rommel whose success he was convinced had undermined his Greek strategy and 'all their glittering prizes in what was for us the supreme sphere of the Balkan War'.*

On 2 July 1941 Churchill appointed General Claude Auchinleck to take command in the Middle East. From the outset the Prime Minister had his doubts about this gaunt, taciturn Indian Army Officer. He had not been impressed when Auchinleck had commanded in Norway† but the speed of his response to the crisis in Iraq when reinforcements had been dispatched was impressive. Auchinleck was Commander-in-Chief in India, and as Wavell was too well known to simply be discarded, it seemed the most sensible solution was to allow these officers to exchange appointments.

Shortly afterwards Churchill also let his views be known over the future of the Commandos in the Middle East. They had not performed in any spectacular fashion, but then those operating from the United Kingdom had rapidly become a wasting asset. There was one successful large scale raid against German installations in the Lofoten Islands in March, and precious little else to justify their existence. Admiral Sir Roger Keyes, as the Director of Combined Operations,

---

*Winston Churchill, *History of the Second World War*, Vol. III, p. 318 (Cassell, London 1957)

† Eric Morris, *Churchill's Private Armies: British Special Forces in Europe 1939–42*, pp. 171/172 (Century Hutchinson, London, 1986).

had been brought out of retirement by his friend the Prime Minister to breathe fire into the war effort through the use of Special Forces. There had been too many failures, and too little action. In comparison with those Commandos at home, the Middle Eastern units had been positively overworked, although constantly misused and mis-employed.

Most if not all of the Prime Minister's closest military advisers, led by the much respected General Sir Alan Brooke, were opposed to the concept of the Commandos and vitriolic in their opposition to Roger Keyes. Nevertheless, Churchill was still convinced that there was a need for such Special Forces and on 23 July minuted General Ismay who was secretary to the Chiefs of Staff Committee:

> I wish the Commandos in the Middle East to be reconstituted as soon as possible. Instead of being governed by a committee of officers without much authority, Brigadier Laycock should be appointed Director of Combined Operations DCO (in the theatre). The three *Glen* Ships and the DCO with his forces should be placed directly under Admiral Cunningham who should be charged with all combined operations involving sea transport and not exceeding one brigade. The Middle East Command have indeed maltreated and thrown away this valuable force.*

The Chiefs of Staff signalled the Prime Minister's missive to Middle East Headquarters, where it created immediate consternation, if not a furore. It was not his condemnation of the HQ which touched a raw nerve, rather the decision that Commandos should be a naval responsibility. The Commandos were the object of much criticism by the Regular Army, but they were *Army* and any thought of their coming under the jurisdiction of another service was quite unacceptable.

In all fairness, much of the internecine battle of memos which now erupted between the Army and Navy passed Auchinleck and the higher echelons by, for they had weightier matters with which to contend. Churchill had discussed the Commandos with Auchinleck in England before the latter took up his appointment, and the general promised to give the matter consideration.

It was perhaps the Prime Minister's concern with special forces which prompted Auchinleck to take a break from the problem of dealing with Rommel and to read a remarkable memorandum; its author was Lieutenant David Stirling.

Stirling had spent the time in hospital putting on paper his thoughts

---

*Winston Churchill, *History of the Second World War*, Vol III, p. 721 (Cassell, London, 1957).

on the role of a special raiding group in the Middle East. He was convinced of the need to conduct small-scale raiding operations. This required a new force, smaller than a Commando and, despite his own personal accident, parachute-trained.

On crutches, Stirling discharged himself and went to deliver the memo personally. He knew that if it was submitted through the 'normal channels' it would probably disappear under a mound of paper generated in Middle East Headquarters.

Stirling's escapade in breaching the security around the HQ has been variously described over the years. The more authoritative accounts recount how he failed to bluff his way past the sentry on the main gate, and stumped around to the rear of the complex. Here he dumped his crutches, hauled himself painfully up and over the high chain-link perimeter fence and found a way into the main building. He was under no illusions that he could reach the Commander-in-Chief, but what he needed was an officer who had direct access to the General.

By this time security were aware of his intrusion and the hue and cry had been raised. After a couple of false starts, Stirling hobbled into an office marked DCGS, lurched up to the desk, saluted Lieutenant-General Sir Neil Ritchie, the deputy Commander-in-Chief, and said, 'I think you'd better look at this, sir.'

Ritchie scanned the memo and arranged for Stirling to return in a few days for a full conference. When Stirling explained his painful predicament, a smiling Ritchie arranged for the security personnel to retrieve his crutches and escort the young officer from the building.

The memo which Stirling wrote so laboriously in pencil has been lost. It was probably burnt the following year when it looked as if Rommel was about to reach Cairo, and Middle East HQ were under orders to decamp into Palestine.

Stirling subsequently produced the gist of his report for Philip Warner's masterful official history of the SAS:

(a) The enemy was exceedingly vulnerable to attack along the line of his coastal communications and on his various transport parks, aerodromes and other targets strung out along the coast. The rôle of No. 8 Commando which had attempted raids on these targets was a most valuable one.

(b) The scale on which the Commando raids had been planned, that is the number of bodies employed on the one hand and the scale of equipment and facilities on the other, prejudiced surprise beyond all possible compensatory advantage in respect of the defensive and aggressive striking power. Moreover the facilities that the Navy had to provide to lift the Force resulted in risking valuable Naval units valuable out of all proportion to the maximum possible success of the raid.

(c) There were considerable possibilities in establishing a unit which would combine minimum manpower demands with maximum possibilities of surprise. Five men could cover a target previously requiring four troops of a Commando – about 200 men. He sought to prove that, if an aerodrome or transport park was the objective of an operation, then the destruction of 50 aircraft or units of transport was more easily accomplished by a sub-unit of five than by a force of 200. Two hundred properly selected, trained and equipped men, organized into sub-units of five, should be able to attack at least thirty different objectives on the same night compared to only one objective using the Commando technique. Only a 25% success in the former was the equivalent of many times the maximum possible result in the latter.

A unit operating on these principles would have to be trained to be capable of arriving on the scene of the operation by every practical method, by land, sea or air. If in any particular operation a sub-unit was to be dropped by parachute, training must be such as to enable it to be dropped from any type of aircraft conveniently available without any modifications; if by sea, then the sub-unit must be transported either by submarine or caiques and trained in the use of folboats; if by land then it must be trained either to infiltrate on foot or be carried by the Long Range Desert Group.

(d) The unit must be responsible for its own training and operational planning and therefore the Commander of the unit must come directly under the C-in-C.*

Stirling returned to Middle East Headquarters a few days later, and at the appointed hour was ushered in to the Commander-in-Chief's presence. General Ritchie was there and so was Brigadier Dudley Clarke.

Auchinleck gave Stirling permission to recruit a dozen officers and 60 soldiers from the remnants of *Layforce* and train them for an imminent operation; he intended to launch a major offensive in November, and Stirling's unit was to parachute behind enemy lines and knock out enemy aircraft on the eve of the battle.

Dudley Clarke had created an organization called the Special Air Service Brigade. It did not in reality exist, but was intended to confuse the enemy into believing in such a force and into wasting their time and resources seeking its purpose. The credibility of such a deception

---

*Philip Warner, *The SAS: The Official History*, pp. 15/16 (William Kimber/Sphere Books, London, 1983).

would be enhanced if there were actually 'men of the ground'! Stirling's unit became 'L' Detachment of the Special Air Service Brigade, and so a regiment and a legend was born.

Auchinleck accepted the last paragraph in Stirling's memo without hesitation. L Detachment came directly under his command and answered directly to his authority; there was to be no repetition of the rule by committee and misuse of specially trained manpower.

David Stirling was promoted to Captain and put in command of the detachment. Their training base was established out at Kabrit, a small village on the edge of the Great Bitter Lake and about 100 miles from Cairo. Stirling might enjoy the patronage of the C-in-C, but this did not make life any easier for him. Stores and supplies were exceedingly difficult to come by, and the first recruits had to rely on initiative and ingenuity as much as anything in the early days.

In true Commando fashion, Stirling first selected his officers and the senior NCOs. Jock Lewes was plucked out of Tobruk where he was serving with the Commando; Stirling liked him for his technical skills and ability as a trainer. Lieutenant Blair (Paddy) Mayne was to prove an inspired but at the time controversial choice, since he was still under arrest for striking his Commanding Officer.

It was team work and in particular those two men that 'formed the most powerful combination of courage, endurance, barefaced impertinence, initiative and leadership that I have ever known, and their combined personalities were almost terrifying in their effect.'*

---

*Virginia Cowles, *The Phantom Major* (Collins, London, 1962)

PART TWO

THE BENGHAZI
STAKES

CHAPTER TEN

Assassins

Auchinleck decided to attack in November, and nothing this time was to be left to chance. There were now vastly superior forces available, enough indeed to create an army. The British Eighth Army, destined to become the most famous of them all, began life at this time with two corps. Auchinleck packed 500 of his tanks into an armoured phalanx called XXX Corps. That left a single tank brigade which together with the bulk of the infantry comprised XIII Corps.

It was a most unsound military deployment, and singularly ill-suited to match Rommel's formations.

Lieutenant-General Sir Alan Cunningham, fresh from his success in East Africa and the defeat of the Duke of Aosta, was brought to Egypt to command the Eighth Army.

There was a role for Special Forces too in the forthcoming offensive. The Long Range Desert Group were required to despatch six patrols behind the enemy lines. Their function was that of reconnaissance and ferry service and they were instructed not to risk their vehicles or engage in battle unless it was unavoidable. The patrols were to monitor the movements of enemy vehicles, supplies and reinforcements from their rear bases to the front lines. These road watches were tedious but nonetheless dangerous affairs, with men watching tracks and monitoring the traffic before signalling their day's findings back to base.

The Road Watch which the LRDG sustained throughout the North Africa Campaign, was for a long while accepted as one of the major contributions to Allied Intelligence, and thereby assessments of enemy strength and likely intentions. We now know that 'Ultra' was the primary source of such information, against which the contribution made by LRDG must be measured.

Since October the LRDG had established two forward bases, one at Kuffra oasis and the second at Siwa, some 200 miles inland from the coast at Sollum.

There were two further operations planned which had strategic objectives. One can only be described as bizarre in content and execution, and, although the second was relatively straightforward, both were to end in failure and heavy loss of life.

It all began earlier in October when in a series of meetings Auchinleck examined the Special Forces that were available in the Middle East. The general carried out a thorough review of the forces and their possible employments, and finally set them upon what his staff assured him would be a more sound footing. It was all to be based on a clear chain of command.

There was a mixed bag of forces around the theatre:

L Detachment SAS
No 51 (Middle East) Commando, due to return from East Africa
The remnants of Layforce
Special Boat Section – Courtney's group which had come out with
Layforce and had since been effective in clandestine operations using submarines based in Alexandria.

The new organization was called the Middle East Commando and Laycock was placed in overall command. The Commando was structured as follows:

Headquarters and Depot Troop (at Geneifa)
No. 2 Troop (originally L detachment SAS)
No. 3 Troop. This was built around C Battalion and comprised 60 all ranks under Lieut-Colonel Geoffrey Keyes.
No. 4 Troop ⎱
No. 5 Troop ⎰ Largely Palestinians from 51 Cdo (when they arrived).
No. 6 Troop (Courtney and SBS).

The new force and its structure looked good on paper and in communiqué with London; it also offered a reprieve for at least part of 51 Commando. However it is hard to imagine that any of its troop commanders or their men took it seriously or believed that it offered a permanent solution. The troops had such widely different operational roles that there could be no sense of cohesion or 'regimental spirit'. Stirling was a captain with 66 men under command, equal as a troop leader to Keyes who was a lieutenant-colonel with 60 men. Stirling had lost that vital feature of access to the Commander-in-Chief and in his view the new structure was wide open to abuse.

For his part, Keyes had so little faith in or sense of identity with the new regiment that he insisted on referring to his unit as No. 11 Commando. The Prime Minister had dismissed his father, Admiral Sir Roger Keyes V.C. from his appointment in overall command of the Special Forces, but nobody thought to curb the independence of his headstrong son.

OPERATION FLIPPER

Keyes assembled five officers and fifty-three men from '11 Commando' for a raid deep behind enemy lines. If it succeeded, it would have the most profound influence on the forthcoming offensive.

The overall objective was to cause paralysis in the enemy high command through the physical removal of Rommel. Historians have tended to tread softly around the incident largely because the operation was so 'un-British' in character, and perhaps too because the Western Desert has gained a reputation over the years as the 'clean arena of battle' with Rommel portrayed as the honourable warrior. Much of this of course is pure cant, particularly in the modern world where military commanders in NATO live with the knowledge that in the event of hostilities they are the personal targets of Soviet Special Forces and KGB assassination squads.

The truth is that British generals in their headquarters and in the field had become so awed by Rommel that they would have welcomed any means which resulted in his removal from North Africa.

The raiding party planned to sail from Alexandria in the submarines *Torbay* and *Talisman* to a point off the coast of the Jebel Akhdar, some 20 miles from Appollonia. The intention was that they should come ashore in canoes or folboats and rendezvous with Captain Jock Haselden and his Arabs who were to act as guides. Haselden was a cotton broker from Miniah in Upper Egypt who had made several trips into the Jebel. The son of an English father and a Greek mother, with his rather swarthy countenance he came nearest of those Englishmen who attempted to pass themselves off as Arabs. But even though Haselden was more successful than others, the quality of the intelligence he gathered was poor – it was haphazard, fragmentary and frequently out of date.

The Commandos were divided into four raiding groups. Italian Headquarters and its communications at Cyrene was assigned to one task force, while a second was to attack the Army Intelligence Centre in Appollonia itself. The third group was to hit German communications at El Faida and the fourth was assigned the German Headquarters at Beda Littoria, and in particular Rommel's HQ at a villa to the west of the village.

It is the last of these missions which is the most intriguing. Was the aim kidnap or assassination? It is hard to imagine how the Commander-in-Chief of the Afrika Korps could have been spirited away from his own Headquarters and taken twenty miles across country to a coastal rendezvous with a submarine.

Colonel Robert Laycock accompanied the raiding party, and his presence provides a vital clue. Accounts of the operation have described his presence as an observer who unfortunately found himself marooned on shore. This smoke-screen hides the fact that this was a raiding party which was less than half the equivalent infantry company, normally a captain's appointment; yet it included a lieutenant-colonel and a colonel in its number.

It is my contention that Laycock was there to sanction a killing.

In this Boy Scout scheme little account seems to have been taken of Rommel's Begleitkommando, a select combat force of about 100 men who provided a permanent Escort Group. This company formed part of Rommel's own Kampstaffel or Combat Group; they numbered about 500 men in total, all hand-picked and thoroughly professional.

However, the British planned that, if by the time they got to the beach (where submarines would be waiting) the hue and cry was upon them, then Rommel would die. Keyes was a lieutenant-colonel, but just twenty-four years of age, and the decision called for a man of mature years. Laycock was there to relieve Keyes of that responsibility.

On the evening of 10 November, HMS *Torbay* and *Talisman* slipped out from Alexandria. The Commandos were in high spirits as the submarines submerged for the voyage westwards into hostile waters.

On the night of 14 November the submarines surfaced and moved towards the shore. The weather had deteriorated and it was now blowing a gale, but Haselden's signal was spotted and the party prepared to disembark. Wiser heads would have postponed the landing, for the weather was appalling, but the Commandos attempted to board their canoes. Even in a calm sea it was always difficult to launch canoes from the slippery casement of a submarine, but in a howling gale and by men who had not practised the manoeuvre beforehand it was a shambles.

Keyes had allowed a maximum of forty minutes for the raiders to disembark. It took ten hours. At one stage HMS *Talisman* came in close to search for more sheltered waters, only to run aground momentarily on a reef. Men and canoes were washed overboard as the submarine keeled over with the force of the swell.

At daylight when the submarines dared linger no longer on the surface. Keyes and Laycock had 26 members of the party on shore. Men and equipment had been lost and the few supplies landed were in a sorry condition. Haselden, who had been infiltrated into the area by the LRDG, told Laycock the latest gossip he had gleaned from his Senussi scouts. Rommel and his senior staff, he now assured them, lived in a house at Sidi Rafa and not at Beda Littoria.

Laycock decided to concentrate on just two objectives; a telephone exchange at Cyrene, part of the Italian Army's communications centre, and Rommel's villa at Sidi Rafa. Haselden agreed to help by cutting communications on the El Fridia Slonta Road and thereby causing a diversion.

Keyes took Captain Campbell, who was fluent in German, and 17 men to attack Rommel. The remainder, under Lieutenant Cork, were to hit the telephone exchange. Laycock decided he would remain at the rendezvous in case the submarines returned the next night and attempted to land the remainder of the party.

It had originally been intended that the raiders would march at night and hide during daylight, but they had already lost time and Laycock was anxious to coordinate the attacks with the opening of Auchinleck's offensive. Keyes and the two raiding parties set out the following evening in torrential rain to cover the 20 miles to their objectives, and despite the appalling weather they found the villa without too much difficulty. Keyes conducted his own reconnaissance for they knew nothing about the building, its geography or the layout of the rooms. It was a large two-storey colonial villa with a courtyard and outbuildings surrounded by a high wall.

Keyes took Captain Campbell and Sergeant Terry with him, deploying the remainder of the party as a blocking group to prevent the enemy from interfering with reinforcements. The German guards appeared to be alert, so the only way in was by bluff.

They hammered on the door and Captain Campbell demanded entry, in his best German. A guard let them in, but put up quite a fight when he saw the British uniforms. Campbell shot him. The alarm was raised and lights went out in all the rooms on the ground floor. A couple of officers dashed down the stairs and dashed back, closely followed by a well directed burst from Terry's Thompson.

There was nothing for it but to search the rooms one by one and three men were not enough for that job. The first was empty, but in the second the enemy was waiting and when Keyes kicked open the door he took the burst from a Schmeisser machine pistol full in the face and chest. He fell back into the passage mortally wounded. Terry emptied his Thompson into the room and Campbell threw in a grenade before slamming the door. Together they carried Keyes out into the courtyard, where he died almost immediately.

The enemy were by now thoroughly aroused and even as he bent over the prostrate Keyes, Campbell was hit by a bullet which shattered the bone in his lower leg. The only course left was to retreat, so

Campbell ordered Terry to gather the party and fall back to the beach. He stayed behind as rear guard, for there was no way they could carry him across such difficult country without exposing themselves to great risk. Campbell knew that the rocks and cliffs of an escarpment face which descended 2,000 feet to the sea could only be negotiated by able-bodied men.

Terry led the group safely and met Colonel Laycock at a cave above the first of the beaches selected for evacuation.

Nothing was ever heard of Lieutenant Cork and his party again, although German records mention a petrol dump being sabotaged that same evening at a cross-roads just south of Cyrene.

On the evening of 18 November *Torbay* hove to off the beach and signalled the party ashore by Aldis lamp; besides Laycock and Terry there were 17 other men awaiting evacuation. The weather eased but there was a heavy swell and the submarine commander, fearing a repetition of the landing, advised they should postpone any attempt to embark for a further 24 hours.

The Commandos had no intention of being bottled up in a cave, so at first light on 19 November Laycock deployed them into a defensive perimeter around the beach. He put a Bren-gun group of three men a little way inland to warn of any approach by the enemy, who had indeed thrown a cordon around the area and begun a systematic beat of the coast line. Discovery was only a matter of time. A large party of Italians and native infantry came upon the gun group and a fire fight developed. The Commandos fell back on the main party and Laycock quickly appreciated that there could be no withdrawal by sea with the beach under fire, whatever the weather was like.

The raiders held off the enemy throughout the day. Laycock divided the Commandos into pairs and at dusk they broke out beyond the enemy positions. They had a number of options. The submarine *Talisman* was due off the alternative beach to the east on 20 November; the LRDG had a rendezvous point inland; or the men could hide out in the Jebel until the British offensive reached their positions.

In the event only Laycock and Sergeant Terry made it back to British lines. All the others were either captured by the enemy, died of exposure or presumably were killed by hostile Arabs. Laycock and Terry marched westwards in another desert endurance epic and 41 days later – on Christmas Day – reached the safety of a British Unit.

In some ways, this operation reads like a schoolboy escapade, divorced from the realities of war. In planning and in preparation it was irresponsible. The way in which high-calibre men were squandered and sacrificed on the flimsiest intelligence was criminal. Neither the villa at Beda Littoria nor the one which was raided at Sidi Rafa was used by Rommel. The General and his staff lived a spartan existence in a complex of caves at Wadi Kuf outside Beda Littoria. The villa attacked at Sidi Rafa was used as a logistics base and a mess for some quartermaster officers, which should have been known at the time.

Even if they had attacked the right target it wouldn't have mattered, for Rommel was not at home; on 18 November he was attending a birthday party in Rome. Another fine detachment of Commandos had been wiped out to no purpose.

Sometimes failure can bring its own rewards. Within a week of his return Laycock had been promoted to Brigadier and was ordered home to England. There he took over all the Commandos which had been reorganized into a new Special Service Brigade.

The remnants of the Middle Eastern Commando were taken over by Lieutenant-Colonel G. H. Graham, the original brigade major to Layforce. By now No. 51 Middle East Commando had arrived back in Egypt after its singularly successful but unsung and unacknowledged contribution to the East African Campaign. But there was no reprieve. The unit was disbanded.

The first operation launched by David Stirling's L Detachment SAS in support of Operation *Crusader* proved equally disastrous. The same fierce storms which had disrupted Operation *Flipper* proved even more lethal for Stirling's men. Fifty-five parachutists set out in five ancient Bombay bombers to attack the Luftwaffe bases around Gazala and Tmimi. The raiders were to move in the night before the offensive and cripple the enemy's air capability. They parachuted into a howling storm which fewer than half survived. Men and equipment were blown across the desert and any thought of attacking the enemy quickly disappeared.

Stirling, Mayne and 20 others made it to the rendezvous points with the Long Range Desert Group for the tedious journey home. Their failure was shared by the Eighth Army which had crossed start-lines on 19 November, after two days of torrential rain had reduced the desert to a bog. Despite their overwhelming superiority in tanks and infantry, it was Rommel, having rushed back to the battle, who came very close to winning what German military historians refer to as the 'Winter Offensive'.

Eventually it was British strength and numbers which wore down the Afrika Korps. Rommel conceded ground and this allowed the siege of Tobruk to be raised; thence the German and Italian forces retreated all the way back to the sands of El Agheila where the campaign had begun just nine months before.

CHAPTER ELEVEN

'Create Alarm and Despondency'

After the departure of Laycock, the character of the Middle East Commando changed considerably. Those who remained under Colonel Graham became more concerned with clandestine operations and worked in conjunction with the Special Operations Executive (SOE). Indeed the title 'Commando' was really a misnomer, but it was retained partly as a cover and partly to satisfy Whitehall and the Prime Minister that his brain-child still lived and thrived in the Middle East.

Stirling too was able to break the link with the Middle East Commando. On the return journey to the LRDG's advance base at Siwa, he pondered the future. Parachuting left too much to chance. He was convinced now that the answer lay in small raiding parties which could be carried to their objectives, or as close as possible, by the Long Range Desert Group – at least until the SAS had learned those very special skills of travel, navigation and survival in the desert.

Stirling discussed his ideas with Colonel Prendergast, who by this time had assumed command of the LRDG in the field in place of the shy and retiring Bagnold, now promoted to a staff appointment at Headquarters.

However, the LRDG were primarily concerned with desert reconnaissance and surveillance; the last thing they needed when deep behind enemy lines was a band of raiders stirring up a hornets' nest. But that month Auchinleck had decided that the LRDG should assume a more offensive role against the enemy. If raiding was now to be the prime requirement, there seemed reason enough to combine forces with Stirling's SAS in a marriage not of mutual convenience but of complementary skills and expertise.

It is hardly surprising that Stirling should look to the LRDG, for by that time anyone who had business in enemy-occupied Cyrenaica booked their passage in the Long Range Desert Group's 'bus service' to the enemy's back door.

They ran their patrols 1,200 miles from Egypt through to Tripoli with satisfying regularity, and except through enemy action they never lost a truck or missed a rendezvous. The patrols were composed of five vehicles, each carrying three men. They drove out of Egypt through the southern desert, which was their undisputed domain, swung northwards in a wide arc and, like raiders from the sea, reached undetected the more populous coastal regions held by the enemy.

The LRDG comprised a free, tireless, efficient and cheerful body of bearded men. The New Zealanders, farmers who had taken so easily to the life of a desert nomad, were still the best, followed by the Rhodesians, British Yeomanry and the Guards' Patrols. But all were extremely good, a true élite in which informal professionalism had succeeded in overriding even the customary ill-natured regimental squabbles of the Brigade of Guards.

On patrol, reveille was at first light. The men were roused, bedding and personal gear were rolled into a compact bundle and loaded on to the trucks. The wireless set was opened up and a quick routine message sent in code to base. Breakfast – a satisfying meal of porridge, bacon, biscuits, jam and tea – was prepared over a makeshift stove. A petrol can cut in two, filled with petrol-soaked sand and set alight, was better than many a portable kitchen range.

The sun rises quickly in the desert, but in the early morning it is cold. Most men would sport their sleeveless leather jerkins and cutback greatcoats, while many an officer wore a long shaggy sheepskin coat, relics of frontier days in pre-war India. Each man's water bottle was filled for the day, the route plotted and the patrol would move off at the Commander's signal.

In the open desert, where there was little chance of detection, they travelled from sunrise to sunset. The lead vehicle was the patrol commander's, picking the route; he would be followed by the navigator and the wireless truck. The fourth vehicle carried most of the passengers while the fitter, in good military fashion, brought up the rear, ready to help any who fell behind with mechanical trouble. Much depended upon the terrain, but the usual formation was single file with the vehicles travelling a quarter of a mile apart.

There were no hourly halts, because there were so many involuntary stops as trucks became bogged down in the sand. When this happened, the whole group would work to get the vehicle out. Sand mats, consisting of strips of canvas stiffened at intervals with rattan cane, were placed under the front wheels. Sand channels, 8 feet × 2 feet steel plates, were pushed under the rear wheels. In low gear and with much pushing and grunting from the rear, the truck would rise out of the hole. It was not often necessary to lighten the load. One useful rule the patrol drivers learned was never to use the the brakes when stopping; it was much better to roll to a smooth halt.

In the middle of the day the patrol commander put out a coloured flag and the trucks pulled in to rest for an hour or two to allow the wireless operator to contact headquarters. The men collected their lunch of biscuits, cheese, tinned fish and pickles. Then until the signallers took down the aerial, they sat on the ground in the shade of their trucks and read; the heat of the day did not encourage talk.

The vehicles would travel on through the shimmering heat of the afternoon until dusk when, at the patrol commander's signal, the trucks came to rest close together and all went with their mugs for the ritual ration of rum and lime powder. Sunset was brief but beautiful. The sandhills and rocks take on every shade of the rainbow, and even the hardened traveller and seasoned desert warrior would pause in his task to take in such beauty.

Suddenly it was dark. The commander and navigator would set up theodolites and consult star tables to pinpoint their position, while the radio operator switched to the broadcast channel in time for the evening news bulletin. The 'Greenwich Mean Time pips' allowed the navigator to fix his position with a chronometer; and the men listened to the BBC and the news read by Alvar Liddell.

On a fire of dry desert brush, dinner of bully beef stew and spices was cooked, followed by a slice and a half of tinned peaches or apricots and mugs of ever-available tea.

LRDG food was the best Army rations in the Middle East.

Patrols were a matter of self-discipline at all times – much routine, some discomfort and occasionally a little boredom. Danger came from the sky. In areas where air patrols were suspected the trucks spread out widely left and right, adopting an arrowhead formation when on the move. A chance encounter with a reconnaissance plane called a 'Shufti kite' could bring a visit from the Luftwaffe within the hour.

Air attack was the single greatest threat because of the almost total absence of cover in the open desert. There is no vegetation, and the sand-charged winds round off or sandblast all the natural features into smooth shapes which afford little or no shadow. But there is plenty of dust and sand, and the plume thrown up by a moving vehicle was easy to spot from the air. Constant listening watch was kept on the sky because an aircraft would be heard, even above the noise of the trucks and the rattle of equipment, long before it was seen. Once an aircraft was heard all the trucks came to an immediate halt. A stationary vehicle, especially those of the LRDG in their pale pink-painted camouflage was exceedingly difficult to spot.

The main problem was not bombing but strafing. In rocky terrain the vehicles laagered close to rock outcrops. Wadis or depressions in the ground were much sought after because of the shelter cast by their shadows. In the open country, even when a patrol was spotted all was not necessarily lost. Identification of friend or foe was virtually impossible, since by this stage in the Desert Campaign each side made liberal use of the others' captured vehicles. Even uniforms were a hotchpotch and often quite nondescript. Most patrol commanders kept an Afrika Korps forage cap in the front of the truck, usually to hand on the dashboard.

The answer lay in behaving naturally. Waving to the pilot, they might keep on the move to see how the enemy would react. Opening fire was the last resort. The trucks were reasonably armed but on the move were not a stable gun platform, and the chances of hitting a fast-moving, low-flying fighter which came out of the sun were very remote.

Until December 1941, LRDG patrols had ranged on a variety of missions as far west as a line from Tripoli to Lake Chad. By that time, Stirling had recovered from his first débâcle, and was preparing to attack again. He planned three raids on enemy airfields to coincide with what he believed was a new British offensive to take the advance beyond the Gulf of Sirte where the German line rested after the 'Crusader' battles.

Two raiding groups moved out with an LRDG patrol to attack enemy airfields at Sirte, Tamont and Aghelin. The raids were planned for the nights of 14/15 December, by which time the LRDG would have deposited the SAS within walking distance of their targets.

To destroy the aircraft the SAS took with them the 'Lewes' bomb. The problem for a sabotage operation was to make a time-bomb which also had incendiary impact.

The boffins had claimed it was scientifically impossible to combine the two characteristics, but Captain Jock Lewes's device was simple to make and, as events were to show, extremely effective. The recipe was as follows.

The Ingredients:
1 lb of Plastic 808 explosive
1 teacup of motor oil
3 ozs phosphorus

The Method
Mix the plastic and the motor oil by hand into a tough plasticine or dough, sprinkle in the phosphorus and roll into a ball.

To use
Place the ball into an army ration bag, add a detonator and a delay time fuse. Place on the wing of an enemy aircraft, close to the fuselage and over a fuel tank, set the time fuse and be well away before it explodes.

The only weak link in the device was the time fuse. The SAS used what were known as time pencils. These worked on the principle of acid eating through a metal wire, which released a metal spring to the detonator. The thicker the wire the longer the 'time fuse'. Acid was stored in a small glass phial which was broken before the bomb was put in position.

The ration bag, neatly tied at the neck, was important. It helped to keep the ingredients together and the plastic explosive safe from human contact. Plastic 808 was a potent mixture which produced an awful debilitating headache if it came into contact with skin. The bombs had to be made by men wearing rubber gloves.

Suitably equipped and armed, Stirling led the attack at Sirte, but drew a blank. The enemy had abandoned the airfield.

Paddy Mayne, however, struck gold in his attack on Tamont. His party had 23 Lewes bombs and there were 24 aircraft; they ran between the planes attaching the bombs and breaking the pencil fuses to set the timing mechanism. Mayne gave an awesome demonstration of his physical strength. Reaching into the open cockpit of the twenty-fourth aircraft, he ripped out the control panel with his bare hands; and as the first of the bombs exploded, he couldn't resist the temptation to empty the magazine of his Thompson into the Luftwaffe Officers' Mess as the pilots came piling out at the sound of the explosions.

Lewes led a raiding party against Aghelin and found that too deserted, which was another black mark for British Intelligence. He returned to the rendezvous, and they drove off down the coastal road to link up with the main parties. Coming upon a brightly-lit roadhouse they spotted tank transporters and petrol bowsers in the adjacent lorry park. Lewes opened fire on the roadhouse, while his own men fixed their limpets to the trucks.

On the night of 21 December, Captain Fraser led a three-man team on a raid against the airfield at Agedabin, where they destroyed 37 aircraft.

In less than a month, Stirling had achieved a complete reversal of fortunes and produced a vivid demonstration and vindication of his tactics. The SAS had destroyed more than sixty enemy aircraft and forced the Afrika Korps, together with their Italian allies, to divert men and resources from the front to protect what hitherto had been regarded as safe areas.

Stirling discussed the future with a delighted Auchinleck who had no hesitation in restoring to him the independence of command and sanctioning the recruitment of a further six officers and forty men. This was easier said than done and, despite the Commander-in-Chief's authority, A Branch, which in those days was responsible for personnel, proved less than helpful. Stirling needed men of the right temperament, with proven qualities of resourcefulness, self-discipline and determination. Such men were not likely to be found in the base depots that littered the Nile Delta and Canal Zone, and the fighting units were very much out of bounds.

While casting around, a persistent Stirling came across a detachment of Free French parachutists. They were the first Allied contingent to have completed the Parachute Training course at Ringway near Manchester and, under their senior officer Commandant Bergé, had been shipped out to the Middle East. Ever since their arrival, they had been kicking their heels in Alexandria.

Bergé was delighted to join and his detachment volunteered to a man. There was only one problem: it was Free French Government policy that no troops were to serve in the field under any but their own regimental commanders.

General de Gaulle was spending Christmas in Beirut at the time, and taking inventory of the latest colony to 'declare' for the Free French, Stirling went to see him. After a couple of evenings of heavy dinners, discreet charm, patient diplomacy and not a little guile, the General relented. Commandant Bergé and his detachment became the first of the redoubtable French SAS tradition.

On the way back through Cairo, Stirling recruited Fitzroy Maclean, who proved to be an immediate asset. Randolph Churchill persuaded Stirling to take him on too; he was fed up with the mindless routine of Middle East Headquarters, but he didn't stay with the SAS for very long.

The December raids had been a remarkable achievement. Stirling had demonstrated the essential principle of successful raiding – which was to hug the element of surprise until the last possible moment and to achieve destruction, not provoke a battle. Nevertheless, this first success was tinged with tragedy, for Lewes and his party were spotted by a low-flying Italian reconnaissance plane as they were travelling across country to link up with the main group at the LRDG rendezvous point. There could be no doubt over identifying friend or foe. The Italian swooped low and machine-gunned the truck and Lewes died instantly.

The heavy loss of aircraft did not deter Rommel.

In January 1942, the Afrika Korps attacked and once again the British were sent reeling back. By early February Rommel had taken Benghazi and Derna too; Tobruk might easily have fallen had not shortage in supply and a frightened Italian High Command been able to persuade the German High Command to curb their rash general.

CHAPTER TWELVE

There were Other Supplicants

THE LIBYAN ARAB FORCE COMMANDO

A further round of the 'Benghazi Stakes' indicated the importance that both armies attached to their long, fluctuating and always tenuous lines of communication. Rommel held Tripoli as the main harbour through which supplies and reinforcements could be unloaded after their short sea dash across the Mediterranean. When the frontline lay at Gazala, it was an 800-mile haul from Tripoli. Benghazi was 300 miles nearer, and also nearer to the Royal Air Force bombers in Egypt. Both Benghazi and Tripoli were on shipping routes which could easily be interdicted from Malta, which explains why it became so important for the Axis Air Forces to pound that fortress into submission.

The pace of the North African campaign was conditioned and set by supplies. For the Axis, the main forward supply dumps and reinforcement camps were located in the area extending from Benghazi to Derna. This was the fertile mountainous Jebel Akhdar of Cyrenaica, peopled by Arabs who had every reason to loathe their Italian overlords. These Senussi Arabs should have been a rich reserve of intelligence to the Allies and it was a source which had already been tapped, if somewhat irregularly and not in any systematic manner. The LRDG ran regular patrols into the desert south of Jebel. On occasion they would detour to leave a couple of Arabs at some spot, then pick them up on the return journey three weeks later with such information as they had been able to collect from local gossip around the camp fires and bazaars.

Intelligence obtained by such haphazard methods was of little value. The Arabs needed careful debriefing by experienced officers and this could be undertaken only upon their return to base, by which time of course much of the information was out of date. Today we would question the validity of such a source, which provided the intelligence for such operations as the Keyes raid to assassinate Rommel!

If the collation and evaluation of such intelligence, together with the ability to respond, could be shifted from HQ into the Jebel itself, then maybe the picture would have been quite different.

This is precisely what Vladimir Peniakoff proposed to his superiors.

After eighteen months of military service in the Libyan Arab Force, he had risen to the temporary rank of Major and even commanded one of the battalions for a short while. Except for one short but hectic period when the unit accidentally found itself in the front line, Peniakoff had found military life frustrating and boring. The future did not appear to hold out any more interesting prospects; at best the battalions of Libyan Arabs seemed destined for lines of communication and constabulary duties.

Like all good ideas, his plan was simplicity itself. Peniakoff would lead a small sub-unit into the Jebel and from there coordinate and direct intelligence-gathering activities throughout the region. It would be his task to pass judgement on the quality of the information, follow through where necessary and above all provide Army Headquarters with a coordinated picture of enemy dispositions and movements on a day-by-day basis throughout Cyrenaica. With him in the Jebel would be a small team of Arabs, trained in demolitions and explosives, who could conduct sabotage operations when there was an immediate requirement to respond.

The scheme received the support of the CO of the Libyan Arab Force; a small Commando drawn from its ranks could produce a couple of spectacular stunts which in turn might cause the powers-that-be to think again. The axe of disbandment hovered over the head of the Libyan Arab Force, for it had no real function within the present needs of the British in the desert. Most of its duties as lines of communication troops could be performed by the equally unreliable Egyptian Army.

HQ Middle East sanctioned the operation because they were in the mood to clutch at straws. Major reverses were following one another with depressing regularity and Peniakoff's proposals offered the prospect of success with very little outlay or risk in terms of men or materials.

Major Peniakoff was authorized to raised a Libyan Arab Force Commando of 22 Arab soldiers, one British sergeant and an Arab officer. He chose Lieutenant Sa'ad Ali Rahuma M.C. as the officer. A cantankerous, vain and often untruthful man, he was nevertheless the only officer, Arab or British, to be decorated for gallantry while serving with the Libyan Arab Force. His battalion had been caught up in the battles for Tobruk and temporarily attached to the 4th Indian Division. Ali Rahuma proved to be exceptionally cool and courageous under fire, for which he was awarded the Military Cross.

Lieutenant Rahuma was a Senussi Arab refugee, already well past middle age. All members of the attachment were trained in the art of demolition before they left Egypt, and Rahuma demonstrated a surprisingly accurate and detailed knowledge of detonators, primers and fuses. He readily admitted that, having fled the Jebel in 1931 after the Italian 'Pacification' programme, he made his living as a mercenary with Palestinian Arab terrorists – services for which he was handsomely rewarded in French gold.

French desire to make trouble for the British Mandate in Palestine shows the world to have been just as complicated in those days and Levantine politics as convoluted as they are today.

On 20 April the Libyan Arab Commando took the field. A patrol of the LRDG led by Captain Hunter carried Peniakoff and Ali Rahuma to the Jebel. The remainder of the Commando remained behind to complete their training under the watchful eye of their British sergeant.

Peniakoff's plan was to spend about three weeks in Jebel on prolonged reconnaissance. He intended to meet the local sheiks and chieftains, secure their cooperation in establishing an intelligence network, and scout some convenient locations for his future base of operations.

Five days after leaving Siwa, Hunter's patrol dumped their passengers at the back door to the Jebel and then proceeded about their own business – a road watch on the Derna-Benghazi road. While Rahuma went off to barter for some camels, Peniakoff established a base camp and came across a couple of British officers who had a radio set. Lieutenants Chapman and Chevalier were also refugees from the Libyan Arab Force who had been sent into the Jebel to build an Arab intelligence network. They worked for Military Intelligence at Eighth Army HQ and, needless to say, neither bunch of saboteurs knew about the other. How could they, when their respective masters at Army and Middle East HQ hardly ever deigned to acknowledge one another's existence? Chapman and Chevalier, however, did agree to transmit any message which Peniakoff might have for Middle East Headquarters.

The Libyan Arab Commando did not run to a radio!

Rahuma proved to be a tower of strength over the coming weeks and obviously enjoyed his position of power and authority around the council fires of the nomad groups. Peniakoff for his part promised the Senussi sheiks freedom from the Italians and independence when the war was won. In the meantime he made a careful note of their immediate needs and requirements. In return the sheiks were committed to help in the gathering of intelligence and to persuade their people to hinder the Italians and to keep well out of the way when the Allies returned to the offensive.

Peniakoff lived the life of an important guest among the Senussi. This had a certain dignity and status, which probably encouraged him to write future British foreign policy for Cyrenaica. Indeed, one cannot escape the conclusion from reading the various accounts of this journey that Peniakoff probably had greater faith in the credibility of his propaganda than did the Arabs. The latter came from far and wide to attend the councils, but never once was Peniakoff betrayed even though he was surrounded by Germans and Italians.

When the appointed time came for Peniakoff to rendezvous with the returning LRDG patrol, Chapman and Chevalier elected to remain behind. They had worked well together and asked if they could join forces with the Libyan Arab Commando. Peniakoff formally accepted them into his command and promised to clear matters with their HQ upon his return to Egypt. In exchange the two young officers were to continue with their intelligence work and radio their findings through to the LRDG at Siwa for onward transmission under Peniakoff's byline.

Peniakoff had no desire to return to that fancy branch of Middle East Headquarters under whose direct command he came. They were simply not geared to respond usefully to clandestine raids and intelligence-gathering behind the enemy lines. Therefore he resolved to sever links with the Libyan Arab Force and join up with Eighth Army.

At Siwa, Peniakoff discussed his ideas with Guy Prendergast who was commanding the Long Range Desert Group. He immediately made some phone calls. Peniakoff listened while Prendergast fixed the appointments, but was confused when the latter talked of 'Popski'. After he had finished Prendergast turned and explained: 'As you heard, we call you Popski. Nobody can understand Peniakoff on the telephone. Do you mind?'

Peniakoff was delighted by his nickname, and remembered that his namesake was the comical hairy little cartoon strip character in the *Daily Mirror*.

The next morning, transport arrived to collect Popski. Eighth Army Headquarters at the time was located at Qambut just to the east of Tobruk. This consisted of a number of austere, spartanly furnished and heavily camouflaged tents and caravans widely dispersed across a dusty, fly-infested plain. It was one of the most miserable places he had ever seen.

Popski left the transport at the Military Police compound and wandered aimlessly in search of 'Operations'. His recent weeks in the Jebel and time spent in the company of the LRDG, of whom he was already an ardent devotee, had done little to prepare him for the shock of the 'Rommel Factor'. It quickly became apparent that an atmosphere of gloom and doom pervaded Army HQ. Nobody had any confidence in their ability to resist a German attack; the prevailing view was that when Rommel chose to advance, there was nothing to stop him reaching Egypt and beyond. Even the Red Sea, it seemed, would part to the appearance of his Panzers!

In contrast to such pessimism, Popski found an immediate willingness to accommodate his demands and to provide all that he required to return to the Jebel. The staff begged him to return urgently and prepare to spread 'alarm and despondency' amongst the enemy as soon as he received the instructions. Popski was told that destruction of the enemy petrol supplies was to have the highest priority for his saboteurs and, so far as the Senussi sheiks were concerned, he had carte blanche to promise a political future of their choosing.

Neither was Popski alone, for suddenly private armies began to appear all over the Middle East. Many were tiny clandestine groups, comprising Balkan nationals, Greeks, Yugoslavs of various hues, Albanians, all locked in some precarious manner into a web fashioned by the Special Operations Executive. In most instances these unfortunates were raised under various forms of patronage to meet the needs of a single operation, and their fate sealed the moment they were dumped on some shore. Most were not around long enough to leave a record of their existence and they vanished without trace.

Others sought to imitate the Special Air Service and the Long Range Desert Group, who were the front runners when it came to raiding. None of those who were to appear subsequently had any lasting value, or indeed made a strategic contribution to the war effort.

In circumstances such as these, it is all too easy to confuse activity and even adventure – of which there was an abundance – with achievement, of which there was precious little.

THE INDIAN LONG RANGE SQUADRON

Some private armies were created largely because of political pressures. In the late autumn of 1941, the Commander-in-Chief approved the creation of a new Special Force. He had been petitioned by Major S. V. (Sam) McCoy, a regular officer in the Second Royal Lancers (an Indian

Army Cavalry regiment) to raise a Long Range Desert Group drawn from the Indian Cavalry. General Sir Claude Auchinleck was an Indian Army officer and sympathetic to such appeals.

McCoy was seconded from his regiment to Syria, where he was ordered to raise the Indian Long Range Squadron. It was a small force, and unique in that the squadron's 16-man patrols were each drawn from a different Indian martial race. The patrols, commanded by 'British' Indian Army officers, were as follows:

'S' Patrol were Sikhs
'R' Patrol were Rajputs
'J' Patrol were Jats
'M' Patrol were Punjabi Mussalmen

There was in addition a small squadron headquarters together with an administrative and support section.

It is not difficult to fashion an argument in support of the unit's creation, and doubtless McCoy was an eloquent officer. The Indian Army had furnished two full Infantry Divisions into the North African War from the earliest days, and more were on their way. The Long Range Desert Group in its reconnaissance, raiding and intelligence-gathering missions represented a new form of cavalry warfare for which it was perfectly proper to expect the Indian Army to acquire such skills. But it was to take six months before the new squadron was considered sufficiently trained to return to Egypt, there to begin the final stages of its operational preparations. Such a diversion of effort and manpower to meet a role which was already more than adequately catered for by an existing force was an extravagant waste in a theatre of war which itself could only be sustained through great efforts and sacrifice from the home base.

THE SPECIAL IDENTIFICATION GROUP

At about the same time another force came into being, and this too was the brainchild of an Indian Army officer. Captain Herbert Buck M.C. was commanding an infantry company in a Punjab regiment when he was captured by the Germans at Gazala. It was a confusing and fast-moving battle, and the German reception arrangements for the prisoners lacked their usual Teutonic thoroughness. Like many others, Buck found it a relatively straightforward matter to escape from his temporary prisoner-of-war cage and strike out for the British front line.

Buck spoke German fluently and his khaki shirt and shorts, which bore the stains of long wear and recent battle, were sufficiently nondescript to have lost all national identity. He found an Afrika Korps forage cap and this was all he needed to complete the disguise. He passed easily through the enemy rear areas and across the 'front line', where he threw away his cap and joined up with Allied troops.

Nobody had bothered him, and Buck could not help but ponder how much damage it would have been possible to inflict had he not been a fugitive.

He quickly capitalized on his sudden fame by proposing the formation of a sabotage unit recruited from anti-Nazi Germans. There were many in Palestine, and others were to be found in the ranks of the French Foreign Legion stationed in Lebanon and Syria.

Such a scheme was a bold affair, and from the outset it had the aura of a suicide unit. Neither did the proposal enjoy the wholehearted support of the military hierarchy. Since the attempt to assassinate Rommel, there were those who felt that such actions were indecent and not at all the kind of operation for soldiers in uniform.

It was a typical piece of British hypocrisy, but the High Command was sufficiently intrigued by the idea to recruit 12 Germans and to enlist the services of a second British officer – Lieutenant David Russell of the Scots Guards who, like Buck, spoke German fluently.

The soldiers came from the Middle East Commando which, having returned from the campaign in Abyssinia, was in process of being disbanded. Others were recruited from the Palmach. The bravery of those Commandos who were prepared to volunteer not just for 'hazardous service' but in a unit where capture was bound to result in their torture and death is hard to comprehend, except that it illustrates the commitment of those who were absolutely dedicated to the downfall of the Nazi regime.

Buck was under no illusions that success – and thus the lives of those under his command – depended upon their being able to carry off their masquerade to perfection. The new force, given the cover name 'the Special Identification Group', was to be trained in the behaviour of German soldiers. Nationality and language were not enough. For the deception to succeed, their language would have to be that of the Wehrmacht and conversation a reflection of the latest topics of interest and barrack gossip. Bearing, dress and mannerisms, drill, the way they carried arms and weapons had to be that of seasoned veterans in the Afrika Korps.

Such an elaborate deception needed two things. Buck reasoned correctly that he had to isolate his unit and to deny them all contact with Allied troops. The members of the SIG needed to live, eat and think as Germans and this was relatively straightforward; physical isolation represented no problem in the open countryside of Palestine and Egypt.

The second requirement was far more controversial: Buck asked the High Command for German NCOs as instructors. Only the genuine article would do, thus the only source of recruitment was from prisoner-of-war cages.

The risk to security was appalling, especially at this stage in the war when the chances of an Allied victory were slim. Buck allowed his enthusiasm to run away with him and the enterprise became all too theatrical and risky. A more balanced appraisal would have recognized that if Germans – and especially their NCOs, the backbone of the Wehrmacht – were essential, then the risks were too great in light of the potential rewards. Nobody was under any illusions that the SIG could win the war at a single stroke, or have any significant strategic influence on the Campaign. But it was clear that they would operate alongside other Special Forces and as part of a larger picture, and it is in this context that the risk to security was unacceptable.

The SIG was a small unit, less than half of an infantry platoon in size, but the effort and the resources now required to meet its needs were very considerable. The various branches in Intelligence and the Military Police were tasked to search the prisoner-of-war compounds and select likely candidates from amongst the German non-commissioned officers. It was a time-consuming process, but eventually two possible candidates were identified; both had served in the French Foreign Legion, and were then conscripted into the Wehrmacht at the time of the French Armistice.

The two men were able to convince their interrogators that they were passionately anti-Nazi, and after repeated screening were presented to Buck.

Intelligence gave them the cover names Brückner and Esser. Brückner was a big fair-haired, broad-shouldered man. Jovial, aggressive and brash, he was a typical product of the Foreign Legion. Esser in contrast was quieter, good-natured and generous, typical too in the sense of the misfits who were strangely attracted to life in the Legion.

It took a time for the Palestinian Commandos – most of whom were Jews – to accept the Afrika Korps in their midst, but as the months passed they settled into a good team. There is no doubt that the strenuous training programme helped to create a common identity. Handling explosives, map-reading, desert navigation and unarmed combat provided the volunteers with the core skills needed to bring them to the level of efficiency required by a special raiding force. Brückner and Esser instructed the Palestinians in the use of German vehicles and weapons. At night and in their off-duty hours they would discuss every aspect of the German Army, so that by the end of their training they had become completely 'indoctrinated' – conditioned to think and to behave as Afrika Korps.

Meanwhile the full resources of the intelligence departments were mobilized to procure those props which would make the deception complete. Buck secured consignments of German Army typewriters and stationery, Wehrmacht forms and documents appeared in sufficient numbers and variety for them to create an Afrika Korps unit orderly room. Every member of the SIG was issued with a cleverly forged *Sold Buch*, which was the German equivalent of the British Army paybook. There were photographs of the bearer in uniform, and the usual maze of stamps, dates and seals to lend authenticity.

BETRAYAL

All of this effort was wasted when the SIG went to war. In May 1942, Rommel was again on the rampage. He had outflanked the Allied defences which stretched from Gazala in a line south to the old Italian desert-like fort at Bir Hakeim. Bir Hakeim was a key feature; as long as it remained in Allied hands, the German supply lines were blocked. The Free French held the fort and in an epic encounter withstood the combined weight of the 90th Light and the Italian Ariete Armoured Division with full Luftwaffe support for nine days before capitulating. This was one of the toughest battles in the North African Campaign.

In the meantime, Rommel outgeneralled the British who frittered away their armoured strength. But although he destroyed four British brigade groups as fighting units, he could not break free of stubborn infantry who fought on in what became known as the Battle of the Cauldron.

Supplies still provided the key to success in battle, and Malta had played its part to the full in interdicting the Axis convoy route across the narrow stretch of the Mediterranean. The enemy had been stung to retaliate and the sustained blitz and air blockade had by June 1942 produced a crisis, with the island fortress and its population reduced to the point of starvation.

The High Command organized two heavily escorted convoys to sail simultaneously to the relief of Malta. In Operation *Harpoon* a convoy set sail from Gibraltar, while in another operation codenamed *Vigorous* a second convoy left Alexandria. It was obvious that the enemy would mobilize all the forces at their disposal in the air and at sea to confront the passage of the supply convoys. So Stirling was summoned, to see what the SAS could do to even up the score by attacking enemy air-bases in advance of the convoys coming within range of the Luftwaffe gauntlet.

Seven airfields were identified as targets. There were two close to Benghazi and three in the area around Derna. Bombers were based at

Barce, which was some 60 miles to the east of Benghazi, and there was the airfield at Heraklion on the island of Crete.

Stirling tasked the new Free French squadron with this, their first operation in the Special Air Service. Eight patrols each of five men were prepared for the mission.

In many respects the SAS were ideally suited to the task since airfield defence created a real problem for the Germans. Security needs conflicted. In order to defend against the threat of sabotage, the aircraft were often grouped close together, but such a concentration presented too great a risk from the more frequent air attacks so the aircraft were dispersed and protected individually. This in turn required perhaps three or four men to each aircraft in shifts through the night, and such a force of guards could not be diverted from the front lines. Mechanics and ground staff were thus dragooned into guard duties which of course reduced their effectiveness or 'productivity' during the daytime.

But there were problems for the raiders too. The most vital airfields were those grouped around Derna; they were also the most difficult to attack, for they were located in the midst of German supply bases, workshops and reinforcement camps. Any approach off the beaten track meant crossing a large expanse of rough and difficult ground, where detection away from the highway would immediately arouse suspicion.

Concerned to find some subterfuge that would allow them a greater chance to reach their target undetected, Stirling contacted Herbert Buck and the Special Identification Group.

A submarine was to convey the raiding party to Crete, while the LRDG performed its now customary but vital role of taking the SAS within walking distance of their objectives.

The raids were planned to coincide for the night of 13/14 June.

Lieutenant the Lord Jellicoe landed on Crete with the French Commandant Bergé and his party from the submarine *Triton*. Theirs was a most successful attack, in which they destroyed 60 Junkers 88 bombers and a number of Stukas. Then disaster struck. Their hideout was betrayed and all the party were either killed or captured, with the exception of Lord Jellicoe and a Greek guide who after many adventures and three days of hide-and-seek were able to evade their pursuers and rendezvous with *Triton*.

Herbert Buck, Brückner, Esser and four members of the SIG went with the main assault groups to Derna, in the hope that they would be able to bluff their way past the guards and lead the SAS on to the airfields.

It was a simple subterfuge. The SIG team wore German uniforms and played their part as guards escorting the SAS 'prisoners-of-war' to the prison compounds in their own captured transport. Buck stayed behind at the rendezvous point to coordinate the operation, and the various attack groups moved off to their targets.

It worked like a charm and at checkpoints along the highway the SIG talked their way past the sentries without arousing suspicion or concern. Once the party had penetrated into the inner cordon of the defences the raiders split into smaller groups and headed off for their designated airfields.

But Brückner betrayed Lieutenant Jordain and his party. He lead them on to the airfield before sounding the alarm and springing the trap shut. The Free French put up a fierce resistance and in a running battle inflicted severe damage and casualties on the enemy. Screaming their hatred and defiance they fought until overwhelmed, and only Jordain made it back to the rendezvous where Buck was waiting; he received the news in shocked disbelief.

Nothing was heard of Brückner again though some say he had been killed in the fire-fight. All hope of surprise had been lost and with the sirens sounding on the airfields the remaining raiders had to press home their attack against a now vigilant enemy.

However, the attacks achieved a measure of success and about 40 enemy aircraft were destroyed. Such valiant efforts were not enough to save the ships heading for Malta, and German and Italian aircraft, warships, submarines and mines exacted a heavy toll. But the enemy did not escape lightly; beside the aircraft credited to the SAS attacks, many more were downed by the ships defences. When the Italian surface fleet attempted to intervene, the cruiser *Trento* was sunk and the battleship *Littorio* badly damaged. The Alexandria convoy, with ammunition running low and facing the very real prospect of annihilation, was forced to turn back. The *Harpoon* convoy, past the point of no return, slugged it out with the Luftwaffe, and eventually just two merchantmen with a much depleted escort reached the Grand Harbour at Valletta.

The Special Forces had been specifically targeted with missions in support of the Malta convoys. It was a valiant effort, marred by betrayal and heavy in casualties. Although a number of enemy aircraft were destroyed, it was not sufficient to prevent the Germans and Italians from exercising their air superiority with devastating effect.

CHAPTER THIRTEEN

The Fall of Tobruk

Fitzroy Maclean was later to write about David Stirling's very special gift of leadership, saying that he brought to his operations, 'what Lawrence called the irrational tenth, like the kingfisher flashing across the pond, a never failing audacity and a gift of daring improvisation which invariably took the enemy by surprise'.*

From the outset, Stirling had grasped the essentials of raiding. When he was in control of events, namely operational planning, he was able to put these essentials into practice with devastating results.

David Stirling saw the SAS as a new weapon of warfare, striking at the enemy with such frequency that there was no respite and much-needed troops would therefore have to be drafted from the front line to reinforce rear area security. The intention was to instil fear and apprehension so that everywhere became like the front line. There were times, however, when problems lay less with the enemy and more with those in the hierarchy who did not share Stirling's views. Some, concerned only with the big battles, resented the excessive demands made by Special Forces on supplies, which had to be fought through convoy routes bombarded by the enemy air forces. They saw Stirling's outfit at best as a temporary phenomenon, and at worst as a thundering nuisance.

There were keen Staff advocates of Special Forces, but confined to

---

*Fitzroy Maclean, *Eastern Approaches* (p. 194, Macmillan Papermac 1982; first published Jonathan Cape, 1949).

the cloak and dagger world of the Secret Service and clandestine sabotage. Stirling was told by a number of well-meaning senior officers that if the SAS were part of the Special Operations Executive, then life would be much easier for everyone. He resolutely resisted such pressures, insisting that his unit should remain a military formation with raids conducted in uniform. His detractors believed that wearing uniforms and behaving like soldiers in accordance with the 'rules of war' lengthened the odds against success and also increased the risks of casualties. Stirling's answer lay in very careful selection of those who volunteered, rigorous training and a ruthless rejection of those who failed to measure up either in performance or as team members. In the case of officer candidates, Stirling relied heavily on the judgements of his senior NCOs.

This was the time-honoured British compromise of careful officer selection based on record of achievement, gut reaction by superiors and acceptability from peers within the unit. Most of the time it worked well and certainly by the end of the campaign in the Western Desert the record spoke for itself. Despite the audacity and frequency of its attacks, the SAS suffered amazingly few casualties.

Stirling and those around him, in particular Paddy Mayne, had a true understanding of the psychology of war.

In the few brief months of operation the tally of enemy aircraft destroyed had passed 150 in total. Any Royal Air Force squadron would have needed more than the usual number of fighter aces in its ranks to produce comparable figures.

Far from satisfied, however, Stirling was convinced that the SAS could achieve even greater things. Their operations suffered from two constraints. The first was the limpet bomb – by any standard a remarkable device, but it had to be placed by hand and by stealth. The bomb's components, such as the detonators or the time pencils, were frequently faulty with the result that many failed to explode.

The second constraint lay in dependence upon others. While they all had the greatest respect and admiration for the professionalism of the Long Range Desert Group, they had to rely on them to provide their 'strategic transport' to and from the target.

The arrival in the arena of the ubiquitous jeep provided an answer to the problem. This remarkably versatile American vehicle – which had been brought to perfection by Wyllys-Overland, a Toledo-based motor manufacturing company – was in quantity production before Pearl Harbor and the United States' entry into the War. Its name is derived from two sources: General Purpose and Eugene 'Jeep', Popeye's rodent pal in the comic strip 'Thimble Theatre'.

The appeal of the jeep to the SAS lay in its cross-country capability and endurance. Four-wheel drive, high ground clearance and a range of 200 miles without additional fuel, combined with its robust construction and rugged durability, seemed an answer to raiding in the desert. Stirling was able to ensure that the SAS leap-frogged others who were waiting in line to receive the jeep, which hardly endeared the regiment to those hard-pressed Staff officers whose military horizons were bounded by ledgers, supply lists and monthly returns.

After a few hours in a base workshop the low-slung, soldier-proof racing jeeps emerged ideally modified for their role as desert raiders. They had a welded array of water and petrol can brackets, the inevitable radiator condenser, machine guns and grooved yellow sand channels clamped to the sides.

Stirling's armourers selected the Vickers-K machine guns to provide the main firepower. This was a weapon which was surplus to other requirements and, with just a few modifications, ideally suited to their needs. The gun, which was the standard .303-inch British calibre, had been used by the RAF with the Gloster Gladiator, the last biplane fighter whose immortality came when already obsolete – in the defence of Malta.

The surviving aircraft in Egypt had been broken up for scrap but those parts and components which were of value, such as the guns, were stored in a warehouse outside Alexandria. The ammunition was loaded in superimposed rounds into a drum magazine, which produced a rate of fire of 1,200 rounds per minute per gun.

In jeeps the guns were mounted in tandem into a steel upright for use by the front passenger, with another pair on the right-hand side at the back. In some instances – and later in the campaign – the front pair of guns was replaced by the American Browning M2 heavy machine gun. This was a belt-fed air-cooled gun which with its .50-calibre bullets packed a heavier punch.

By the time the SAS had completed its re-equipment and was once more ready to take the field, the strategic position had changed again – and this time very much in favour of Rommel.

The largely immobile British infantry and artillery had delayed the Germans for a while in the so-called 'Battle of the Cauldron', but by the middle of June the Eighth Army was in considerable disarray. Rommel needed ammunition, food and fuel to sustain his advance and these he found in abundance at the huge supply dump built up and abandoned by the British at Belhammed which lay between Tobruk and Gimbut.

Once the spearhead of the Afrika Korps, 21st Panzers, 90th Light and the Italian Ariete Armoured Division had been suitably replenished, Rommel advanced on Tobruk. On 18 June the garrison was surrounded and the remnants of the Eighth Army not locked inside streamed in considerable confusion back to the Egyptian frontier.

Rommel resisted that temptation, for it was Tobruk which beckoned. Plans were hastily improvised and everything made ready for the attack. Batteries of artillery moved into position and the Germans were amazed to find that ammunition supplies which had been stockpiled during the previous siege had not been removed by the British. This welcome contribution was an important factor in the speed with which Rommel was able to launch his offensive against the garrison.

The scene was set for the most calamitous defeat of British arms in the Western Desert Campaign. Arthur Braine was a part of that disaster. A Londoner and a regular soldier, he had left school and joined the London Radio College; having a yen to go to sea, he decided to train as a ship's wireless operator. However, the bright lights and the good life proved too much of a distraction to the youngster who flunked his course, left the College and then drifted from job to job. He joined the Territorial Army, experienced a summer camp and found that he enjoyed the life. On 2 December 1936, and aged just eighteen, he enlisted in the Regular Army and joined the Royal Signals where he thought his basic knowledge of wireless would stand him in good stead.

Pre-war service took Braine to India and eventually into the Signals Headquarters of the 5th Indian Infantry Division. He served with the Division through the East African Campaign and thence into the Western Desert. In the summer of 1942, by now a hard-bitten veteran, Braine was caught up in the flotsam and retreat that was carried into the supposed haven of Tobruk.

Braine lived and worked in the 'Gin Palace', Army slang for the radio truck used in the HQ of larger formations. It was a pre-war vehicle of elderly vintage, slabsided, chunky, slow and past its prime. Special wide-tread tyres were the only gesture made to desert mobility. Otherwise, for the crew it was a hot and sticky existence with the constant hum and static of the radios. In those early days only the driver enjoyed the benefit of air-conditioning, for his was an open-topped cab.

At the time, Braine was a member of a 'Jock' Column. Named after Major General Jock Campbell, Royal Horse Artillery, these ad hoc all-arms battle groups had been around since the very early days of the campaign. The Jock Columns had proved remarkably successful against the Italians, but in no way compared with the German battle groups. In 1942 there were two Jock Columns operating with the 4th Field Regiment Royal Artillery; they were mainly guns with a small lorried infantry and armoured car escort, and a signals element. The columns were sent out to harass the enemy, and Headquarters claimed that to belong to one was something special. Braine did not agree. It was not a case of volunteering, so it couldn't be special. Now he found himself in one, and he never volunteered.

The two columns were code-named *Ham* and *Eggs* and Braine was in the latter. The idea was to drive around and unlimber the 25-pounder guns when the enemy were spotted, fire off as many shots as possible and then limber up and away. It was quite exciting when it worked, because by the time the enemy realized what was going on and could return fire, the Jock Column had disappeared out of range.

However, it did not always work according to plan. In their retreat from the Cauldron, the gunners failed to limber up fast enough and the 'Gin Palace' became stuck in the sand. Braine sat there high in his perch and watched through the canvas slats as the rest of the column drove away. The fitter kept grinding away with the clutch and gears, but the beast didn't respond.

'Well, we've had it,' Braine thought. He had three weeks' pay in his money-belt and began to look for somewhere to hide it from the enemy. Fortunately rescue was at hand. The Gunner Battery Sergeant-Major had spotted their predicament and, despite the dust which signalled the approach of enemy armour, had turned back to help.

There was no time for finesse. The Sergeant-Major rammed his fifteen-hundred utility straight into the back of the 'Gin Palace' and thrust her free and on to firm ground. Braine heaved a sigh of relief as they chased after the column but their reprieve was short lived.

On 17 June they received a message from Corps Headquarters. It came over in voice and was not coded:

> The road has been cut between Tobruk and the main 8th Army. To avoid capture you must retreat on Tobruk and join the garrison there. Goodbye and good luck.

Braine ripped out the sheet from his message pad, acknowledged with the standard 'Roger out' and handed it to the Signals officer who sat behind him.

They found Tobruk in chaos. By all appearances no one had expected it to be in the front line again so soon. What had once been a formidable garrison which had inflicted a first defeat on Rommel had become one large NAAFI storehouse and depot. Though some of the defences were still intact, most had been allowed to fall into decay. Even worse, nobody knew what was happening.

Besides their officer, the crew of the 'Gin Palace' comprised a corporal, two signalmen, Braine, another pre-war regular called Lee and a fitter who also doubled as driver. Nobody wanted to be bothered with them and their officer left to find instructions with the words, 'Just hang around and make yourselves useful'.

It was the last they saw of him.

Having parked the 'Gin Palace' behind a ruined building down on the eastern perimeter, they brewed up and then bedded down for the night. After supper they sat in the truck and listened to the radio. Braine tuned into the various broadcasting stations before settling on the BBC in London.

In those days Major-General Fuller, a famous soldier philosopher who had been forced into premature retirement, gave a regular war commentary on the Home Service. That evening they listened as he talked about Tobruk and, although London was one day behind with the news, his comments were uncannily perceptive. Fuller believed there would be no repetition of the long-drawn-out siege of the previous year; in his view Tobruk would either be relieved or would quickly fall to the enemy. Neither did its capture matter, concluded the general, for its importance was largely symbolic and its loss of no great military consequence. Many men in Tobruk that night heard the broadcast and wondered at the futility of it all.

Then came the dawn. At 05.20 hours on the morning of 20 June, Rommel unleashed the Panzers. Tobruk was commanded by Major-General H. B. Klopper, recently promoted to lead the 2nd South African Division which in turn comprised the larger part of the 'formed' element in the garrison. Klopper had no experience of any command in battle, and indeed his last command had been a battalion back in South Africa. He had gladly followed Ritchie's advice to strengthen the south-west quadrant of the defences, for there he was assured Rommel would attack. As a consequence, the bulk of the division was deployed in the south-west and an additional minefield laid to their front. The mines were taken from the south-eastern quadrant.

Rommel directed the main weight of armoured assault against the south-eastern corner.

The Stukas signalled the start of the battle by bombing the shipping that had crammed into the harbour. Arthur Braine was about three miles away, but paused to watch the magnificent spectacle of the gull-winged bombers peeling off to dive screaming down on top of their targets, until succeeding waves of Stukas turned their attention to the perimeter where Braine had spent the night.

The crew huddled for cover behind a low wall as the ground heaved and shook to the blast of the bombs. By the time the air raid had finished, their corporal had become a casualty of shell-shock and the fitter had disappeared.

The defenders in the south-eastern corner gave a good account of themselves and it was not until about noon that the perimeter was breached. Assault pioneers bridged the anti-tank ditches and the enemy spearhead – Mark III tanks of the 21st Panzer Division supported by lorried infantry – then drove over the positions held by the luckless 2nd/5th Mahrattas, whose centre company was wiped out in a gallant last stand.

Thereafter the defences just melted away. Braine watched with all the contempt of the regular soldier as officers who should have been trying to organize resistance packed their valises and hot-foot led the retreat to the harbour. Buttonholing one fleeing commissioned member of the Royal Signals, Braine pointed to the 'Gin Palace' with its radio, codes and cyphers.

'What shall we do about it, sir?' he asked.

'Well, what do you think? I mean what the hell can we do with it?' was the reply.

'Surely we can blow it up or do something, set light to it or something?'

'Well, look, good idea that – and here's a Mills bomb.' So saying, the officer thrust the pineapple-shaped grenade into Braine's hand and disappeared into the crowd.

Braine had spent the war in the 'Gin Palace' and had never seen a Mills bomb in his life; he had even less idea of how it worked. The young soldier opened the rear door of the vehicle, retreated a few yards, took careful aim and threw in the grenade.

Nothing happened.

A little Gurkha stood watching, highly amused. 'Pull the pin, sahib!'

'I hadn't thought of that.'

'Well,' he said, 'it won't go off.'

Braine, red-faced, scrambled into the 'Gin Palace' and retrieved the grenade. The Gurkha having shown him how to pull the pin, he followed the advice and seconds later the vehicle disintegrated in a ball of flame.

Braine turned to Lee and the corporal. 'Come on, let's make our way with the rest.'

The corporal had remained where they left him, morose and with-drawn, hunched against a wall. 'I'm sitting here,' he stated.

'Well, I'm not waiting. I'm off with this lot,' said Braine, losing patience. Lee and Braine picked up their small packs, rifles and helmets, and joined the crowd moving in a slow relentless mass towards the harbour. To Braine it was for all the world like coming out of West Ham on a Saturday afternoon after the home team had been defeated.

They passed the South African HQ, where inside a miserable Klopper was completely out of his depth. His immediate staff were just as inexperienced, his brigadiers and battalion commanders were already advising capitulation. To their jaundiced eyes, the situation was beyond recovery and Klopper's duty was clear. There was no virtue in the sacrifice of 'Afrikaans blood', and every need to save the flower of her manhood. This transcended the requirement of defeating Rommel!

Braine found himself by the harbour's naval HQ where an RN Commander – a big man with a large black bushy beard – had grabbed a Lewis gun and was outside exhorting men to follow him and stop the Germans.

Braine was a regular soldier who had lived by the time-honoured code of never volunteering. Instead, he and Lee joined the queue which had formed for evacuation by sea. By this time the Stukas had returned and concentrated their attention on a couple of ships which, heavily loaded with men, were moving through the outer harbour to the sea. Despite the intense barrage of anti-aircraft fire Braine watched the Stukas dive through the bursting shells to hit a destroyer crammed with soldiers. The warship disintegrated and sank without trace.

Braine decided that that way out was certain death, so he and Lee pushed back through the crowd and headed inland. Afrika Korps motor-cycles came down the road off the escarpment and in the early afternoon Rommel arrived at Kings Cross in the centre of Tobruk. From his command car he looked down on the harbour and at the long file of dejected Allied soldiers who were trudging past into captivity. Braine walked by, unaware of the German's identity; he had never seen his own general as close to the battle.

At the far end of the eastern perimeter, the enemy had hastily prepared a barbed-wire enclosure which was guarded by some swaggering Italians. Braine was searched, his watch was confiscated and his money-belt went too.

That night it was a simple matter to walk out and Braine and Lee headed east, keeping close to the coast in the hope of finding a British unit before their water-bottles ran dry.

Having walked all that night and well into the next morning, they were just beginning to question the wisdom of their decision when they spotted a warship close into shore. They could see no flag, but the sailors waved and appeared friendly and Braine decided to take a chance.

The two men took off their boots, knotted them about their necks and waded out to sea.

It was the *Beaver*, a South African minesweeper. The ship had left Tobruk and then sailed inshore picking up stragglers.

By this time it was all over in Tobruk. Even while the bulk of the South African Division – fresh and untouched by battle – eagerly awaited the order to counter-attack, Klopper succumbed to the defeatism of his advisers.

'Ultra' picked up an uncoded German signal transmitted on the evening of 21 June: *Mit unbedingte Kapitulation der Garrison zufrieded* (I agree to the unconditional surrender of the garrison).

It is said that when a huge white flag was raised above headquarters to greet the sunrise, a great moan of anguish and despair could be heard throughout the western part of the defence.

For most of the 30,000 Allied officers and men who surrendered that morning, the capitulation was a disgrace and a bitter humiliation. Many men felt a sense of betrayal by their own commanders, and such feelings were not without justification.

Churchill was in Washington when he received the news and he told the President immediately. General Marshal, the American Chief-of-Staff, then set in train that critical reinforcement of three hundred Sherman tanks which was to have a crucial effect on the Desert Campaign from El Alamein onwards.

The *Beaver* landed its human cargo at Mersa Matruh, where Army bureaucracy once again assumed responsibility for its lost souls. Within the day Braine found himself at the Royal Signals Reinforcement Depot at Cairo – which was just as well, for Rommel captured Mersa Matruh shortly after.

The great trophy had been won by the Afrika Korps, but an even more tempting prize lay ahead: the Nile Delta. Within hours of taking Tobruk Rommel ordered his mobile forces and his armour, now replenished, to strike hard for Egypt.

The flap was on in Cairo and bonfires of burning archives were a daily sight in the sedate gardens of the British Embassy. Civilians, Europeans and rich Arabs alike were scrambling away to the Congo, South Africa, India and some even as far afield as Australia – wherever they could find a ship or a plane to take them.

When Rommel drove deeper into Egypt, the Staff in Cairo panicked and Middle East HQ set about burning its documents. In an incident which became known as 'Ash Wednesday', the Staff in its zeal started so many fires that Cairo was coated in a fine layer of charred paper.

Egyptian merchants and vendors refused to accept English paper as currency, and prostitutes dusted down their Italian phrase-books.

The fleet scattered; the Royal Navy abandoned Alexandria and redeployed to Port Said, Haifa and Beirut. But ripples of consternation, if not panic, spread further afield than the Nile Delta. When it seemed as if the Germans would invade Palestine, the Hagannah drew up the so-called Carmel Plan which called for fortifying and concentrating most of the Jewish community on Mount Carmel. It was their intention to fight the Germans to the end, in much the same way as the defenders of Masada had fought the Romans in AD 70.

Braine had been at the Reinforcement Depot for about a fortnight when it was announced over the tannoy that all first-class operators were to report to the orderly room. There weren't many, about half a dozen, and they were called in turn to a side office. When it was Braine's turn, he stepped inside and saluted; a major looked up from the file he was reading which Braine could see was his own.

'My name is Major McCoy. What is your health like?'

'Very good.'

'What are you like if your set breaks down and you are out in the blue somewhere – could you repair it?'

'Yes.'

'Would you like a rather unusual job? I can't tell you much about it, but something a bit out of the ordinary?'

'Yes, sir,' replied Braine, who by this stage was prepared to accept anything to get away from the drudgery, boredom and petty fatigues of the Depot.

'All right, get outside and in to the truck.'

CHAPTER FOURTEEN

A Legend in his Lifetime

The fall of Tobruk brought Rommel international fame, exultation from the German nation and a Field-Marshal's baton from his Führer. At 50, he became the youngest Field-Marshal in the German Army, but by all accounts he would have preferred an extra division of Panzers. Before him stood the glittering prize – the Nile Delta, the Suez Canal and even Palestine. With few exceptions the Italian infantry was worse than useless; a fresh German division introduced into the battle at this stage, he later maintained, quite probably would have secured that success. Instead, all he received from his grateful Führer were the resources which had been earmarked for the now postponed invasion of Malta, and a new name. All the German forces serving in North Africa became known as Panzerarmee Afrika,* but this is confusing because it included some – but not all – of the Italian units, who of course had their own commanders.

The Arabs of the Jebel Akbar greeted the fall of Tobruk with alarm and dismay. It meant that the British could not win and therefore the Italians would remain their masters for a long time to come. Some of the sheiks began to consider reaching an accommodation with the strutting Fascists while they still had something with which to bargain. Even those who were resolute in their resistance agreed with the waverers over one matter: Popski had become an expensive liability.

---

* The 15th Panzer Division and the 21st Panzer Division originally comprised the tactical formation known as the Afrika Korps; but all German troops who served in the theatre for a minimum of two months were allowed to wear the Afrika Korps cuff-title on their uniform.

During the four months that he had been operating in the Jebel, Popski had established an Arab network of sorts which allowed him to feed his superiors with sufficient data and intelligence to make it all worthwhile. A regular road watch was maintained and every evening Eighth Army received a report of traffic movements during the preceding 24 hours. Rumours reached him that Mussolini had been spotted in Qubba, but Popski discounted them until a man he trusted came personally to his camp and told him that he had seen Mussolini disguised as a sergeant, not once but several times, in the bazaar in Qubba. This man had seen Mussolini on numerous occasions before the war and swore he was not mistaken.

Popski was loath to forward the information to Army headquarters, for he feared his credibility would suffer. But he did not check personally, because he drew the line at assassination, which would have been the only positive course of action to him at the time.

Instead, he moved closer to Derna and there monitored movement on the airfield. On a single day he counted 42 Junkers transports taking off empty; six hours later they returned – from Crete his informants told him – loaded with troops and petrol. This appeared to be a daily occurrence until Popski radioed the information. A few days later, a squadron of RAF Beaufighters ambushed them on the return flight and 38 were destroyed.

Popski also attacked enemy targets and the saboteurs in the group carried out one small raid which resulted in the destruction of a dump at Kaf El Kifra. An unexpected bonus was that the Arabs also delivered a number of Allied military fugitives – downed airmen on the run and those more determined souls who had made a break from the POW compounds and were trying to get back to Allied lines.

The fugitives' presence caused other problems besides the more obvious difficulties such as feeding and concealing them. Re-supply came by way of the LRDG patrols who would drop off rations at a prearranged rendezvous. On one of these occasions another officer was sent out to join him, though Popski had not asked for this. His name was Grandguillot, a pre-war French international tennis player who lived in Alexandria and who liked to play the part of a stage Frenchman; he shouted, gesticulated and generally got very excited. There was an immediate clash of temperaments. Grandguillot also belonged to a clandestine organization called the Ecapados, which he had set up to help POWs escape. His superiors sent him into the Jebel with orders to establish a chain of food depots along the routes which the escaping prisoners might take, and to induce or bribe the local natives to guide them from one depot to the next until they reached a point where a rendezvous might be effected with the much-put-upon and overstretched LRDG.

The Frenchman brought with him a truck-load of specially packed bags containing scientifically prepared rations. He also had plenty of lira to bribe the Arabs. It is curiously touching that there were those at Headquarters naïve enough to believe that the Arabs would not take the bribe and then loot the dumps at every available opportunity.

Grandguillot's boss had given him strict instructions to keep this operation well out of the way of Popski's Commando. The Ecapados were a new formation and they needed all the credit and kudos for themselves.

However, the two officers, Grandguillot and Popski, agreed a personal compromise: they would cooperate to help release more POWs and all the credit could go to the Ecapados.

Popski knew that he had outstayed his welcome amongst his Arab hosts. Moreover, the fall of Tobruk had reduced the importance of the Jebel, for the front had moved 200 miles to the east and the region had become a quiet backwater.

The arrival of the Allied fugitives encouraged Popski to investigate the possibilities of organizing a jail-break en masse from the compounds which at that time had been established at Derna. These would be flooded with captives from Tobruk and security depended not on the perimeter wire and watch-towers, but on their remoteness, hostile environment and the massive deterrent posed by the desert.

The fall of Tobruk marked the end of Ritchie's tenure of command in the Western Desert. The austere Auchinleck dismissed his Army Commander and sent him home – a step which many including Winston Churchill believed was long overdue.

Auchinleck assumed command, moved into the desert and ordered his forces to dig in along a line which represented the last feasible defence positions west of the Pyramids. In the south the position was anchored deep inland at the Qattara Depression, while on the coast the defences rested on a hitherto little-known way station called El Alamein.

Hardly pausing to draw breath, the 90th Light Division was sent forward by the exuberant Rommel to harry the Eighth Army in its retreat. The Germans swept forward in confident style, their minds set firm on the delights which they believed awaited them in the fleshpots of the Nile.

Although he did not know it, Rommel had taken the road to his own defeat. Armies on the march are ravenous consumers of supplies. The loot taken at Tobruk was sufficient to take him into Egypt provided that the British did not stand and fight, but at the same time, the further west he advanced, the weaker he became. This far west, the Luftwaffe could only support Rommel by withdrawing its attacks on Malta. Once the island was reprieved, it could return to the offensive and send its own bombers and submarines to interdict Rommel's supply convoys.

The British fought back, and advance elements of the 90th Light walked into a storm of artillery fire and air bombardment. The South Africans in the Alamein box stood firm and the German advance faltered, then stopped. The first of a series of bloody encounters, which through the summer of 1942 comprise the battles of Alam Halfa and first Alamein, had begun.

Auchinleck was to inflict upon Rommel and the Afrika Korps a stinging defeat in a series of actions which Montgomery was later too churlish to acknowledge. In these brilliant engagements of manoeuvre he called upon the Special Forces to play their part. Stirling was asked to ease the pressure by attacking enemy air bases in the forward area, concentrating upon the Junkers-52 transports, for it was those aircraft which were the key to easing Rommel's logistical problems now that his lines of communication extended all the way back to Benghazi and to Tripoli.

Between them Stirling and Mayne had hit upon a way to increase the tempo of their raids against the enemy. They believed the answer lay in establishing a forward patrol base, a stronghold behind enemy lines from which the jeep task force could sally forth and attack their targets.

Early in July, while the big set-piece battles erupted along the Alamein line, Stirling took to the field with 100 members of the SAS in jeeps and three-ton trucks full of supplies. Two patrols of the LRDG navigated them around the edge of the Qattara Depression and behind the enemy lines to establish their patrol base in some caves about 60 miles to the west.

Once they were established, Stirling and Mayne sallied forth on their first raid, the target being a Luftwaffe landing strip at Baguish. While Stirling stood guard and covered the withdrawal, Mayne led a dismounted party on to the field to place their limpet bombs on the enemy aircraft. This part of the operation was completed without any problem and, undetected, Mayne led his men back to the rendezvous. They retreated some distance, then stopped their jeeps to watch the results of their handiwork.

The night sky was lit up with the comforting 'whoomph' of the Lewes bombs, but on this occasion the number of explosions was less than a third of the bombs planted. The detonators were probably faulty, but Mayne was too angry to consider the problem rationally and instead cursed and raged in an awesome display of anger.

Stirling and Mayne were always a dangerous combination and never more so than on occasions like these. They aroused the competitive instinct in one another and took risks that might easily have ended in disaster had they not carefully considered the odds and assessed the situation.

They could see from their vantage point that the enemy were aroused but confused. Judging this to be the moment to try something different, Stirling gave instructions to the jeep crews and then led the raiders back on to the airfield. There were four jeeps in the attack group and one left back at the perimeter in reserve, to cover their withdrawal. The four jeeps were enough for what Stirling had in mind. In the glare of the burning aircraft, the massed firepower from 32 machine guns reduced the remaining aircraft to matchwood. By that time, Stirling judged it appropriate to depart the scene.

The experiment worked, and the machine guns proved more effective than the limpet bombs used alone. In combination, these two methods of attack promised a rich harvest in aircraft which the Germans could ill afford to lose.

Stirling left a small force at the patrol base and returned to Kalmit for more men and supplies. It was not an easy journey, for the Germans had now blocked the route around the Qattara Depression and the only way home lay across this forbidding feature. The Depression was a deep vast bowl of salt-flats and oozing bog below an escarpment and sea level. It measured 150 miles long and 70 miles wide.

Within days Stirling had collected his forces – 18 jeeps and 20 three-ton trucks – to return the same way, using a route pioneered by the Long Range Desert Group.

The objective was Sidi Haneish.

RAID ON SIDI HANEISH

Sidi Haneish lay just across from the Egyptian border and close to Fuka on the coast. The Italians called it Landing Ground 12 and in the early autumn of 1942 it was Rommel's main staging area for flights bringing vital supplies and reinforcements.

Stirling decided to attack by night and with every jeep that he had available. In a carefully orchestrated demonstration of mass fire he intended to destroy all of the Junkers-52 transports that he could find on the field. Their destruction, it was estimated, would have an immediate impact on the land battle six times greater than the seemingly more menacing Stukas.

The attack was to occur on a night when the moon was full. Hitherto both LRDG and SAS raiders had confined their raids to the darker, moonless periods. The Germans would not be expecting an attack, so surprise would be even more complete, while the moonlight would help the jeeps to keep formation.

Stirling explained his tactics to the assembled crews in the deep cavern which still served as their forward base. Sidi Haneish lay about 40 miles to the north. The main fear was obviously the risk of damage from their own side, which Stirling intended to avoid by rigid fire discipline and tight formation driving.

As they approached the airfield perimeter, the jeeps were to move into an extended line abreast so as to provide maximum firepower across the perimeter wire, through the defences and on to the airfield itself. Line abreast would also help to confuse the enemy by creating the impression of a very large attacking force.

Once the defences had been swamped, Stirling would fire a green Very cartridge which would be the signal for the jeeps to change formation into an arrowhead.

'Like this,' said Stirling, drawing a design in the sand on the cave floor:

In arrowhead formation they were to drive between two rows of parked aircraft. The guns on the three leading jeeps would fire ahead of the column and the remainder would fire outwards. Stirling's jeep was in position 1 and the navigator 2 was directly behind; the latter would be the only vehicle not to fire. Even so, with 17 jeeps in action the combined weight of 34 twin Vickers machine guns worked out as something in excess of 80,000 rounds a minute. Many have since questioned the wisdom of the British for keeping faith throughout the war with the .303 rather than switching to guns like the American .5 which packed a heftier punch. In this maelstrom of fire, such argument was academic.

The intention was to move slowly and sedately in formation up and back across the field and between the lines of aircraft. Speed was not important, since the sheer volume of fire would obliterate any defence post which was foolhardy enough to resist.

What mattered most was for the jeeps to keep their formation and discipline their fire. The vehicles had to be five yards apart, which meant that the drivers, always an officer or NCO, had to concentrate hard and in the face of obvious distractions, for the risk of losing formation and drifting into another arc of fire was extremely high. When it was dark, Stirling led the column out into the desert until he found a suitable piece of flat ground, and there they practised the changing formations until he was satisfied they had it right. Only then, with the sky already beginning to lighten to herald another day, did he lead his exhausted crews back into the shelter of the caves.

The raid was to take place the next night and Stirling planned to hit the airfield at one o'clock in the morning. At that hour the sentries would be at their least vigilant, and it would give the raiders sufficient time to complete the operation and scuttle away before daybreak brought the howling wrath of the Luftwaffe about their ears from other fields. Even so there would not be sufficient time for them to return straight to the cave, so his orders were to disperse into small groups and find somewhere to hide throughout the day, returning to the cave after dark.

In the meantime there was much to be done before the raid. Jeeps were checked and serviced by their crews – the fitters on call for those maintenance problems that needed an expert hand. Gunners cleaned and loaded their weapons and stored the vehicles. Only then did the men grab what remained of the day to eat and catch up on their sleep.

In the late afternoon, the cooks produced a mighty meal and by sundown the crews were mounted and ready. An air of suppressed excitement was pervasive. For many it was their first operation, and, although seasoned soldiers tuned to battle, they had found it difficult to rest even for those few hours.

Once it was dark, Stirling led the column of jeeps out across the desert. He had allowed over four hours to travel the 40 miles and in the event they needed every minute of that time. There were frequent punctures, and it took five minutes to change a wheel. Navigation was crucial and Stirling had absolute faith in Mike Sadler, his navigator. He needed to stop and take an accurate fix so as to plot their course and calculate the distance precisely, and Sadler would not be rushed. These were the most anxious moments when everybody else could only sit and wait, eyes and ears finely tuned to desert sounds. By now it was bitterly cold.

Shortly before midnight Sadler called a halt, and walked across to Stirling's jeep. 'The airfield is about a mile ahead.'

That didn't seem possible, for in the moonlight the ground ahead looked as barren and deserted as that which they had just crossed. In that wild and featureless desert, there were those who silently questioned Sadler's navigation.

Stirling did not. He ordered the jeeps into extended line abreast.

Each driver tried desperately to keep the engine revs down and then reduce the noise to a minimum as they inched their way forward into the scrub. Suddenly night became day: the desert ahead burst into view as floodlights exposed the airfield and its installations.

It could only mean they had been spotted!

Then realization dawned, as the raiders heard that distinctive irregular beat of unsynchronized aero-engines so typical of German planes and a laden trimotor Junkers came in to land.

'God! It's like Southend Prom,' breathed one voice in awe.

Stirling did not hesitate. He ordered his gunner to fire as he accelerated forward and immediately 36 machine guns fired as the jeeps crossed the perimeter and bumped on to the field.

The first casualty was the lumbering Junkers. The pilot, on final approach, was already committed to a landing and a touchdown just 100 yards ahead of the jeeps. Probably he never knew what hit him. The aircraft simply disintegrated in a hailstorm of fire and flaming chunks somersaulted like burning Catherine wheels across the strip.

The lights went out and Stirling fired his Very pistol. With practised ease the jeeps changed formation to move in slow motion down between the lines of parked aircraft. The noise was incredible. Hardly pausing to change ammunition drums, the gunners fired long, long bursts – for some aircraft seemed to take an awfully long time to burn. In the heat and the excitement, even while the formation was impeccable the gunners lost their discipline and used up their ammunition too quickly and too wastefully.

At last the ground defences began to respond and a Breda heavy machine gun started to pump out in defiance. This was joined by a mortar which with unerring accuracy dropped its opening salvo in front of Stirling's jeep. Riddled with splinters, the jeep shuddered to a stop in a cloud of steam and smoke.

The raiders halted while Stirling and his crew transferred themselves and their equipment to other vehicles. In the meantime the gunners concentrated all their fire on the single defiant weapon's pit, which was quickly and effectively silenced. If there were other defences, they had no intention of betraying their presence.

Stirling took this opportunity in the midst of battle to review their progress to date. The drivers switched off their engines and the gunners ceased their fire; the only sound was that of burning aircraft and exploding munitions and aviation fuel. Checking for casualties and ammunition, Stirling was alarmed at the expenditure of the latter. At his command the column started up and moved off once again on the rampage. They completed their circuit of the field, destroying dispersal huts, buildings and stores as well as parked aircraft en route. Stirling noticed in the glare of the flames a clutch of the big Junkers transports which were dispersed out on the far perimeter of the airfield. He led the raiders in that direction and disposed of his prey before heading out into the desert.

Once they were beyond the range of the airfield defences, the raiders split into 'penny packets' and sought cover for the daylight hours. As Stirling had predicted, the enemy reaction came with the dawn and many of the men spent a hot, uncomfortable day lying cramped and still beneath their nets while enemy aircraft flew low and slow overhead scouring the desert. On this occasion they were fortunate; only one gunner had been killed in the raid, and during the course of the day the enemy were able to find and destroy just two jeeps, though their crews survived.

Night eventually came and the SAS headed thankfully for the rendezvous in the cave. Elated by success, and with the promise of a good hot meal, they were ready to enjoy their triumph.

In the debrief which followed, such euphoria was rudely shattered by their leader's opening remarks.

'I believe we probably destroyed 25 aircraft and damaged a further 12 more. Frankly, that isn't good enough.' Stirling paused to allow his words to take effect before continuing, 'We could have achieved a total success if you had followed instructions and kept fire discipline.'

They knew he was right. In the heat of battle the raiders had allowed their own exuberance to overcome even the most basic rules which they had learned on first joining the army. Short but well-aimed staccato bursts of machine-gun fire are more economical and equally as lethal as sustained bursts.

Rommel, nevertheless, had certainly counted the raid as an Allied success and was particularly angry at the loss of the transport aircraft. Only a couple of weeks previously, his Junkers-52 fleet had suffered an even bigger loss at the hands of Popski.

Shortly after his success, Popski's radio failed, but undaunted he pressed ahead and set up camp on the outskirts of Derna. His scouts had learned that there were two large transit camps where the prisoners captured at Tobruk were held before being shipped west to Benghazi. He had a couple of weeks before his scheduled rendezvous with the LRDG patrol.

Popski walked boldly about the streets of the enemy garrison. The faded khaki of his British uniform and a battered forage cap was sufficient disguise to take him right up to the prisoner-of-war cages.

An Arab network of couriers was quickly established and messages relayed into the camp via the tea boys who were allowed in daily by the lax Italian guards to sell their wares. The messages detailed a series of RV points, first in the town where guides would wait to lead the escapees out and into the desert. Popski established his reception area about 40 miles from Derna.

Five days after the first message had been taken inside the compounds, a group of prisoners walked into Popski's camp; they were South Africans, 20 of them. The escape had worked according to plan; getting beyond the perimeter wire had been no problem, the guides met them and led them out in the desert, although they had shown scant sympathy when it came to providing food and water during their desert hike. Grandguillot's special packs had, by all accounts, very quickly disappeared.

More men came on successive nights, but in nothing like the numbers Popski had anticipated. Brutally cynical of what he dismissed as weakness, Popski was all too ready to blame the apathy which affected those who had found in the safety of prison life a more acceptable alternative than the rigours of battle.

Even so, it became quite a problem to feed the men who did come and Popski soon ran out of money. By the time it came for him to leave, there were 50 POWs and half a million Italian lire in IOUs and debts.

An LRDG patrol arrived – two days early and cautiously – for nothing had been heard from Popski for a couple of weeks. The news they brought was good. The Axis had been halted at El Alamein and there were plans afoot to coordinate all the operations of the Special Forces currently working behind enemy lines. The word was out that if Popski was alive and free, he was to be brought in by whichever patrol found him, no matter how much he protested or argued. Popski was required for new operations.

Cheered by the prospect, the maverick Popski dismissed any thought of remaining native in the Jebel and gladly agreed to his return. The 50 escapees, together with Grandguillot, Popski and his Arab Commando, clambered aboard for an uneventful but cramped journey back to base.

CHAPTER FIFTEEN

Enemy Special Forces

British Special Forces were always surprised by the manner in which the enemy reacted to their attacks. It was only on rare occasions that German or Italian mobile patrols pursued them deep into the interior. Instead the enemy used his air forces to track down and destroy the raiders – but usually in retaliation and after a raid.

There were a number of reasons for this apparent weakness. In the first instance, and probably not until the betrayal of Brückner, the enemy did not really know what they were up against.

Although the Italians had in the Auto-Saharen Company a special force of sorts, the Axis were most reluctant to mount operations on their desert flank at any great distance into the interior.

From the summer of 1942, Rommel was forced to acknowledge the threat by diverting troops from the front to counter British raids. But the main difference was that, whereas the Germans and Italians feared and disliked the vast empty waste regions, there were always sufficient British and Commonwealth troops fascinated by the desert to provide the better Special Forces with a steady flow of good recruits.

Compared with the British, the Axis use of special forces in the North African Campaign was modest.

The German High Command and the Abwehr* had not given any

---

* *Abwehr: Amt Auslandsnachrichten und Abwehr* was the information-gathering and counter-espionage service of the German Armed Forces which under the direction of Admiral Canaris was an efficient, effective organization. Rivalry with the SS and its operations caused friction which ended in victory for the SS and the incorporation of the Abwehr's activities under their control.

real thought to the use of agents or the need for deep penetration intelligence gathering, let alone raiding in North Africa, prior to the despatch of Rommel and the Afrika Korps.

However, considerable thought had been given by the Abwehr and the Operations Department of the Army Headquarters (OKW) to other areas in the Middle East. The British presence in the Persian Gulf had aroused Arab sensitivities and feelings of nationalism in both Iran and Iraq. By the same token, in the years immediately prior to the outbreak of war Jewish immigration into Palestine had sparked off an Arab revolt in the Mandate. Arab sentiment did appear to be strongly anti-British, and Berlin felt that because of its anti-Jewish politics it was particularly well placed to mobilize such emotions to German advantage.

As early as the summer of 1941, plans were set in motion to raise a Special Force which could operate behind British lines among the oil-fields of the Persian Gulf. This new unit, known as Sonderverband 288 or simply as SV288, was a special force comprising twelve independent company-sized battle groups. In July 1941, the first members of SV288 reported to their depot in the Höhenlohe barracks in Potsdam. At that time, the Vichy forces in Syria were staunchly pro-German and it was believed that the units could be airlifted to Damascus and there equipped for battle. Their first commanding officer, Oberst Henton, intended to emulate the tactics of the Long Range Desert Group.

It took time to find officers and men of the right calibre and background for the special unit. The Wehrmacht and the Reich were scoured for soldiers who had some experience in the Arab world; ex-Legionnaires, merchant seamen, engineers who had worked on oil rigs etc were all recruited into the new formation.

By the time the advance party of SV288 arrived in Tripoli, in October 1941, the strategic situation had changed drastically. The British had taken a firm hold in Iraq and, as we have seen, after a messy campaign Syria was now lodged in the Allied camp.

There was no nonsense and little delay over the decisions that needed to be taken. Sonderverband 288 was reorganized as a three-battalion regiment named Panzergrenadier Regiment Afrika and attached to the 90th Light Division, where it was to distinguish itself in action throughout the Desert Campaign.

In marked contrast to the British – where the requirements and conditions of the desert campaigns pointed to the need for Special Forces, and probably spawned too many in the process – the Germans could afford to redeploy SV288 into a conventional war role because they already had such elite formations in being and as part of their order of battle.

The Brandenburgers were a special unit under the command of the

Abwehr in 1939, whose function was to operate behind enemy lines in Commando-style raiding operations. By 1941 and the invasion of the Soviet Union, the original battalion had become a regiment and it had achieved divisional status a year later.

The Brandenburgers had proved to be an effective elitist force which had made a significant contribution through its clandestine operations in all the German campaigns in Europe. Great use had been made of men with local knowledge and this talent was also available in the North Africa Campaign. There were soldiers whose families had settled in German South-West Africa, others who had been brought up in the Cape and East Africa; there were even a few who had lived for some years in Palestine.

In February 1941, Brandenburgers formed the Afrika Kompanie of some 60 men, all of whom had experience of living and working in Africa. Oberleutnant Von Koenen, a man of wide experience in the African continent, was appointed to command and he wasted no time in training and preparing his formation for desert warfare. In October 1941, Von Koenen arrived in Tripoli with the first contingent and by January 1942 the Kompanie was up to strength and declared operational.

The role of the Afrika Kompanie was to carry out short penetration raids behind the British lines and to conduct intelligence and reconnaissance. Every man spoke English fluently – at least well enough to be mistaken for an Afrikaaner – all had command of Arabic and Swahili and many in addition could speak assorted African dialects.

The Brandenburgers were indeed superbly trained volunteers and politically committed. The only ingredient they lacked which would have put them on a par with the quality of man who volunteered for the British SAS or LRDG was combat experience in the desert.

So specialized were they that no attempt was made to redeploy them to other tasks; and so the Afrika Kompanie waited around for weeks on end in the hope of gainful employment. In June 1942, they were stood by ready to follow through Rommel's defeat of the remnants of the British Army standing at El Alamein. They were briefed to exploit the breakthrough by infiltrating the lines dressed as South Africans to seize and hold the bridges across the Nile and the Suez Canal. This was precisely the sort of operation at which the Brandenburgers had excelled in the past; in Poland, the Low Countries, Scandinavia and Russia, they had moved in ahead of the Panzer blitzkrieg to seize and hold vital communications facilities.

Even while the main force of Brandenburgers waited for the Panzerarmee Afrika to achieve the magic breakthrough, another group set out on a long-range reconnaissance mission. For some reason,

German military intelligence were convinced that the Allies had trail-blazed a grand trunk route across Africa from the West Coast to the Red Sea. They could not accept that the resources which sustained the Eighth Army, and indeed the whole of the Middle East, in men and materials were solely dependent on the sea and the long voyage around the Cape. There just had to be a short-cut across land, and intelligence specialists even suggested that somewhere on the Gulf of Guinea or even Lagos was the western terminal. Port Sudan seemed the obvious candidate for the eastern terminal in Egypt.

The Brandenburgers were ordered to find the route and plot the ways and means by which it might be interdicted with a larger force.

Jake Easonsmith and the Long Range Desert Group had under-taken some epic journeys across the desert, but even they would have been impressed by this enterprise, both in the 3,000-mile trip and the care that was taken in preparation.

Oberleutnant Von Leipzig was given command of this reconnais-sance mission, which began to assemble in June 1942 at the Bran-denburgers' base to the south of Tripoli. The group was to wear British uniforms and travel in captured vehicles to give the impression they were a LRDG patrol. To this end the following captured vehicles were made ready:

> 12 × 15 cwt utility trucks
> 12 × White half-tracks, each armed with a Breda 20mm cannon
> 4 × Jeeps with multiple machine guns
> 1 × Large Humber open-topped staff car
> 1 × Bedford wireless truck
> 1 × Ex-RAF petrol bowser
> 1 × Scammel workshop repair truck

It was also intended that they should have the use of a captured RAF Spitfire to provide longer range reconnaissance.

In the last week of June 1942 the column drove south first to Marzuq in southern Libya, where the Italians maintained a small and isolated garrison. There the vehicles were serviced and repaired before they headed further south across the Sahara Desert and into French Equa-torial Africa. At an oasis called Gatrun, Von Leipzig established his main base camp and prepared a landing strip for the Spitfire.

The aircraft left Tripoli, but it never reached Gatrun. The Bran-denburgers waited a while, but once it became clear that the plane had been lost Von Leipzig reorganised his force to conduct the reconnaissance by land.

Gatrun remained their base and rear link. The crews in charge of the radio truck, rations and petrol remained, protected from the depredations of raiding Bedouin by a couple of half-tracks. The rest were split into three parties. One group under Von Leipzig headed for the most likely location which the intelligence specialists had suggested – the Toummo Mountains and the Tassit Plateau. A second party searched the Tibesti Mountains, while the third group under Leutnant Becker searched as far as the frontiers between Algeria and Chad.

Each of these missions represented a considerable achievement. The Germans travelled vast distances through unknown and hostile terrain, in the knowledge that they were totally dependent upon their own resources. The country through which they travelled was patrolled by the French who had declared for de Gaulle. Had anything gone wrong, there was no hope of relief or rescue.

The three missions were completed and the teams, exhausted by the ordeals of their journey, reassembled at Gatrun. They had drawn a blank, for there was no 'Pan African trunk highway' feeding the Eighth Army in the Western Desert. There was a trans-African air route which roughly followed the same path as German Intelligence indicated. Ferry service crews piloted replacement aircraft to the Middle East and further.

Von Leipzig and the Brandenburgers retraced their steps to Tripoli. The lessons learned could hardly be put to good use, for it was not intended that other patrols should undertake such expeditions. Carefully husbanding their resources they shed vehicles en route, cannibalizing for spares until the party reached the sanctuary of German lines.

Their achievements and the report of their mission made little impression on Rommel. By this time the Field-Marshal was losing the best of his Panzerarmee in the vicious fire-fight at Alam Halfa. He needed to know what reserves the British had over the hill, and there were no plaudits for those who could only tell him what was happening 1,000 miles inland, or around some flyblown oasis in the middle of nowhere.

The Brandenburgers did have other uses. They were called upon to provide a bus service, on the lines of the LRDG, to ferry agents into Egypt. This had been a recurrent problem for the Germans which so far they had been unable to solve. The Abwehr had attempted to establish a clandestine commando unit to infiltrate spies and agents into the rear areas of the Eighth Army, but previous attempts had ended in failure. On one occasion a small team had headed out in the desert and disappeared without trace; they are still listed as missing.

It was now to be the turn of the Brandenburgers. Under the cover of an operation code named *Salem* they were to drop Abwehr agents deep behind British lines.

Coordinating the Abwehr effort was Hauptman Von Steffens, an experienced African traveller who spoke English and Arabic fluently. The Brandenburgers provided Hauptman Count Almasy to lead and guide the Abwehr team. An arrogant Junker and by all accounts an insufferable bore, he nevertheless had enjoyed an international reputation before the war as a desert traveller; like Von Steffens he was multilingual.

Count Almasy intended to swing south and make a wide detour below the Western Desert battleground to deliver the agents to the Yapsa Pass which was next to Assiyut on the Nile. From there it should be possible to evade any security checks and catch a train through to Cairo. The Count would then return with the main party to the German lines by the most convenient and safest route.

This was to be another 4,000-mile voyage into enemy country, but unlike the LRDG the Brandenburgers had neither the experience nor prearranged supply dumps to aid them in their mission. Von Steffens' solution was to take a leaf out of the LRDG book. The party took a number of trucks which were dumped en route, ready to serve as a supply point on the return journey when they would be cannibalized and abandoned. He also adopted the stratagem of appearing like an LRDG patrol, but at the same time paying scrupulous heed to the conventions of war. The usual captured British trucks and vehicles were acquired, each now painted with a straight-sided (rather than the more pronounced Maltese) German Cross on the side, and then all but obliterated by the sand, wear and tear. The men were given Luftwaffe desert drills which were very similar to the British khaki.

There is nothing like German military confidence to make light of a desperate and dangerous journey, but then pride always came before a fall. Von Steffens led the party out into the desert in May 1942 and they were very soon in trouble. Remarkably for Germans, their preparation had not included equipping the trucks with sand channels. The exertion of digging bogged-down trucks out of the sand proved too much for Von Steffens who suffered a heart attack and had to be rushed to the nearest field hospital; fortunately they were still within German lines. Neither had their desert hygiene achieved a high standard, for a number of the party were laid low with cholic and dysentery.

This was hardly an auspicious start to the operation, but Hauptman Count Almasy now took a grip on things, assumed command and led the party on its way. Their route took them through mountains which the Count had last explored ten years before; with unerring skill he guided them straight to a water supply he had cached on that previous occasion.

Having detoured far to the south and crossed into British territory, Count Almasy led the party northwards once again until they reached the military road that led eastwards into Lower Egypt. From then on it was a matter of bluff, nerve and a large measure of luck as they passed through the perfunctory road blocks and sentry posts. Count Almasy played the part of an Afrikaan officer and his men laughed and joked in English, giving the impression of light-hearted relief after a long-range patrol into enemy territory. The rear-echelon troops on sentry duty at the check-points were treated with that studied mixture of contempt and pity that the fighting elites always displayed towards non-combatants and they were waved through without question.

Two agents were dropped at the Yapsa Pass, where Count Almasy tarried just long enough to spruce up their appearance before returning down the Military Road. Now they were a special group about to embark upon a long and dangerous mission behind enemy lines, the men grim-faced and taciturn as befitting hardened veterans who knew what lay ahead.

There were no incidents on the journey home and Von Almasy signalled the successful completion of Operation *Salem*. Shortly afterwards the first coded messages were received from the two agents now ensconced in Cairo. Unfortunately for the Abwehr, it was not quite as simple as it appeared. The two agents had been spotted in Assiyut, shadowed on to the train and picked up in Cairo, where they were made an offer it was difficult to refuse. Turned by British counter-intelligence, they radioed information which was carefully doctored by their new masters.

PART THREE

EL ALAMEIN TO TUNIS

'The mildest manner'd man that ever scuttled ship or
cut a throat.'

Winston Churchill on Stirling,
from *Don Juan*.

CHAPTER SIXTEEN

The Seeds of Disaster

Popski did not return to fame and acclaim. After five months of operation behind enemy lines, he was completely unknown in Headquarters. In those same five months of flaps and retreats, all the records and documents relating to his operation had been mislaid somewhere between the Nile Delta and Palestine. The Libyan Arab Force, his original unit, had been disbanded, and he was no longer the responsibility of the Eighth Army.

Orphaned and alone, discarded by the Eighth Army, Popski walked the corridors of HQ Middle East in search of a sponsor. There he came upon a new branch called MO/4 which had been created to coordinate all the military activity behind enemy lines. The department was led by Shan Hackett, a bright young regular cavalry colonel.*

Hackett listened to Popski's version of events, and then proceeded to put the record straight.

'Now, Popski, for private reasons you fade into the desert. You go and fight a private war with your private army for your private conscience, taking orders from no one, and when you choose to come back you expect HMG to pay for all your fun and honour your debts.'

There was a lot of truth in these remarks. Popski was willing to fight and, if necessary, to die for the Allied cause in the war against Germany. We have already seen how he prepared to go to war by first

---

*Destined to rise to High Command in the post-war British Army of the Rhine before retiring to become Principal of Kings College, University of London.

setting all his affairs in order, including his marriage. Yet he belonged to that breed of soldier who fought wars in a selfish fashion. He had a clear view on how best his talents should be used and what form his contribution should take, and nothing was to deviate from that course. Popski had no doubts about the correctness of his actions, and the intellectual arrogance of such men makes it difficult if not almost impossible for others to work with them. Men like Popski found in battle a stimulant unique in their emotional experience; they did not expect to survive the war so lived life to the full and for the moment. Theirs was a potent but restless energy which needed appropriate employment. The more able and sensitive generals realized that they did have such men, filled with a crusading zeal, under their command. If that energy could be harnessed and directed, they were capable of inflicting awesome destruction to the enemy. Conventional soldiering for the Stirlings and Maynes of this world is stifling.

Hackett suggested that Popski attach himself and his band of desperadoes to one of the big raids being planned at the time. Upon his return they would then agree what form his future contribution to Special Forces and the war effort should take.

The operations in question were being planned from the outset by the administrators, the staff officers and chairborne warriors in Headquarters. In one sense, it was all up to Stirling. Earlier he had suggested a raid against Tobruk and HQ had been filled with enthusiasm for the proposal; they had taken his original concept and expanded it out of all proportion. It was a sound idea. Rommel was known to be planning a major assault on the defences at El Alamein, and so a series of coordinated attacks from land and sea against his main logistic centres made military sense.

But this was to be a raid with a difference. Instead of a lightning thrust – a quick attack and away – Benghazi and Tobruk, which were the main targets, were to be captured and held. Stirling was tasked with a raid on Benghazi, a port whose defences the SAS had penetrated on a couple of occasions previously to attack enemy shipping, but damage and material destruction had been negligible. Now he was to take under command a force of 200 whose main mission would be to liberate 16,000 men said by Intelligence to be held as prisoners-of-war. These men, armed with captured weapons, were then to take over the defences and hold the port for anything up to a week until a landing party from Malta could be brought over by the Navy.

The purpose of the landing party, whether it was to hold the port indefinitely or simply to provide reinforcements prior to evacuation, had not really been considered, so it was hardly surprising that David Stirling should raise strong objection to the operation. The size of the raiding party meant that the chances of surprise were much reduced.

Even worse, the majority of the men who comprised his raiding force were not SAS but Commandos. The latter had not received any special training similar to those who served in the SAS; they were a disgruntled and much abused unit, remnants of the ill-fated No 1 Special Service Regiment, whose reputation, perhaps unfairly, was still sullied by their past record of misdemeanours.

The raid on Tobruk was the special responsibility of John Haselden. Now promoted to lieutenant-colonel, this romantic figure – even more a Second World War version of Lawrence – intended to take Tobruk from land and sea, seize it, hold it, destroy it and escape by sea.

There were to be other operations too. The Sudan Defence Force was to assault the Italian garrison at Jalo, a fort deep in the desert which could attack some of the raiding columns, particularly on the return leg, if left unmolested.

Finally, the Long Range Desert Group were to attack the airfield complexes around Barce.

In his memoirs Popski wrote scornfully of the operation:

> The rooms occupied by MO/4 in Middle East Headquarters were not lacking boyish enthusiasm. Every young man developed mad schemes to make an end of Rommel and the Afrika Korps. With a few hundred men armed, it seemed to me, with little more than peashooters, they were going to capture the whole of Cyrenaica from Benghazi to Tobruk and leave the enemy troops on the El Alamein line without a base in their rear to die of fright, I assume. John Haselden, who was my age and should have known better, showed a more youthful spirit than anyone.*

Haselden's plan was to drive into Tobruk using a bluff which the SAS had already tried once, and with tragic consequences,. The 80 men in the party, for the most part Commandos, were to pretend to be POWs but with weapons concealed beneath their greatcoats. The SIG were to be the escorts and the three trucks to be used would be driven by German Jews in German uniforms masquerading as German soldiers.

The intention was to bluff their way past the outer perimeters and down to the waterfront, where security would be at its most rigorous, to capture the coastal batteries. It was essential for those guns to be silenced, for the next part of the plan required the Royal Navy to bring in a landing party of Royal Marines to capture the town and liberate the prisoners.

Haselden wanted Popski to join with his operation on Tobruk. As far as Popski could see, it comprised 10 per cent planning and the rest wishful thinking and he told Haselden he would have no part of such

---

*Vladimir Peniakoff, *Private Army* (Jonathan Cape, London, 1950).

a harebrained scheme. He listened to the plan for Stirling's raid on Benghazi and pointed out that to his certain knowledge there were no prisoners-of-war held anywhere near the town. All the camps were much further away. Nevertheless Intelligence had decreed that the prisoners were in Benghazi and nobody on the staff was prepared to take Popski's word on the matter.

Popski opted to join the LRDG raid on Barce partly because he admired them so much, and partly because it was the one operation which was not the subject of Headquarters gossip. The bright young creatures of the Middle East HQ were far too excited by their own cleverness to hold their tongues. But it was worse than that during the evening when they gathered in the bars and night-clubs and continued their senseless chatter; later some were easy prey in their pillow-talk to prostitutes in the pay of enemy intelligence.

The gossip spread even further afield and at Alexandria a drunken Royal Marine was heard boasting in a bar that he was off to Tobruk. A Free French officer picked up some startling information in Beirut where a barman in a waterfront hotel – generally thought to be a Vichy sympathizer – seemed too well informed.

Later, when the Italians changed sides, they were to admit that they had every detail on all the raids except the precise time of the attacks.

'The whole plan,' Stirling wrote, 'sinned against every principle on which the SAS had been founded.'

It was to his everlasting regret that he allowed himself to be persuaded into taking part. Against even his better judgement at the time, he listened to those who advised that the SAS should be seen to be cooperative rather than obstructive, for it was a time of great changes in the Middle Eastern theatre.

Auchinleck had gone. The Prime Minister – en route to Moscow and a first meeting with Stalin – had broken his journey in Cairo specifically to review the questions of command. There he had been joined by Generals Smuts and Wavell.

Churchill's impatience with Auchinleck and the factors that led eventually to his dismissal were both strategic and personal. Whereas most attention was directed to the need to defeat Rommel, the Middle East theatre of operations did encompass a vast area which included the northern front and the Persian oilfields. If the Russian defences failed and the Germans broke through into the Caucasus, then these resources vital to the war effort would be under immediate threat. Neither were there divisions of troops available to fight a war on two fronts simultaneously, for Britain would then be like a Continental power.

The Prime Minister could not rely on the Russians to protect the oilfields; his answer was to defeat Rommel decisively, to clear and to secure as much as was necessary of Italian North Africa in the shortest possible time. Once that objective had been achieved, attention could be given to securing the northern front and the oilfields if the need arose.

All the indications from the 'Ultra' intercepts were that the Germans intended to launch a new offensive on their southern Russian front in October; while Auchinleck was adamant that he could not contemplate an offensive against Rommel until the middle of September.

The Prime Minister was accompanied by General Brooke, Chief of the Imperial General Staff (CIGS), who had already advised that Auchinleck should be dismissed. After two days of discussions in Cairo with his advisers and senior military personnel in the theatre, Churchill found that his views conformed to those of the CIGS. Auchinleck no longer enjoyed – or so it seemed – the confidence of the Eighth Army.

Moreover the Prime Minister did not like Auchinleck. This big, bluff general lived a spartan existence in the field and made few concessions for visiting VIPs, even the Prime Minister.

This view was not shared by the enemy. The Germans certainly rated Auchinleck highly; General Bayerlin, who was Chief-of-Staff at both Afrika Korps and the Panzerarmee and an astute observer of military talent, commented after the war:

> If Auchinleck had not been the man, and by that I mean the best Allied General in North Africa during the war, Rommel would have finished the Eighth Army off.

General Alexander was Churchill's second choice. He had first offered the appointment to Brooke, who reluctantly turned down this chance to return to an operational command. Not only had he been in his present appointment for less than a year, but also he felt it would appear unseemly to inherit the mantle of a man whose dismissal he had recommended.

The new Commander-in-Chief would need a new Army Commander, since Auchinleck was still fulfilling both appointments.

General Montgomery was Churchill's second choice.

'Strafer' Gott was everyone's preference for command of the Eighth Army – everyone, that is, except Brooke, who demurred because he believed Gott to be worn out after so many months of divisional and thence Corps command in the desert. Gott had been in the Western Desert since the outset, was an outstanding commander of the Seventh Armoured Division, the Desert Rats, and had since enjoyed mixed fortunes with XIII Corps.

Churchill wanted Gott and so did Eighth Army.

On Friday 7 August Gott was killed en route to take up his new command when the aircraft in which he was flying was intercepted by German fighters. The pilot managed to crash-land his badly-damaged plane in the desert, but one fighter came in low on a strafing run and Gott was killed in a hail of fire as he helped other passengers out of the aircraft.

Montgomery was nominated to take command in the desert, and he was very definitely Brooke's choice.

During his stay in Cairo the Prime Minister enjoyed the princely hospitality of Sir Miles Lampson, the British Ambassador. Every evening there was a lavish dinner party to which the brightest and the best amongst the rising stars were invited. David Stirling and Fitzroy Maclean were summoned, but a member of Colonel Hackett's staff who delivered the invitation advised Stirling not to discuss the Benghazi raid with the Prime Minister.

'Why on earth not?'

'Because he is insecure, of course. We cannot run any risks.'

After dinner Stirling had a chance to meet the Prime Minister personally. Wondering what they had come out to Egypt to do, and at this stage little realizing that the visit betokened a complete change in the High Command, Stirling and Maclean took the opportunity to put in a word for the SAS.

Maclean had not seen the Prime Minister since he had become a Member of the House of Commons; he had been elected as MP for Lancaster, but had done this purely to get into the war. At the time, Maclean was a career diplomat and thus barred from Military Service, as it was a reserved occupation; it was equally incompatible for a civil servant to be a Member of Parliament. Maclean made his intention known to the Foreign Office, from which he had to resign immediately, and also equally clear to the good burghers of Lancaster. The Prime Minister had been highly amused at his stratagem.

'Here,' he said, dragging Maclean before General Smuts, 'is the young man who has used the Mother of Parliaments as a public convenience.'

Their presence must have been a success, for both Stirling and Maclean were back the following evening and again had a long discussion with the Prime Minister. Stirling was able to explain that his unit was only a detachment and lived in constant fear of disbandment.

After a few days of court life, the two young officers thankfully escaped into the desert and back to the war.

CHAPTER SEVENTEEN

The Betrayed

Besides its symbolism as a fortress and bastion, the importance of Tobruk lay in its use as a forward supply base. Some 300 miles behind the front at El Alamein, it stood midway between the battle front and the main logistical areas to the rear. Indeed its role as a forward supply point, especially for such items as petrol, was vital if Rommel was going to build his forces up at the front, either to launch a new offensive or to withstand a British attack.

The Afrika Korps had never stood so far east and it was hurting. The Luftwaffe squadrons based in Sicily had been withdrawn to support the offensive on the Eastern Front at Stalingrad, which meant that the few remaining German squadrons could not support the front line in the desert and neutralize Malta as had happened previously. Marauding strikes from Malta by the Royal Navy and Royal Air Force were reducing the supply flow to Rommel. If the British could also hit the supply bases in North Africa, then Rommel would be in a desperate plight. The original idea, which had been Stirling's, was sound.

Tobruk was an obvious choice for a raid. John Haselden's operation was code-named Daffodil, and he took with him a very mixed bag of people and assorted skills. Together with those who were allocated from the SIG, Haselden recruited two British officers; Captain Bray was an Oxford Scholar and fluent in German, and Lieutenant David Lanark is reputed to have spoken six German dialects. Their role was obscure. The SIG could provide all Haselden's needs for German speakers since that was their prime purpose. Clearly Bray and Lanark were two very talented officers in a British Army which then as now was not over-endowed with linguists. To risk these skills on such an enterprise seems a foolhardy business and serves once again to underline the amateur boy-scout type of approach which all too frequently punctuated Special Forces operations in the war.

The raiding party left Kuffra on 5 September to cover the 800 miles across the desert to Tobruk. The LRDG under David Lloyd Owen led the way with a patrol of five trucks, while the Commandos and the SIG – about 80 men altogether – travelled in lumbering, heavily-laden three-tonners. The Commandos were not trained to withstand the rigours of desert travel, especially in summer, and the three-tonners were most unsuited to the task. It was with these considerations in mind that David Lloyd Owen set a leisurely pace and made a wide detour to the south; this allowed him to move at times when they thought they were unlikely to be seen by patrolling aircraft.

Lloyd Owen had chosen an oasis called Hatiet El Etla to lie up and rest the soldiers before the raid. Almost 90 miles and due south from Tobruk, it afforded reasonable cover and was often used by the LRDG. They reached the oasis undetected on 10 September and, with the raid planned for the night of Sunday 13th, this allowed the Commandos ample time to rest.

At first the plan worked perfectly. Allied Intelligence had radioed the German password in Tobruk for Sunday, and the raiders penetrated the outer perimeter defences without any problems. Royal Air Force bombers arrived exactly on time to attack the harbour area and to distract the defences from scanning the sea.

It was the Royal Navy which was late and it was at this point that the operation began to go wrong. The amphibious assault forces came in four groups. A company of the Argyll and Sutherland Highlanders, a platoon from the 5th Royal Fusiliers, which was a machine-gun battalion and some sappers trained in demolition, were to land from eighteen small craft on to the south shore.

The main force, 20 officers and 360 men of the 11th Battalion Royal Marines Light Infantry, had been formed as a 'Commando' just for this operation. They were to land on the northern shore from the big Tribal class destroyers *Sikh* and *Zulu*, escorted by the elderly converted AA cruiser *Coventry*.

Had the Navy been on time, perhaps the raiders could have come ashore undetected. But there was a delay after the raid and the Germans, thoroughly alerted and alarmed, flooded the harbour with search-lights and caught the two destroyers (thinly disguised as Italian warships) in the full glare of their beams. At that precise moment the ships were stopped and had lighters alongside into which the Marines were being transferred.

They were sitting ducks, stationary and close in shore – the kind of target gunners dream about. The shore batteries opened fire and within minutes HMS *Sikh* was a smouldering wreck; only one turret and the close-range weapons remained in action. Some Marines made it ashore, most did not. What made matters worse was that a heavy sea was running that night, which was more than enough to swamp the few lighters which escaped the shells.

The Germans then sprang the trap shut. Haselden and his party, together with a few of those who had managed to reach the shore, were surrounded by the enemy. By dawn it was clear, despite their spirited defence, that all hope for success or even relief had faded and the order was given to break out and escape. Haselden died in the first counter-attack. In the ensuing confusion some men escaped to the desert, but nobody knows how many; they died a lonely death, from exposure and thirst or at the hands of marauding Arabs.

Two better organized groups set out on yet more epic marches. David Lanark had three men with him. Tom Langton, an Irish Guards subaltern, had Sergeant Steiner SIG, Sergeant Evans and Private Walker. For two months they lived in the desert, succoured and helped by friendly Arabs. On 13 November they reached the safety of British lines. Five days later Lanark, the sole survivor of his group, was found more dead than alive by a squadron of British armoured cars.

On the day following the raid, the Luftwaffe found and sunk *Zulu*, *Coventry* and eight of the coastal craft.

Only 90 of the Royal Marines made it back to their base.

Once Haselden's Commandos had moved into the perimeter, David Lloyd Owen was supposed to attack the landing field at Tobruk and an enemy radar station before making good his escape into the desert. But the enemy defences proved too diligent; therefore, convinced there was little he could do to affect the battle, Lloyd Owen reluctantly withdrew into the desert. He returned to Hatiet El Etla and there radioed Kuffra for fresh orders.

BENGHAZI

Snowdrop was the code name given to Stirling's raid at Benghazi. Again their approach march involved crossing 800 miles of open desert to a destination some 600 miles behind the front line. Here they met Bob Helot, a Belgian cotton broker who had been a fighter pilot in the Great War before settling as a merchant in Alexandria. In 1940 he had offered his services to the British, since he spoke Arabic and knew the desert and had spent much of the war behind enemy lines on intelligence missions. Helot's scouts reported that the defences had been strengthened and were on alert, while all the talk in the bazaar was of the impending attack by the British Commandos.

Stirling radioed Headquarters with this intelligence and asked for instructions. He considered they should postpone the raid perhaps for a couple of days, and thereby catch the enemy off-guard. It wasn't much of a hope, but there was nothing else they could do in the circumstances except cancel the operation.

HQ ordered them to ignore the bazaar gossip and to carry out the attack in accordance with the original timetable.

The jeeps moved into the attack on time and against the cover of a bomber raid as a diversion. It didn't work, and it soon became abundantly clear that the SAS were expected. They drove into a cleverly concealed and expertly executed ambush in which Italian Breda automatic weapons were more than a match for the jeeps' machine guns.

They attempted to rush the defences, relying on their mobility and firepower, but simply lost jeeps in the process and to no avail. The element of surprise had gone and with it all chances of success. Stirling dared not be caught in the open come daylight and so ordered a withdrawal.

The raiders barely had time to make it to the foot of the escarpment which lies inland of the port before it was dawn.

Enemy aircraft rose like locusts from the plain. Jeeps and trucks scuttled for cover and endured a day of absolute misery and fear. To open fire might have downed a plane or two, but the remainder would have identified the exact location of their targets. For the same reason, any attempt to move would have been disastrous; there was nothing to do but to lie low and hope for the best. There were inevitably casualties, though fortunately only amongst the vehicles, but their loss – especially one truck which carried the bulk of the spare ammunition – was bad enough. Everything now depended on their being able to restock at Jalo on the way home, for they were low on food and fuel.

Unfortunately, the Sudan Defence Force had experienced the same reception at Jalo as had awaited the raiders in Tobruk and Benghazi. By the time the remnants of the SAS had arrived at the oasis, the fire fight was still in progress. It was a classic business, with the SDF laying siege to the Italian garrison and neither side strong enough to affect the outcome. The SAS were able to receive some supplies from the SDF, enough at least to press on towards their base at Kuffra. The Sudan Defence Force continued with their battle; if they could not subdue Jalo, at least they could keep the enemy occupied while the other attack groups came by on their way home.

Only the attack on Barce achieved any measure of success and even then there was a heavy price to pay. The LRDG took two full patrols on this operation. The New Zealanders were to attack the airfield, while the Guards Patrol attacked military installations in the dirty, one-eyed town; these included the local HQ and any supply dumps they could find.

Jake Easonsmith led the raiders deep into enemy territory (Barce lay 500 miles west of El Alamein) and again they were undetected. Popski's role was to take a party of his Arabs into the town ahead of the main attack to carry out a last-minute reconnaissance of the likely targets.

In the event it didn't take the Arab scouts to tell the LRDG that Barce was better defended than Intelligence had led them to believe. There were freshly-laid minefields covering all the approaches off the main track and a number of enemy tanks and armoured cars were in evidence. The armour was more than a match for the soft-skinned LRDG Chevs.

Nevertheless the attack went ahead on schedule. The New Zealanders shot up the airfield and accounted for some 30 aircraft, while the Guards shot up the town in grand style and put the fear of God into the garrison.

Getting away was another matter; for they ran into a cleverly-laid ambush in which a number of trucks were destroyed and some of the men, including Popski, were wounded.

After a short, sharp and inevitably confused fire-fight in the dark, the raiders broke clear and headed out deep into the desert in the hope of putting as much distance as possible between them and the enemy by daylight.

It soon became disconcertingly obvious that there was trouble in store. As the skies lightened to dawn, they espied Arab horsemen on the skyline plotting their route. Easonsmith decided to keep moving until the aircraft were spotted. There was no advantage to be gained from camouflaged concealment; neither could they evade the nimble, mounted horsemen. The only answer was to put as much distance as possible between themselves and the enemy air bases. Easonsmith threw caution to the wind and the trucks pressed on at their best speed deeper and deeper into the desert.

The Luftwaffe found them just after midday.

The LRDG tactic was to lie low, and never to respond to an air attack no matter how great the provocation. Perhaps on this occasion Easonsmith had got it wrong. The radio truck was an early victim and thereafter a number of vehicles were destroyed and men hit. By the time darkness had fallen and the enemy had called it a day there were 40 men alive, 6 of whom were wounded, some seriously. All the vehicles were destroyed except for one Chev and a jeep; another jeep was salvageable. There was some water and fuel for perhaps 200 miles. Kuffra was 600 miles to the east. The nearest emergency dump lay 150 miles away at LG 125, a disused RAF air-strip.

The wounded travelled ahead in the vehicles. Popski, who had been shot in the hand in the ambush and had a finger amputated by the LRDG doctor, took command of the wounded and the medical team. Everyone else marched with Jake Easonsmith.

It was not quite the desert epic which was a regular feature of the Western Desert Campaign, but it was a formidable challenge. Popski reached the landing ground in five days, where they found food and supplies. In the event Easonsmith and his party had the easier time, for quite fortuitously they fell in with a Rhodesian patrol of the LRDG returning to Kuffra. It was still very much business as usual for the Long Range Desert Group.

Easonsmith radioed Kuffra, who in turn contacted David Lloyd Owen at Hatiet El Etla and told him to make for the landing ground which lay about 80 miles away. They arrived within a few hours and that same day, 17 September, found the wounded survivors. The next morning a Bombay aircraft lumbered to the landing ground to evacuate the wounded back to a hospital in Cairo.

David Lloyd Owen waited for a further twenty-four hours for stragglers and by the morning of 20 September he had collected a total of 60 men and 11 vehicles, including some of Stirling's party from the Benghazi raid. There seemed little point in waiting any longer and so Lloyd Owen set out for Kuffra which they reached three days later.

Tragically, the raids had conformed to the pattern of Special Force operations – executed by brave and determined men who had endured hardship and danger to press home their attacks with skill and great courage. But the results were negligible. Rommel's supply lines remained intact and though some forces had clearly been diverted to reinforce the threatened garrisons, their numbers did not influence any outcome at the front. Faulty intelligence, bad planning, an unprofessional approach and a lack of security which bordered on the criminal by Staff Officers at Headquarters resulted in the special forces being betrayed to the enemy.

And the Germans had not finished yet. On the morning of 21 September, Luftwaffe Heinkels swooped low over the palm trees of Kuffra in a surprise bombing attack which caught the defences, such as they were, totally unprepared. The elderly Bombays of 216 Squadron which performed such an excellent service in casualty evacuation were destroyed on the landing strip. The enemy then turned their attention at leisure to the crowded encampment around the oasis, which they strafed in turn with machine guns and cannon fire. By the time they had finished, there was considerable damage and David Lloyd Owen was among the more seriously wounded.

CHAPTER EIGHTEEN

The Special Air Service Regiment

The Special Forces had failed to achieve their objectives and Rommel, unhindered, was able to consolidate his position at El Alamein; though some front-line units had been diverted to protect the more vulnerable rear areas and the lines of communication.

Their headlong advance that summer had taken the Axis further east than at any time in the past, and it now seemed that one last effort would be enough to ensure victory. On the Allied side, all the forces had retreated behind the new defence lines. The Long Range Desert Group had been forced to leave Siwa in a hurry and that encampment was now occupied by a detachment of Mussolini's Fascist Youth – sent across from Italy in readiness for the victory parade which even at this time was occupying Il Duce's time and attention. Mussolini was sure Rommel was about to secure the great victory which would make all the sacrifices and failures of past years worthwhile.

The loss of Siwa had led to terrible overcrowding at Kuffra. There was the usual garrison of French and British troops occupying the old fort which, situated on a hill, looked out over the oasis and the surrounding countryside. The LRDG had their operational HQ and a training facility, while the SAS had moved in support elements as well. The Sudan Defence Force maintained a presence and there were always plenty of visitors.

In September the Indian Long Range Squadron moved. The unit was now considered ready to complete the final stages of its preparation, which entailed understudying the LRDG on active operations.

It had taken a little while for Arthur Braine, the Indian Army regular who reckoned he knew all the angles, to become used to soldiering in an unconventional unit. His period of adjustment had begun on the very first day when, returning from the cookhouse, he encountered Major McCoy. Anxious to create the right impression, he gave a parade ground salute.

McCoy called him over. 'There's no saluting in this unit,' he said. 'We just get on with our job and we can cut all that out.'

'All right, sir,' said Braine as he walked away. This was a brand-new experience.

He teamed up with Guardsman Cox, who had been with the unit since its inception. Braine also encountered some instructors from the LRDG and he asked Cox what a cavalry unit was doing with them.

'How do you mean?'

'Well, the London Royal Dragoon Guards?'

Braine had never heard of the LRDG, nor of their desert exploits. Most private soldiers serving in the Western Desert hadn't either. However, his years of service in India did stand him in good stead, especially in this unconventional formation where the British and Indians were forced to live cheek by jowl. Thus the perceived homosexuality of the Sikh – they were forever holding hands, and that was good enough for the British soldier – did not disturb him in the least, nor did the Sikh custom of using a rather pungent body oil. While others tittered, Braine respected them as fine soldiers whose personal habits were none of his concern.

The Punjabi Mussulmen were cold, hard men, dedicated to their religious beliefs and not people to encourage too close a relationship with the British. The Jats, in contrast, were everybody's favourites – nice fellows with shaven heads and just a pigtail at the back; a little like the Gurkhas, friendly and laughing but fearsome warriors. The Rajputs were more serious.

There were problems. Some of the British troops had never served with Indians before and had no idea how to behave off-duty. One minute they would all be joking and laughing together; then when the Indian started to treat the British as his equal there was often friction.

David Stirling spent just a short time at Kuffra upon his return from Benghazi. The raid had been the detachment's only failure since their very first operation more than twelve months previously. Such was his temperament, however, that he allowed no time for brooding let alone post mortems. Thus, when summoned to GHQ in Cairo, he was brim full of confidence and looking forward to a future in which his organization could play a more positive role in winning the war in the desert.

For once the fates were kind and even Stirling must have been taken aback at his reception. The SAS were no longer to be a detachment, but a regiment in their own right. Colonel Hackett was the first to point out the significance, for it was something the British Army did not do lightly. The Second World War had seen an enormous change in the Army, in some respects even greater than the changes wrought by the Great War. But there had been very few new regiments. A new Corps had been created in the Royal Electrical and Mechanical Engineers (REME) to meet the needs of a machine-age war, and the Parachute Regiment was in its infancy together with the Glider Pilot Regiment and Army Air Corps.* All these new formations numbered men in their thousands.

Although it was Hackett who broke the news to Stirling, the latter could not help but remember the evening which he and Fitzroy Maclean had spent in the company of the Prime Minister, for it could only have been his intervention which produced such a result.

Stirling was now promoted to the acting rank of Lieutenant Colonel and placed in command of the new regiment. This was a remarkable achievement for it showed that, for the present at least, the ideas of a 25-year-old lieutenant (his substantive rank) about how war should be fought had at last gained a measure of acceptance. Even Churchill's intervention would not have worked had there not already been a climate of opinion which was receptive to Stirling's unconventional approach.

Hackett, whose job was to coordinate the regiment's raids with the Eighth Army's offensive, recognized the need to bring the regiment up to establishment as quickly and as carefully as possible. Stirling knew what he wanted – the opportunity to hand-pick new volunteers, access to those volunteers from the Army's battle-hardened, desert-experienced fighting formations, and a high proportion of non-commissioned officers and officers.

An appointment was made with the Army Commander; only with Montgomery's blessing would Stirling be allowed to pillage his way through the fighting regiments.

It was not a meeting of minds. Montgomery's battle HQ was located just ten miles behind the front line at Alamein, consisting of a series of camouflaged tents and caravans strung along the coast.

Hackett and Stirling were ushered in to meet Montgomery in his caravan. There were few polite informalities. The prim little general with his clipped moustache, his clipped military ways and his over-large slightly ridiculous twin-badged Tank Corps beret asked Stirling to state his business.

---

*The Reconnaissance Corps had been created from the outset for wartime service only.

Stirling described in simple terms the role of his regiment in raiding behind the lines and how this could best assist the Army in its forthcoming offensive. There was little to disagree over until he approached the question of requirements and his particular need to recruit from those regiments which had experience in desert warfare and, moreover, to take their best.

Montgomery's charter was clear: to destroy the enemy forces opposing the Eighth Army. To do so, he intended to trap the Panzerarmee in its positions; the few who escaped westwards as remnants would be dealt with later. The Army Commander knew precisely what needed to be done to achieve such an objective and nothing was about to deflect him from achieving that end. Virginia Cowles in her account of the SAS* has recreated the conversation that now ensued between the puritanical Army Commander and the rather large, languid but urbane acting-Lieutenant Colonel.

'If I understand you clearly,' said Montgomery, 'You want to take some of my men from me. Indeed my best men, my most desertworthy, my most dependable, my most experienced men.'

Montgomery had gone straight to the root of a problem which few Special Force commanders had ever considered, or given much thought to; namely, the effects of their demands for manpower upon other peoples' regiments.

'I'm very proud of my men,' continued the general. 'Very proud indeed. I expect great things of them.'

Stirling failed to heed the warning signs and change tack. Instead he felt only anger and resentment against this 'Johnny-come-lately' – this funny little man who hadn't been in the theatre more than a month and who had no experience of desert warfare. What he failed to appreciate was that Montgomery was different from those who had gone before. During the short time that he had been in command, Eighth Army had fought and won at Alam Halfa in exactly the way their Commander had said it would happen. Remarkably Eighth Army's morale, which previously had been at rock bottom, had been completely re-established. The nature and the conduct of desert battles changed at Alam Halfa; there was to be no more failure and no more retreating.

Stirling thought the recipe would be more of the same – albeit on a bigger scale – now that more men and guns were available. He could not have been more wrong. What he did not know was that the Allies were on the eve of seizing the strategic initiative in North Africa.

---

*Virginia Cowles, *The Phantom Major – The Story of David Stirling and the SAS Regiment* (Collins, London, 1962).

Montgomery didn't need Stirling; what he needed was massive material superiority over the enemy and a leavening of battle-trained desert-wise regiments.

'What makes you think, Colonel Stirling, that you can handle my men to greater advantage than I can handle them myself?'

'I don't know what you mean, sir. I need to bring my regiment up to strength and I need experienced men otherwise I won't be able to carry out my immediate plans. It would take too long to train recruits.'

'But I need experienced men too,' replied the Army Commander. 'How long will it take you to train fresh troops?'

'Perhaps a couple of months,' said Stirling, 'whereas if I get seasoned troops, then three or four weeks at most.'

'But I am planning to open my offensive in a fortnight,' replied Montgomery. 'If I keep my experienced men myself, I can then use them. If I give them to you, they won't be ready to play any part in the action.'

There was no escaping the relentless logic of Montgomery's argument, and his grasp of the situation. Now was the moment to bow out gracefully, for there only remained one blunder to make and that was to question the Army Commander's faith in his own assuredness of victory.

Stirling did precisely that.

'Perhaps they won't be ready for the next offensive,' he responded, 'but they will be ready for the one after that.'

'I don't intend to have one after!' Montgomery retorted, 'I intend the next offensive to be the last offensive.'

The Army Commander looked hard at Stirling. 'What's the matter with you, Colonel Stirling? What's the matter with you? Why are you smiling?'

'Nothing, sir; its only that we heard the same from the last general – and the one before.'

Stirling had won a moral victory, but it was cheap, and that last withering comment of a seasoned warrior to a soldier new to the desert was to win him no favours from the Army Commander. The latter brought the interview quickly to a close.

'I'm sorry, Colonel Stirling, but my answer is no – a flat no. Frankly your request strikes me as slightly arrogant. I am under the impression that you feel you know more about the business than I do. Yet you come here after a failure at Benghazi demanding the best I can give.'

Montgomery paused and then continued, 'In all honesty, Colonel Stirling, I am not inclined to associate myself with failure.'

Montgomery got to his feet. He was not above the cheap comment either, but could also be magnanimous in defeat.

'And now I must be on my way. I am lunching at the Guards

Brigade. I shall be pleased if you and Colonel Hackett will lunch in the Officers' Mess as my guests, even though I cannot be there. I am sorry to disappoint you Colonel Stirling, but I prefer to keep my best men for my own use.'

It was game set and match to the Army Commander in more ways than one. Hackett did arrange for Stirling to meet General Sir Harold Alexander, the Commander-in-Chief who, more mindful of the Prime Minister's directive, moved the Greek Sacred Squadron and the Special Boat Section across to join the Special Air Service. For the remainder, however, Stirling had no choice but to consider falling back upon those most depressing of military establishments, the Infantry Reinforcement Depots, to meet the bulk of his needs for new recruits.

Other than the Long Range Desert Group which Montgomery used as a means of strategic intelligence, there was no role allocated for Special Forces. Montgomery had no intention of taking on the Panzerarmee on equal terms, neither did he intend to let his own tanks out of his sight. There would be no armoured phalanxes swanning off into the desert with Yeomanry officers beating taps on the turret rims with riding-crops and bunting streaming from aerials. Montgomery had no need to search for the open flanks, and even less intention of repeating the errors made by Wavell, Ritchie and Auchinleck. Nor did the master plan call for raiders to attack the enemy rear and force him to divert troops from the front. The plan in fact called for the very reverse. Montgomery wanted the bulk of the Panzerarmee in place at the front at El Alamein. There it would be destroyed methodically, piecemeal, in a meat-grinder battle that ensured him sufficient reserves to leave nothing to chance.

At Alamein Montgomery sent an army into battle which not only had an overwhelming superiority but an absolute confidence in its capabilities and its Commander, and it moved forward supported by the biggest artillery barrage since the Somme.

Though their defences were cleverly sited and in depth, there was little comfort for the Panzerarmee. Rommel described Alamein as a 'battle without hope', and was actually away from Africa when the offensive began. There are some who would maintain that strategically the battle was unnecessary. In November 1942, the Anglo-Americans landed in strength along the North African coast from Casablanca to Algiers. With an enemy to his rear, there was only one way for Rommel to go and that was backwards, where he could consolidate his forces and protect their lines of communication. However, that is to take too simplistic a view of events. A decisive victory in the desert was essential to convince the Vichy French in North Africa to cooperate with the Allies when they came ashore, and to dissuade Franco from allowing the Germans access into Spain to counter developments in the Mediterranean.

Politically, of course, Alamein was essential, for the North African landings marked the opening round of alliance warfare and the British needed a decisive victory on land to help balance their inferiority in numbers.

Winston Churchill particularly had desired a significant victory before the British war effort was absorbed into the American alliance, and a great many men died in granting him that wish.

So in Britain the church bells were rung for El Alamein, though as a battle it can never rank with Blenheim or Waterloo where large field armies were defeated. At El Alamein a minor German expeditionary corps was forced to concede defeat and conduct an orderly retreat. Though at home the public, so weary of defeat, treated the news with great joy.

The result of the Allied landings in North Africa was an immediate response on the enemy side. The Germans swept aside French protestations and garrisoned Tunisia, seizing ports and airfields including those with hard surfaces near Tunis and Bizerta which would guarantee them air superiority through the ensuing winter.

General Oberst Jurgen von Arnim was sent to command. His forces in Tunisia were separated from Field Marshal Rommel's Panzerarmee Afrika by some 1,200 miles. Even so, Rommel must have been not only envious of the men and supplies which were made available to von Arnim but also confused by the strategy adopted by the Führer. Thousands of men were poured into a theatre which had, by virtue of the Allied landing, been lost. Had but a portion of those been spared after the fall of Tobruk, then the map of North Africa might have looked entirely different.

In Operation *Anton*, the Germans in France put into effect their contingency plan to occupy the Vichy rump. They moved quickly, although they lost the race to secure that most valuable of prizes, the French Mediterranean Fleet. In Toulon and in Marseilles battleships, cruisers and destroyers were scuttled at their moorings and nobody, neither Allied nor Axis, got them.

Meanwhile nothing would stop the flow of troops and fighter aircraft from Sicily and Italy to Tunis. The British advance from the North African ports eastwards was slow and cautious, while the French squabbled and stalled for time. Thus all hopes for a speedy resolution of the war in North Africa disappeared and the winter campaign in western Tunisia settled into a stalemate. It settled too into a pattern of small-scale actions by Allied task forces usually under strength, indifferently directed and always under-experienced against tough and tenacious German opposition.

Montgomery pursued Rommel's Panzerarmee Afrika westwards seeking to maintain the advantage strategically and sustain the pressure. In this relentless war of attrition, the Army Commander had use for the Long Range Desert Group as desert navigators, but those other Special Forces did not figure in his order of battle so long as he retained the initiative.

Rommel abandoned all intentions to hold at Gazala as he had on previous occasions, and ordered a fighting withdrawal all the way to El Agheila – twice already the back-stop to which the Axis forces had fallen. The 90th Light, together with the 15th and 21st Panzer Divisions, proved masterful in retreat. The war in North Africa was anything but over.

In the meantime, as a result of his meeting with Montgomery, Stirling had been forced to split his forces and his command. Under the circumstances he had little choice, for there was not the manpower available to launch the sequence of concentrated and coordinated attacks which he had envisaged would cause maximum damage to Rommel.

Stirling was determined that those who were ready should be deployed in battle without any further delay. The old hands that remained, which numbered 80 men, were therefore sent out under Paddy Mayne.

As the crow flew, the German front line was only 40 miles from Alexandria, yet the raiders had to journey 1,000 miles to get into the battle. Their route lay southwards from Cairo to Kuffra and thence by way of the Sand Sea to cut across the coast behind Rommel's lines; just as they had done for the Benghazi Raid.

At Kuffra, Mayne paused only long enough to establish a patrol base. There he left some of his forces and the three-tonners while he pushed on with the jeeps to a forward base to the west of the Sand Sea. He chose a position about 150 miles south of the Matruh railway track, and some 200 miles behind the enemy front at El Alamein. From this stronghold the jeeps set out, three or four at a time, to raid the enemy airfields, supply convoys and other targets of opportunity.

David Stirling stayed behind to tour the reinforcement camps and depots for men of the calibre he required to bring his squadrons up to strength. Kabrit became the renewed focus of frenzied activity as SAS instructors hammered the new recruits, ruthless when it came to rejecting those officers or men who failed to measure up to standard. Nor did the pace slow when Stirling was forced to go into hospital for treatment to suppurating desert sores; the hospital ward simply became regimental HQ.

It was a daunting task to bring the regiment up to the 800 men agreed by the establishment. Besides his original forces, there were 14

Erwin Rommel

Long Range
Desert Group on
patrol

Left to right: Leese, Alexander, Churchill, Alan Brooke and Montgomery

Below left: The camouflaged HMS Glengyle   *Below right:* Stirling

Below: A successful raid

Popski and his gunner

Slim at Mandalay

Left to right: Sandford, Haile Selassie and Wingate

Below left: Stilwell and Mountbatten

Below right: An improvised sunhat

A recalcitrant Missouri mule

Wingate on board a mule transport Dakota

A glider bound for
'Broadway'

Wingate and Cochran

Bombing raid combined
with Chindit attack

Chindits carrying a
wounded comrade

officers and 80 ranks of the Greek Sacred Squadron, together with a few dozen in the Special Boat Section.

Stirling needed another 10 officers and 100 ranks to come up to strength, and the quality of soldier from the Reinforcements Camps was indifferent to say the least. Eventually, after some careful politicking and lobbying, he was permitted to recruit from the Middle East Commando – all that was left from the days of *Layforce*. Some had been taken by the LRDG on small-scale raids behind the German lines, while many more had disappeared in the disaster of the recent Tobruk and Benghazi operations. Others had shivered in the mountains along the Turkish-Syrian frontier, deployed in case the Germans broke through at Stalingrad and swung south through the Caucasus. Then after Rommel's last successful offensive the bulk of them – by now renamed the 1st Special Service Regiment – had been brought back to man defences in the Delta. They scanned the skies for parachutists and the Canal for frogmen, guarded vulnerable points and provided escorts for important people. Dispirited and demoralized, this remnant of 30 officers and 300 other ranks came within Stirling's orbit.

David Stirling was singularly unimpressed with the quality of 1st Special Service Regiment. He selected the best and sent the remainder packing, where they were quickly swallowed up by the Infantry Reinforcement Depots.

CHAPTER NINETEEN

Late in the Field

In October 1942, the Indian Long Range Squadron deployed to Kuffra. McCoy had succeeded quickly in welding a team identity out of many disparate components. The men, British and Indian, had all been made to feel that they belonged to an élite force. The British had certainly enjoyed that special feeling in Cairo before departing for the desert. Usually it was a bar where another soldier would come up and ask, 'What's that ILRS?', pointing to the shoulder flashes.

'Indian Long Range Squadron.' A minimal response added to an air of mystery.

'What sort of mob are you?' Replies to this question were always non-committal, since Sam McCoy had impressed on them the need for secrecy. But it added to the mystique and, when in the company of lesser mortals such as base area troops, it did make them feel special.

Even so, there were things which took some getting used to, especially for the regulars. They served in the knowledge that a misdemeanour carried the threat of being 'RTU' (returned to unit). Regulars of the pre-war Army had lived with defaulters and punishments – it had been part of their life – but this was a brand-new experience. So was the relationship with officers, which again was dramatically different from that of the Regular Army. Braine was in the Royal Signals, a technical branch where the officers had many of the skills and mechanical bent of their soldiers, but even so the relationship was never other than stiff and formal.

In the Indian Long Range Squadron the relationship was an easier one based on mutual respect. Perhaps it was also the case that the

British officers would have a close affinity with the few British rankers in the squadron. Braine got to know all the Patrol Commanders well, especially Captain Birdwood who was a member of a famous Indian Army family and a regular officer. Birdwood commanded the Sikhs. He never said very much and had a hot temper, but he encouraged the men to get on with things without the constant 'bull' so often the hallmark of a regular battalion on a peacetime station.

The Jats patrol was led by Captain Read, a tea planter in civilian life who had joined the Army for war service. Lieutenant Cantlay was a dashing young officer and a fluent French speaker, which was to come in handy later; he commanded the Punjabi Mussulmen. Finally there was Captain Hangle, who led the Rajputs. Braine found him a most interesting man; one night on patrol, he confided that he had fought as a volunteer in the Spanish Civil War on the side of Franco and the Fascists.

At Kuffra the ILRS were anything but special. Here they rubbed shoulders with the sun-beaten veterans of the LRDG and the desert toughs of the SAS whose reputation by now always preceded them.

In the short time available, Braine learned more about radio work in the desert than he would ever have thought possible. He also found himself naturally drawn to the LRDG, for they were the acknowledged experts. He especially enjoyed the company of the New Zealanders and the Rhodesians, outgoing and friendly men always ready to share their knowledge and experience with a newcomer to the exclusive 'club'. It was all rather masonic. The Yeomanry patrol were all right, but a bit clubby and exclusive with their own line of chat. The Guards' patrol were fine, but even down there in the middle of the desert, guardsmen still seemed to Braine to have that little bit of snap and 'bull' which made him feel he was still in the Regular Army.

They worked hard and learned fast. The heavy patrol of supply trucks ventured out from Kuffra to replenish the secret supply dumps deep in the desert which gave the LRDG its mobility. An ILRS truck would be attached on these occasions to a column of three-tonners complete with Scammel for heavy recovery and jeep escorts. A typical supply run lasted about fifteen days.

By the time the opening artillery salvoes marked the beginning of the battle at El Alamein, Braine was out with Captain Birdwood and the Sikhs. Their task was to patrol the rim of the vast emptiness that marked the Qattara Depression, to watch for any attempt by Rommel's light armoured forces to probe the Eighth Army's desert flank.

One night, an Italian aircraft sneaked through the defences and attempted to bomb targets along the Suez Canal; it was chased away by fighters and reportedly damaged. The plane was last seen flying

141

south and their patrol was radioed to keep their eyes open for survivors or wreckage. Braine acknowledged, then took the message across to Captain Birdwood. They were all relieved to have something to do after days of tedious patrolling. The trucks started up and Birdwood led them in the usual search pattern, a great circling motion in every decreasing circles.

They came upon the body of an airman, in a horribly mangled state and still attached to a partly-opened parachute. It was terrible business burying the body, which had been in the sun for some time, and the pungent smell had the weaker brethren retching.

Captain Birdwood insisted on a proper burial. There was no way of telling whether this man was part of the crew they had been sent to find, but the uniform showed him to be Italian. A wooden cross was fashioned from the lid of a ration box. It was the first wartime military burial that Braine had witnessed.

Captain Birdwood read a short piece from the bible over the grave, then he solemnly saluted the cross.

Later that day Corporal Collins and Braine, together with a couple of Sikhs and the radio truck, were detached from the main party to an area where the dunes came down to the edge of the Sand Sea. There was a track which they were ordered to watch; it was to be a static patrol, not a road watch. If they spotted movement, they were to radio Kuffra immediately.

Captain Birdwood left them a Boys anti-tank rifle as additional protection against enemy armour. The little group watched the area for day after day, but nothing happened. Sometimes in the heat a rock would appear to take on a new form – shimmering in the relentless sun, it could look like an armoured car. Even though everybody knew what it was, they were so convinced that they would rush to erect the aerial while the Indians prepared to man the anti-tank rifle behind a small rampart of sandbags.

Everyone, Indian and British, prayed that they would not have to use the gun, which had a kick like a mule and could not penetrate wet newspaper at anything over 100 yards. But they didn't have to worry.

Meanwhile Popski, on his discharge from hospital and whilst con-valescing, had called on Colonel Hackett to discuss his failure. Hackett outlined the plans for the coming offensive and stressed that Rommel would soon be reeling in retreat, but must not be allowed to gain strength. There was to be no repetition of the Benghazi stakes; General Montgomery was determined to break the mould. The ground was crossed by Eighth Army in one direction, once westwards and in advance. A contribution which the Special Forces could make was to destroy the supply lines to the enemy rear, make their positions untenable and thus harry Rommel into retreating even further west.

In such an operation the Jebel figured prominently and Popski's knowledge of the area and his relationship with the Senussi were an added bonus for what Hackett had in mind. He offered Popski the opportunity to raise his own motorized force of raiders. It may seem strange that Popski, whose record to date had been erratic, should be supported by Middle East Headquarters when the Army Commander had already flatly refused to accept that the one available force with a proven track record had any real contribution to make.

The obvious answer was to award the SAS this particular mission. Stirling had more than sufficient men available. Maybe the personal clash between Montgomery and Stirling had clouded the issues, but then Colonel Hackett had attended that meeting and made no such proposal.

However, at first Popski turned Hackett down. He wanted to join the LRDG, his preference being to raise a raiding squadron as an integral part of that unit. The problem was that his feelings were not reciprocated. Jake Easonsmith was most apologetic, and explained that the LRDG establishment simply did not allow for another squadron.

Popski was forced to accept Hackett's offer and raise his own independent command. He too entered the market-place in pursuit of spare manpower.

A War Establishment, No. MEWE 866/1 was hastily produced which allowed for 23 men; one major, one captain, three lieutenants and 18 other ranks. The unit was allocated four armed jeeps and a couple of three-ton trucks for their stores. Popski was in command with the acting rank of major, though in numbers it did not match a respectable platoon in a line battalion. War Establishment MEWE 866/1 was provisionally called No. 1 Demolition Squadron.

Hackett pressed Popski to select a decent name for the new formation; the Desert Raiders, the Jebel Rats and others came to mind, only to be discarded. The colonel was running short of patience and summoned Popski to his office. 'You'd better find a name and very quickly – or we shall call you "Popski's Private Army",' he said in feigned anger.

'I'll take it,' Popski replied. 'I would like it to be known as that.'

And so it came about that a new unit joined the British order of battle alongside other more exalted formations of the past such as Hobson's Horse and Skinner's Horse, which had begun life as irregular units named after their founder.

Popski rushed into town to an Indian tailor who quickly ran up some shoulder-flashes. At first they were dark blue with the letters

PPA picked out in red* He had already chosen the emblem for a unit badge. The astrolabe was the name given in the fifteenth and sixteenth centuries to a navigational instrument used to measure the altitude of the stars – it was replaced by the sextant at sea and theodolite on land. Popski used an Italian design as a book-plate for many years, and in the pre-war days had named his sailing boats *Astrolabe*.

A Jewish silversmith off the Shareh El Manakh in Cairo fashioned a cap-badge.

Popski had a name, a shoulder-flash, a cap-badge and a month to find his men, train and equip them, and take the field in order to beat the Eighth Army into the Jebel.

He found two General List officers who had served with the Libyan Arab Force. Since their disbandment they had been filling in time on the Staff while waiting for gainful employment. Bob Yunnie came from Aberdeen, and was a married man; he was old for a subaltern and Popski promoted him to Captain. Jean Caneri was a Frenchman and a lawyer by profession. He lived in Damascus and, on the outbreak of war, had been drafted into the French Army of the Levant. When France surrendered, the intrepid Caneri fled south into Palestine where he offered his services to the British. Strangely Caneri preferred to stay with the British Army rather than to join the Free French under de Gaulle.

The establishment allowed for one sergeant. Here Popski secured the services of Regimental Sergeant Major Waterson, a regular soldier in the Kings Dragoon Guards, an armoured car regiment with which Popski had spent some time earlier in the desert war. Waterson had only recently been released from hospital and there was no slot for him with his regiment, since it was up to strength in readiness for Alamein. Rather than wait for a place to become vacant through casualties, Waterson accepted Popski's offer and the regiment agreed to release him.

It was a fortunate choice. Popski had someone who not only had experience in armoured car warfare in the desert, but also as a long service regular knew his way round the Army system. The establishment did not allow for any quartermaster staff and so they could exist only by begging, borrowing and living off their wits.

There was little choice when it came to the soldiers. Time was short and Popski had to make his selection from the Reinforcement Depots that dotted the Canal Zone. The best on offer were mediocre, those who were any good and with a proven record had long since been snapped up by the line units. The most promising for Popski's needs

---

*He later altered the flashes to white letters on a dark background.

came from Royal Army Service Corps Camps; at least these were men who could drive and had some idea of vehicle maintenance in the desert. When it came to warfare, however, they were innocents. Life in the Eighth Army had involved convoying supplies from one dump to the next, and always in the rear areas. None had seen any action except the occasional air raid, nor heard a shot fired in anger.

It was all done in too much of a rush. Popski took some men on approval, but he had a knack for selection and made few errors. He quickly found twelve soldiers who together with Waterson and the officers were given a crash course in handling explosives by the SAS at Kabrit. At least that gave them a rudimentary knowledge of sabotage.

Under the indulgent eye of Hackett, Popski arranged to draw equipment on LRDG scales. The paperwork was one thing but, with a major offensive in process, in the end they had to take what was available. The British Army supply parks had no jeeps to spare, but the Americans had plenty and these could always be obtained by barter, usually Scotch from the officers' mess accompanied by some lurid tale of 'derring-do'. The Americans were still new to war and at this stage suckers for the Special Forces, especially if the barter also included a cap-badge or a German Luger.

The SAS helped to outfit the four jeeps that Popski acquired by these and other devious means. They were armed with the twin Vickers-K on swivel mounts, with racks to carry a dozen four-gallon cans of petrol. In theory the jeeps had a range in excess of 700 miles.

The stores were loaded on to a couple of elderly three-ton Bedfords; they had a ton of explosives but rations for only 11 days. Each truck had a single Vickers-K and a two-man crew. Popski, Yunnie, Caneri and Waterson took the jeeps with their selected gunners, while the rest clambered into the back of the trucks together with a couple of the Arabs that Popski had managed to retain from his Commando.

They were short on rations for a trek into the desert, but there were no other stores available. The seasoned SAS and LRDG took six days to reach Kuffra; Popski allowed for eight, and still had three days' spare rations in case of emergencies.

By any stretch of the imagination the PPA was at least only partly trained, but he dared not tarry any longer in Cairo. It was going to be a closerun thing to reach Kuffra, re-equip and then press on to the Jebel in time to be of any use.

CHAPTER TWENTY

Pursuit to Tunisia

Popski's Private Army took twelve days to reach Kuffra. They got lost, the trucks frequently became bogged down and they experienced that most frightening of desert phenomena – the sand-storm.

By the time that the PPA had a moment to draw breath at Kuffra, the reason for their existence had disappeared. Montgomery had broken Rommel at El Alamein. The Army had taken the field and won a great victory and now the enemy was in headlong retreat. The 'Desert Fox' fought a series of brilliant rearguard actions while the surviving remnants of his Penzerarmee withdrew. Lacking mobility, the bulk of the Italians in static infantry deployments along the central and southern sectors of the front were not able to disengage in time to escape. A similar fate befell the Ramcke Brigade. This brigade of paratroops taking its name from its commander, Major General Bernard Ramcke, were an elite body, rigorously selected and trained. They were originally earmarked for the invasion of Malta, but when this operation was abandoned the High Command had no hesitation in keeping them gainfully employed. The Brigade was despatched to North Africa and went into the line at El Alamein as ordinary infantry.

Though initially overwhelmed, Ramcke and the bulk of his brigade made good their escape. In the confusion of battle they marched westwards into the desert until, close to the limits of their endurance, they came upon and surprised a British supply column – easy pickings even for a much debilitated outfit. Replenished and mobile, Ramcke kept south of the main advance until they made contact with Rommel's rearguard. It was a brilliant achievement and a foretaste of times to come. For the Allies, even with their vast superiority of firepower and resources, still found the German Army in retreat more than a match.

In North Africa Wehrmacht pioneers destroyed bridges, blew in culverts and sewed the ground with cleverly concealed mines, but Montgomery's advance was cautious in any case. He did not trust his armour sufficiently to give them their head; neither did he intend to be lured into any rash moves. Nevertheless, Tobruk and Benghazi, gutted and abandoned, fell after a token resistance. The Germans yielded up the Jebel. It was not until the British came up to El Agheila, where Rommel's entrenchments stretched from the coast to the salt marshes inland, that they encountered a more stubborn defence.

Shan Hackett had sent the PPA into the desert to raid the Jebel, but that once critical ground was again a British backwater. Such was the pace of battle that Popski was out of a job without having even left Kuffra.

The oasis itself had now become obsolete for the first time since the Desert War had begun. It was simply too far from the front and too remote from the action. The LRDG prepared to abandon Kuffra, which reverted to its previous existence as a religious shrine of the Senussi sect. A new main base was established 500 miles north west at Zella, an oasis in the Fezzan, with an advanced outpost 100 miles further on at Hon.

By common consent the area of decision lay 600 miles west, beyond Tripoli and deep inside Tunisia. Years before the French had built a series of fortifications, called the Mareth Line, against the Italian threat from Tripolitania. The Allied landings in North Africa had caused the Italians who now occupied Tunisia to turn the defences round and face the threat from the west. Rommel, however, appreciated that once he had failed in Egypt, the theatre was destined to become a sideshow in which he could never compete for resources with the Eastern Front. Nor could he hope with the forces available to him to fight every inch of the way and defend what remained of the Italian Empire in North Africa. Tripoli in time would fall. The best he could hope to achieve was a bridgehead in Tunisia. Rommel ordered the Mareth Line to be restored and strengthened to the limits of the resources available.

At last General Montgomery had need of the services of the Special Forces. This suited David Stirling, who was eager to take the field once more and with a full complement to his regiment. Nor was this all. Winston Churchill had taken Stirling's message very much to heart during their earlier meetings. When the new British First Army had landed in North Africa it was considered important that it should have the same capabilities as those afforded to the veteran Eighth. Accordingly the nucleus of a Special Force travelled out to North

Africa under the command of David Stirling's brother Bill. He established a training depot at Philippeville and looked to the Commandos for recruits. They had returned in a new role as the shock troops of amphibious warfare, revitalized under the direction of Lord Louis Mountbatten and commanded in the field by Robert Laycock. For the latter in particular it was a triumphant return to a theatre of war which had humbled and abused his previous command. Bill Stirling also had to prove himself. He moved quickly to complete a crash training programme and to take the field with the 2nd Special Air Service Regiment. At first he attempted to emulate the achievements of the senior regiment, but this proved very difficult in the cluttered terrain of North-West Africa to infiltrate jeep raiders behind the lines in the mountains and to attack enemy airfields.

However with First Army ashore and Eighth Army advancing, not just with a clear superiority of firepower but with the feeling of inevitability about their success this time, Special Forces were at best an adjunct to the main event. Even so, David Stirling was determined that his SAS should play a significant role in the final battles in Tunisia; he composed a paper on the subject which he sent to Colonel Shan Hackett at Headquarters. The intention was to infiltrate a force of some 200 men behind enemy lines, with sufficient supplies to allow them to operate independently of the main base for a sustained period. Their target was to be the coastal highway, Rommel's artery for supplies which ran from the port of Tripoli to the front line at Agheila. This 400 miles of highway would be attacked night after night. The aim was not just to destroy enemy supply columns, but rather to make it so expensive that the enemy would be forced into running convoys during daylight hours. This of course would make them immediately vulnerable to attack by the Allied Air Forces.

There were new risks and dangers for the Special Forces as they concentrated their efforts on the borders of Tunisia and Tripolitania. The wide and open desert had given way to a terrain where broken ground denied mobility, and there was a decidedly unfriendly native population. The local Arabs hated their French masters even more than the Senussi had hated the Italians, and the Allied conquest hardly promised to improve their lot. Guerrillas cannot operate effectively if the local people are opposed to them, but this is a lesson which it seems has to be learned afresh on each occasion. An added complication in this instance was the loyalty of the French community, mostly farmers, who again had no particular love for de Gaulle and less for the British.

It must have been a relief to David Stirling to have his plan endorsed by the Army Commander. Having met General Montgomery on a number of occasions since that first frigid encounter, by all accounts Stirling had come to revise his opinion and now held the general in high regard. Montgomery for his part, though the model of civility, showed not the slightest warmth.

One evening over dinner at the Mess with Colonel Hackett present, Montgomery revealed his true feelings to those of his inner circle of advisers:

> 'The boy Stirling,' [began Montgomery after the meal had finished] 'is quite mad. However, in war there is often a place for mad people. Now take this scheme of his. Penetrating miles behind the enemy lines. Attacking the coast road on a 400-mile front. Who but the boy Stirling would think up such a plan! Yet if it comes off I don't mind saying it could have a decisive effect, yes, a really decisive effect on my forthcoming offensive.'

But Montgomery needed all the help he could muster, for Rommel was continuing his brilliant withdrawal westwards along the North Africa coast. It was stalemate as the winter rains turned Tunisia into a sea of mud. As Montgomery encountered stiffening resistance in the east, the Allied advance in the west had lost all momentum. Eisenhower's troops, the British First Army and the American IInd Corps were at the end of a long line of communications. A poor rail-link, bad mountainous roads, atrocious weather, indifferent command and poor staff coordination all comprised to reduce the effectiveness of the fighting troops at the front. However, nothing could disguise the feeling that victory now was just a matter of time and this encouraged those at the front not to take too many risks.

David Stirling was already thinking beyond the North African Campaign. In late November 1942 the battle at Stalingrad reached its first critical point as the Soviet counter-offensive encircled the Germans under General Van Paulus. There were no details available in the Western Desert, but Stirling was well aware of the potential for disaster if the Germans proved victorious and then swung south through the Caucasus for Persia. Paddy Mayne and his squadron had been on continuous operations for some time and were much in need of a rest and a refit. As soon as the new squadrons were ready, he decided that Mayne should be pulled out of the line and sent to Lebanon. Stirling wanted the men trained in skiing and mountain warfare.

General Montgomery had his sights fixed on the more immediate target of the Mareth Line. Intelligence sources had already indicated that this would be a formidable nut to crack.

Was there a way round the landward flank? Would it be suitable for armour? The LRDG was tasked to find the answer to these pressing questions.

Finding the answers was going to take some time. It was more than

1,000 miles from Kuffra to the Mareth Line and the new bases were still to be prepared and stockpiled before long-range operations could be conducted into Tunisia.

Stirling and the LRDG now had missions to plan, but Popski had been left out in the cold. The PPA had been created as a force of saboteurs trained to destroy the enemy's petrol supplies; but the battle front had shrunk and the Axis supply lines now measured just a few hundred miles, so the destruction of petrol was no longer such a critical factor.

Popski decided that his answer lay in operating alongside the LRDG. One method would be to detach his men to join the reconnaissance operations which were now being planned. This would also give them much needed battle experience.

The only problem was that the LRDG was not at all enthusiastic about this plan, and had no desire to play nursemaid.

Popski, however, had an ace card. The LRDG needed jeeps for the reconnaissance missions that lay ahead. The long-legged 30-cwt Chevrolets and Fords with their sawn-off cabs and clapped-out engines were fine in the desert, but in the rock and scrub of the Tunisian hinterland nothing could match the agility of the four-wheel-drive jeep. Today it seems incomprehensible that with its track record the LRDG should have had to go, cap in hand, to a bunch of freebooters with a romantic image and little else to give them legitimacy. But the problem was that at that stage of the war there was neither an effective chain of command nor an overall commander. Colonel Hackett had a staff appointment in a directorate which administered to the needs and attempted to coordinate the various activities of a gaggle of independent Special Force units. He was also required to ensure that their actions complemented conventional operations, but it seemed he had no authority to intervene directly in the internal affairs of these various organizations.

The result was that Popski had a remarkable degree of independence. There was no immediate commander to order him to surrender his vehicles because of the pressing needs of a tried and tested formation. Instead Popski struck a deal with Jake Easonsmith and the LRDG; he would attach his jeeps to the LRDG patrols, which would give the latter the mobility they lacked and provide the PPA with the combat experience they needed.

CHAPTER TWENTY-ONE

Tunisian Tears

In January 1943, the Allies held a Summit Conference. Code-named *Symbol*, the leaders met in the faded opulence of the forty-bedroomed Anfa Hotel and its surrounding villas, near Casablanca in Morocco. General Eisenhower, who had overall responsibility for the security arrangements, voiced his concern, but now that the Allies had taken the initiative in the war it was considered politically important that the meeting should be held on liberated territory.

Stalin refused to attend since the battles at Stalingrad had reached a critical juncture. So all the decision-making was left to Churchill and Roosevelt, together with their retinues of staff. It was eventually agreed that once the campaign was over in North Africa the Axis should be pursued into Sicily and the Mediterranean secured as a vital channel for logistics and supply both to the Soviet Union and for the war effort in the Far East.

The Casablanca Conference also recast the Allied High Command structure yet again. While Eisenhower, US Supremo, prepared for the next operation, General Alexander assumed command of the newly constituted Eighteenth Army Group in Tunisia, which embraced the British First and Eighth Armies and the IInd US Corps. The final battles for North Africa were to be conducted in a tight and highly centralized fashion. In the search for greater coordination and efficiency, some considered the command structure had become too centralized and rigid. That acerbic commentator, General Fuller, called it a 'decline from generalship into ironmongery!'

General Kenneth Anderson, in command of the First Army, had failed to achieve very much once winter had visited the Tunisian

151

mountains. The Germans, who occupied favoured positions in the hills, first blocked the cautious British advance at Tebourba and then inflicted a conspicuous defeat in the pouring rain and the mud of the Battle of Longstop Hill. Though there was some skirmishing and small advances for tactical objectives, the main advance from the West had come to a complete halt. For the duration of the winter, it was to be trench warfare with all the misery and discomfort that was so reminiscent of the Western Front in the Great War.

In the east it was a different story. Montgomery out-generalled Rommel and in late November drove him from the defence line which he had established at El Agheila. The Eighth Army spent Christmas at Sirte, where Montgomery regrouped and resupplied his victorious and by now supremely confident formations.

Logistics still exerted a crushing and sinister influence over Allied progress. Tripoli lay tantalizingly close, but so long as the enemy held the port then the main supply base for the Eighth Army rested on the Nile Delta. Distances were vast. It was the equivalent of fighting a battle on the outskirts of Moscow while using London and the Thames as the main port of supply. Benghazi had come into operation, but that was still 750 miles from the front – or to put it another way, the equivalent of the distance between London and Vienna.

The Long Range Desert Group had established a forward base at Hon, an attractive little oasis some 300 miles south east of Tripoli. Popski was there, and the PPA was ready for operations.

In January the PPA moved off as junior partners of a New Zealand patrol of the LRDG under Captain Tinker, their mission being to reconnoitre a route around the Mareth Line. Compared with the desert of Cyrenaica, the Tunisian landscape was positively pulsating with unfriendly natives as well as the enemy in ever-increasing numbers, forgetting other special and 'friendly' forces. Before their departure Jake Easonsmith warned them to keep an eye out for the SAS who were operating in the area, but precisely where and with what aim nobody knew. David Stirling kept his own counsel and preferred not to disclose his plans to possible rivals.

Desperate to establish a reputation and stake claim to a role in any future campaign, Popski knew he had only limited time. Therefore he took virtually his whole unit into the field. He had agreed to 'assist' the LRDG by making his jeeps available for the reconnaissance of Mareth; once that task was accomplished, he intended to break into the enemy rear areas and raid across Tunisia before linking up with the British First Army.

The main defences of the Mareth Line extended inland as far as Matmata. Montgomery had instructed the LRDG to conduct a reconnaissance of the ground to the south of the town and into the foothills of the Jebel Tebaqa Range. Captain Tinker and Popski established a base camp in a wadi some 60 miles to the south of Matmata. It was fiercely rugged country; the heavily laden three-tonners were being torn apart, and could only make very slow progress cross country. They decided to press ahead with a small jeep force for the final stage of the operation.

Captain Bob Yunnie was left in command back at the wadi, hardly an ideal location. The wadi was a fissure in an otherwise flat plain, a shallow crack between sandstone walls with a soft sandy bottom and a few stunted bushes. Yunnie dispersed the three-tonners and the LRDG trucks near to the bushes and overhangs where they were camouflaged from the air. A defensive perimeter was set up, mines laid further down to the wadi to give warning of enemy armoured car patrols, and a guard set.

The reconnaissance of the Mareth Line was completed without incident. Tinker and Popski took four days to examine the ground and to chart a route. It was just about possible for armour provided that combat engineers were on hand in a number of critical places to ease the progress for the tanks. They were also able to map and plot some recently completed defence works and pill-boxes without the enemy, who were uncharacteristically lax, becoming aware of their presence.

The LRDG's experience and knowledge resulted here in one of the most important contributions by Special Forces to the land battle in North Africa: a route around the Mareth Line.

The party quickly retraced their steps back to base to radio their success to Eighth Army, only to find the camp a smouldering ruin. Its location had been betrayed by the local Arabs, and every vehicle, PPA and LRDG, was destroyed. The incident emphasized once again the vulnerability of Special Forces operating as guerrillas in a countryside where the local inhabitants are hostile.

Yunnie had earlier spotted the Arabs watching from the lip of the wadi, and although he suspected they were up to no good had feared to intervene lest he cause offence. When the Luftwaffe arrived they knew the position of every vehicle. Irrespective of the camouflage, they set about the bombing and strafing of each vehicle in turn until there were none left.

A couple of New Zealanders were wounded in the initial attack, but thereafter Yunnie was able to extricate the remainder of the party and they hid in some cover nearby until the raid was over. The enemy made no attempt to follow up the attack by sending patrols into the area. Yunnie and the others returned to scavenge among the debris, but there was very little left.

Popski was furious and not unnaturally blamed Yunnie for the disaster. They were now in a most desperate plight. The PPA had been associated with the LRDG in a memorable operation, but now fate had snatched the fruits of that success from their hands. Not only did they have no means of letting HQ know of their findings, but the complete vehicle and supply complement of the PPA had been wiped out in a single devastating raid.

The nearest friendly base was the French fort at Tozeur, 200 miles west across country. Between them lay Italian outposts, hostile Arabs and marauding enemy aircraft. There was less risk of enemy motorized groups since the Italians did not operate so far into the interior, but they did have mounted patrols of native cavalry and camel troops who would prove more than a match for a dismounted and largely unarmed body of men. A further worry was the French Camel Corps; these native Goums had a reputation for shooting first and asking questions later, and for being rather indiscriminate in their choice of enemies.

The jeeps had returned from the reconnaissance low in fuel and supplies. Yunnie's base party had lost everything, even their weapons and warm clothing. However, a thorough search did produce some additional food and by pooling the petrol there was enough to send Tinker ahead with three jeeps. He was to reach Tozeur, radio through the information and return with transport.

Popski took command of the walking party, which consisted of 37 men; they had an escort of two jeeps for as long as their petrol lasted.

It was to be another epic march. Most of the men who were at the camp site had sandals for footwear and no socks, or soft-soled desert boots made of suede. Thus it was impossible to cover more than fifteen or twenty miles in a day. Those in sandals chose to go bare-footed, reckoning the discomfort from torn and bleeding feet was slightly less. In sandals, sand got between the toes and the leather acted like sandpaper and stripped away the skin in layers.

There were also Arabs to be handled and this was a delicate task. Like all tribesmen of the region, the men they encountered were destitute and lived miserably off thin, sickly cattle for which they had no decent grazing. The French and the Italians had settled the decent land to the north, and had slowly squeezed the Arabs out of the rich pastures. It was hardly surprising therefore that the Arabs at the bottom of the social pile harboured such a smouldering resentment for the Europeans.

Popski bought food off some Arabs they encountered, for which they paid exorbitant prices. With others they pretended to be Germans with promises of reward for assistance. After four days there was no petrol left for the jeeps, so the vehicles had to be abandoned at an Arab encampment, but somehow Popski kept his footsore party alive and together for a further three days before Captain Tinker found them. The French had refuelled his jeeps and a neighbouring American Army unit had obligingly allowed him to borrow a couple of extra jeeps. Tinker radioed his report to Eighth Army and then immediately set out on the return journey. By this stage, Popski calculated they had marched 150 miles.

Six to a vehicle, they arrived in Tozeur the next day. The French garrison arranged a special lunch at the Hotel Transatlantique, and it was there that the continued existence of the PPA was assured. They were among the first – if not the very first – units from the Eighth Army, to link up with those forces which had landed in French North Africa. War correspondents bored with the inactivity of the First Army's front descended upon the hotel. The strange glamour of Popski's name and this recent escapade, together with their survival, was more than enough to brew up a good story. Reporters plied the weaker brethren of the PPA with whisky; loosened tongues then fabricated wonderful tales of derring-to for a wide-eyed press.

Suddenly the PPA became part of the Desert War mythology and the censors, who in turn recognized easy political propaganda, allowed the accounts to be printed. Such notoriety was as offensive to many in the Special Forces as it was to Popski, although as a good opportunist he was the first to acknowledge that it did no harm in keeping a stake in future operations.

CHAPTER TWENTY-TWO

Out of Africa

On 15 January 1943 Montgomery launched an offensive aimed at Tripoli, even though this meant denuding his reserve formations of supplies and transport in order to make the attacking divisions sufficiently mobile.

The SAS harried the German lines of communication and David Stirling was as good as his word to the Army Commander. But this required them to fight and to raid in difficult country along the coast road between Gabes and Sfax. There was little room for concealment other than what the night could offer, and surprise was no longer possible to achieve. After the first few incidents, the Germans provided a heavy escort for their convoys. Even though the jeeps packed a mighty punch, with more than enough firepower to knock out soft-skinned transports, they were no match for German armoured cars with 20 mm-cannon.

Captain Jordain and the Free French squadron pressed home their attack with great vigour and suffered severe casualties as a consequence. Such was the ferocity and persistence of the German response that the French patrols were forced to separate. Captain Jordain was eventually cornered; outnumbered and outgunned, he was compelled to surrender.

Though German convoys had been shot up and significant damage inflicted, the SAS had seven of their patrols destroyed, which was a high price to pay.

The German Command had been sufficiently concerned by these attacks to deploy a Feldgendarmerie unit from Italy into North Africa; their express purpose was to coordinate efforts in hunting down Allied

Special Forces operating behind their lines. Other formations were also sent out as reinforcements after a raid; they would help to search particular localities for base camps and hideaways.

Geography was now in the Germans' favour, since to reach their targets Allied Special Forces had to pass through a feature known as the Gabes Gap – a natural bottleneck, no more than 5 miles wide at its narrowest point. There was no other way round. The French SAS squadron had stirred up a hornets' nest and the enemy were particularly vigilant.

David Stirling had been sniffing around the Mareth Line when he attempted to negotiate the Gabes Gap. He was with a patrol of four jeeps and they were spotted from the air. Fortunately, it was late in the day, so the enemy could not respond. Stirling kept moving throughout the night and by morning the patrol had put 20 miles between them and the Gap. The plan was to attack the railway at Sousse that night, so the patrol scattered at first light to find concealment and rest. They were to rendezvous at dusk.

This was to be the day when Stirling's luck finally deserted him. Feldgendarmerie were out on exercise together with other troops, mostly rear echelon units roped in to help in a cordon and search operation. By chance they focused on the very wadi in which David Stirling and three others had bedded down for the day. For some unaccountable reason, although the enemy and three soldiers came face to face, Stirling's men were not challenged and made good their escape.

Their leader, asleep in a nearby cave, was less fortunate. He awoke to the pressure of a Luger to his temper, the weapon gripped by an understandably nervous and excited young soldier. Stirling, the scourge of the Afrika Korps, had been captured by a dentist who joined the exercise just to vary his usual routine.

At this stage, however, the enemy were quite unaware of the identity of their captive, though they searched the surrounding country with renewed vigour and flushed out other members of the patrol.

There were 10 captives and late the next day, when the enemy considered the area to be swept clear, the prisoners were taken away in a truck with a Field Police half-track as the escort. At dusk the convoy stopped and the prisoners were locked into a large empty barn for the night. The sentries were lax and David Stirling and a Lieutenant McDermott made a break for it and escaped into the darkness. At first, all went well, and they made good time heading across country. Navigating by the stars, Stirling intended to head back to an area which he knew the SAS were likely to frequent. Somehow in the early hours of the morning, tired and weary, they became separated.

Stirling pushed on alone, but he had neither food nor warm clothing and was forced to make contact with the local people. Belatedly the enemy realized whom they had captured and lost. A hue and cry was raised and there a price put on his head. A young shepherd boy offered Stirling assistance, and led him straight into the arms of an Italian search party.

This time there was no escape. David Stirling was quickly taken to Italy and imprisoned. After his fourth escape attempt, the Germans had him removed to the Reich and incarcerated in Colditz.

Rommel wrote in his journal: 'The British lost the very able and adaptable commander of the desert group which had caused us more damage than any other British unit of equal strength.'*

At about the same time and in complete contrast to the frantic activities of the other Special Forces, the Indian Long Range Squadron was detached on separate duties. They set off to reconnoitre the tracks which led through the interior of Tripolitania and towards its southern borders. At the time this region deep in the interior was called Fezzan. In their only active operation in the North African campaign the IRLS were to find General Leclerc, who had left Lake Chad in Equatorial Africa with a column to join in the final battles of the North African Campaign. The Indian Long Range Squadron were dispersed across their anticipated line of march to lend assistance and escort the Frenchmen to the coast.

Half a patrol was detached under Braine and another corporal called Collins. A Liverpudlian from the King's Regiment, the latter was a good navigator, a hard-fighting and hard-drinking soldier who could never enjoy himself on the drill square but found unconventional soldiering entirely to his taste.

They were ordered to take their trucks to a place called Sevare which was near to Murzuq. Nobody was sure who held the town – Italians, Free French or Vichy French. Perhaps it was deserted.

A recognition signal had been arranged with the French authorities, who had until recently controlled the North African Colonies in the name of Vichy. Instructions had supposedly been transmitted to all their isolated outposts. It was a simple enough signal; about half a mile from a fort, the approaching patrol was required to have two men standing up on a vehicle with a blanket held out between them.

When they came within half a mile of the fort at Sevare, two men clambered on to the back of their truck, faced the front and held up a blanket between them.

There was no response.

A flag was flying over the fort, an ancient weather-beaten pile with

* *Rommel Papers*, p. 393, trans. Liddel Hart (Collins, London, 1953).

crumbling walls, ramparts and a solitary watch-tower. The flag looked like the French tricolour, but in the hazy light of the late afternoon, and at that distance, it could just as easily have been the Italian tricolour.

They took a chance and moved closer.

The flag was French, but the fort was deserted, so they settled into the place and made themselves at home. Nevertheless it had an uncanny feel. Pieces of equipment and uniforms lay discarded; there was even a legionnaire's kepi, and Braine could not help but recall a popular film called *Beau Geste* starring Gary Cooper.

They waited for a week – one of the most boring weeks Braine could remember in his entire military service. The Indian havildar or NCO took responsibility for all the chores and the guards, so time hung heavily on the shoulders of the two British soldiers. What made it even more tedious was that they ran out of cigarettes. Braine and Collins took to spending their afternoons a little distance from the fort taking pot-shots with their rifles at empty tin-cans and bottles.

One afternoon a cloud of dust moved towards them, heralding a convoy of vehicles. It was impossible to identify them, but assuming it was Captain Birdwood with the remainder of the patrol, the two young men walked out into the desert to meet the column.

Collins looked at the vehicles and shaded his eyes. 'They're not ours, you know,' he said.

'What shall we do?' asked Braine.

'Run off back to the fort.'

'They're too close for that now. If we start running back they'll shoot us in the back; better bluff it out.'

The column came nearer and about a hundred yards away it stopped.

A man scrambled from the leading patrol car. He was dressed in the most bedraggled outfit, but wore the distinctive kepi and had a carbine in his hand.

He was indeed a Free French officer and the men with him were mostly Senegalese. They were the advance guard of the long-awaited column which had completed the 1,500-mile journey from Lake Chad. Strung out behind them were a further 3,000 who had fought their way northwards, destroying Italian outposts on their line of march and replenishing their pitifully inadequate supplies from plundered storehouses and petrol dumps.

The French officer lost no time in contacting General Leclerc. Unbeknown to Braine and Collins, the French claimed to have liberated Brach!

There were 20 vehicles, a single officer, a few French NCOs and the

Senegalese in the advance guard. Braine radioed their presence and they were ordered to abandon the fort and lead the column northwards. They met Captain Birdwood at a rendezvous the next morning and a couple of days later made contact with Leclerc's main column which was being led in by one of the LRDG Rhodesian patrols. Screening the column's advance was Leclerc's picturesque Camel Corps detachment.

The 'conquest' of the Fezzan was completed on 21 January 1943 with the capture of Murzouk, the capital, and Sebha, the main military base. In almost every case the Italians offered only a token resistance and capitulated with indecent haste. After a short refit, Leclerc took his column to Ghadames.

The Indian Long Range Squadron, together with the Rhodesian LRDG, pulled out of the line as the Free French columns linked in with Montgomery's left or landward flank.

The Eighth Army continued their offensive and in a brilliantly executed manoeuvre flushed Rommel out of the defence positions he had built at Buerat. At dawn on Saturday 23 January 1943, an advance guard of the Eighth Army symbolically comprising representatives from those desert veterans the 7th Armoured, 51st Highland and 2nd New Zealand Divisions entered Tripoli. The enemy had razed the harbour in an effort to prevent its use, but the British were not to be denied their moment of triumph. A Valentine, the first tank in the column, was piped into the town by a Gordon Highlander preceded by a Bren-gun carrier manned by New Zealanders. It was three months to the day since the offensive had begun at El Alamein 1,400 miles to the east.

The last remaining capital of Mussolini's former African Empire passed into British hands. Technically this marked the end of the Desert Campaign.

At noon on 23 January General Montgomery received the official surrender of Tripoli from the Vice-Governor of Libya at a point just outside the city walls. The Army Commander then entered the city at the head of more columns of tanks and armoured vehicles which filed in from the suburbs, and thence past their commander who stood on a hastily erected review stand in the main square.

The fighting soldiers moved on out of the city, for though the Desert Campaign was won the enemy was not beaten yet.

By the end of January 1943, the Eighth Army had pushed about 200 miles beyond Tripoli. Just 200 miles now separated the Allied Armies and there was very little requirement for the Special Forces. Those which were operating were deployed to the landward flank of the Eighth Army, checking out the occasional and invariably abandoned forts and encampments.

The Indian Long Range Squadron moved ahead to the flank of the Eighth Army. They were given clearly defined areas in which to make a detailed reconnaissance so that should the need arise to switch the advance further inland, information was available.

Still enjoying the benefits of the popular press, Popski managed to have his unit completely re-equipped and re-armed by an overawed and over generous quartermaster's department from the American IInd Corps supply depot. The excellent American combat jackets and waterproof clothing was especially welcome protection against the miserably damp conditions of the Tunisian spring. Their new jeeps were armed with belt-fed Browning machine guns whose .50-calibre shells gave them a fighting chance against German armoured cars. The Dodge six-by-six truck enhanced their cross-country capabilities and was so new they could smell the paint.

The much vaunted Mareth Line still stood between Montgomery and the Allied forces in the west. Rommel, ever the opportunist, decided to have another attempt. He proposed therefore to hit Montgomery with a spoiling attack, catching the Eighth Army as it deployed to attack the Mareth Line. This, Rommel believed, would give sufficient breathing space to turn the full weight of the still significant German forces against the western salient and inflict a withering defeat on the Anglo-Americans. So long as the fighting continued in North Africa, the Allies would not be able to do much more than contemplate an invasion of the European mainland.

British Intelligence interpretations and 'Ultra' intercepts provided ample forewarning of the impending attack even down to the date. Pausing in their advance, the 51st Highland and 7th Armoured Division deployed an anti-tank screen and ambush at Medenine.

On the 6 March three veteran Panzer Divisions were repulsed and forced into ignominious retreat with the loss of seventy tanks and armoured fighting vehicles.

Sick in body and spirit, Rommel left Africa for ever on 9 March and Von Arnim assumed the command. Montgomery renewed his advance and assaulted the Mareth Line. Rarely in the annals of military history could a commander have known more about the objective which lay ahead of him. Senior French officers and engineers who had designed and first constructed the defences were on hand; there were prisoners whose interrogations revealed even more details on defences; there was aerial photography, where interpretation had by now become a most sophisticated skill. Finally Montgomery had the results of the detailed reconnaissance carried out by the LRDG and PPA, as well as SAS reports in abundance. The LRDG had found and reconnoitred a route which would allow the Mareth Line to be outflanked on the landward side. It is therefore difficult to explain why Montgomery launched a frontal assault against the centre of the Mareth Line and the very heart of the enemy stronghold.

That part of the line was held by the Italians, for whom Montgomery had a well-founded contempt. Even so, the battle is remarkable for its complete rejection of the recommendations of those Special Forces whom the Army Commander had tasked to find the open flank.

The attack ended in disaster. The Italian Young Fascist and the Trieste Divisions put up a surprisingly tenacious defence against an abrupt British infantry assault which had moved up behind an over-generous artillery barrage. Tanks and Panzer Grenadiers from the 15th Panzers led the counter-attack which hurled the British back in dismay.

Montgomery was forced to switch his assault to the left flank far inland. The New Zealand Corps – which comprised the veteran 2nd New Zealand Infantry Division, the 8th Armoured Brigade and the regrouped Leclerc Division – advanced along the route which the LRDG and PPA had reconnoitred. Joined by the First British Armoured Division, in a brilliantly directed operation, the Corps outflanked the defences and forced the enemy into full retreat.

Even as the Tunisian Campaign drew to its now inevitable close, Popski led his PPA once again into the field. With the Mareth Line ruptured, the Anglo-Americans in the west cautiously resumed the offensive and Popski was able to break behind the enemy lines and for a few days at least experience the exhilaration of shooting up convoys and retreating columns.

Popski led his little band of jeeps eastwards, moving very cautiously on the lookout for the advance elements of the Eighth Army. It was at times like these that accidents could easily occur, when mistaken identities between advancing spearhead units on a collision course could end in tragedy. The PPA came out of the Tunisian hills on to the coastal plain, made themselves known and thence linked up with the forward elements of the First British Armoured Division. They then joined forces with the armoured car screen of the advance guard and for a couple of days were employed in a minor reconnaissance role.

In early May the surviving enemy, Germans and Italians, were penned into a 70-mile perimeter at Cape Bon; it was left to the conventionally armed formations to complete the submission. Some attempt was made to evacuate the remnants of the Germans. The Royal Navy controlled the narrow waters and despite Luftwaffe and Italian air bases on Sicily, went to work with a will to fulfill Admiral Cunningham's order of the day to, 'Sink, burn and destroy. Let nothing pass.'

A few enemy escaped in an airlift, but the vast majority of the lumbering transports which attempted the passage were shot down.

In this final act there was no room nor role for special forces. The LRDG, together with the Indian Long Range Squadron, returned eastwards towards the Delta. A long convoy of battered Chevs, Fords and jeeps with the three-ton Bedfords trying manfully to maintain the pace threaded their way through the garbage of war and out on to the coastal highway.

Elements of the SAS remained in Tunisia. The sudden removal of their leader caused considerable difficulties, for the Special Air Service Regiment in 1943 was a reflection of David Stirling's persona; he alone had a vision of the future, but he confided those thoughts to none of his contemporaries. Paddy Mayne stepped into the breach. This outstandingly able commander was to lead the regiment brilliantly in the field for the remainder of the war, but he lacked the lobby skills and 'drawing room diplomacy' which Stirling possessed. Mayne had neither the inclination nor the intention to fight the long, exhausting intrigues required to hold the disparate groups together. Even before the fighting had ceased, the Special Boat Section broke away under Lord Jellicoe, while the Free French Squadrons sought regimental status. Shortly afterwards, the Greek Sacred Regiment followed its own path.

Popski kept the PPA in Tunisia while he sniffed around Allied Headquarters seeking future employment.

The war in the desert had been a unique experience. Popski and the other private armies in Tunisia had a foretaste of what war in inhabited countries could be like, and none had enjoyed the experience. In the desert the Special Forces and the conventional battalions and regiments had fought a clean conflict exclusively between soldiers. With nothing to ravage, they had left no trail of burnt houses and inflicted no miseries upon the innocent.

Neither was the country defaced by the war.

The Special Forces had also epitomized an Eighth Army attitude collectively held towards opponents. They had fought one enemy they despised, the Italians; and another, the Germans, whom they respected and even liked to some degree. But even they were aware this was a sideshow, and that in the spring of 1943 the real war – the war for Europe – had yet to begin.

Some of the Special Forces had started to prepare for this new phase of fighting and there was a fair concentration of exotic formations along the more desirable stretches of the Levantine coastline.

A thousand miles and more to the west on 13 May 1943, the surrender of the Italian Field Marshal Giovanni Messe, nominally the Commander-in-Chief of Axis Forces in North Africa, marked the end of the Campaign. General Von Arnim and 200,000 men in Army Group Africa capitulated.

General Alexander cabled Winston Churchill:

'Sir,

It is my duty to report that the Tunisian Campaign is over. All enemy resistance has ceased. We are masters of the North African Shore.'

PART FOUR

DEFEAT IN THE EAST

CHAPTER TWENTY-THREE

Japanese Sunrise

After El Alamein, Special Forces were able to contribute little, even though the final defeat of the Axis in North Africa took a further six months. The pace of battle and the entrenched attitudes of senior commanders, who saw little virtue in taking risks and everything to be gained by playing safe, swept the private armies to the sidelines. In truth, some had already outlived any usefulness and even those with an enviable track record of success had to lobby for their continued existence. The loss of Stirling occurred at a particularly crucial time in the unit's history, but his loss may not have materially affected a trend which suggested as the war progressed that the powers that be had less need of such elite special units.

When it comes to the war against Japan, the circumstances are remarkably similar.

In the Far East, the Allies ought to have been better prepared, both in terms of conventional war and the role of the unconventional. There, the war clouds had been gathering for some time when in the summer of 1941, the Japanese descended upon Indo-China and the Vichy French, humiliated, bowed to the inevitable. The Japanese Imperial Navy sailed into Camranh Bay, the finest natural harbour in the Orient. Thirty thousand Japanese soldiers and marines landed at Saigon and Haiphong. In Washington, President Roosevelt's response was immediate, and thus the fate of Asia was sealed.

Presidential decrees froze Japanese assets in the United States, denied the Panama Canal to Japanese shipping and slapped a crippling embargo on the export of strategic materials – rubber, oil and metals to Japan. Britain and the Netherlands' government-in-exile followed suit.

War between Japan and the Western powers was now a matter of timing and it opened with a series of spectacular victories for the Japanese. The Anglo-Americans together with assorted Allies, despite months of warning and ample time in which to prepare, were humiliated and expelled from their colonies by an Asiatic foe who proved their master when it came to fighting a machine-age war in the jungle and at sea.

On the face of things the demise of Western conventional force of arms ought to have provided the opportunity for irregular warfare, and indeed some guerrilla groups did emerge out of the shambles of defeat. In the Philippines fugitive Americans joined with the local populations, civilians and soldiers, in guerrilla bands, a few of which survived until liberation three years later. Elsewhere amongst the Pacific Islands Americans and Australians established a clandestine network of coast watchers. In Malaya, and at the eleventh hour, a number of stay-behind parties were organized.

In all of these instances, very few survived and none can be said to have made any significant impact on the war as guerrillas. The reason is that the difficulties were well-nigh insurmountable.

In December 1941 the Japanese invaded the territories of three Imperial powers: Great Britain, the United States and Holland. If the truth be known all of the Imperial powers were unpopular, some more than others. For the Americans who lived and worked in the Philippines, that island archipelago was like India to the British – a hot and enervating land rich in servants and other amenities of colonial life. Pampered and closeted from the grimy realities of the industrial world, over the years the rigidly stratified society had spawned an imperial aristocracy with a life that few of their countrymen at home would have recognized. It was a land where living was opulent yet cheap, so that hard-earned fortunes need not be squandered in support of 'standards'. Even those in more humble occupations among the white community could afford servants and the best the islands had to offer.

For the British in Malaya, Burma, Singapore and Hong Kong, life was a Victorian dream in which Europe's war dared not intrude. For the most part, the Malays accepted British authority with polite indifference and reserved what reverence they had for their Sultans. The Dutch in the East Indies lived in their own fools' paradise in which the occupation of their country seemed only to act as a stimulant in the search for greater compensations. Yet even before the outbreak of war, all were confronted by nationalist inspired oppositions which in some cases flared periodically into open rebellion.

The Japanese were also able to benefit, at least initially, from the cosmopolitan nature of the societies they sought to conquer.

Throughout south and eastern Asia there was a tremendous mixture of races, religions and tongues; many of these peoples were mutually antagonistic.

Even more importantly, most of the Asian peoples – with the exception of the Chinese communities – had little dealings with or experience of the Japanese. Therefore the defeat of the Europeans in such a convincing fashion, and by an Asian power using European weapons, shattered the illusion of white supremacy seemingly once and for all. It was the same story from Manila to Rangoon. The triumphant arrival of the Japanese was greeted by those Asians who had the wit and understanding to comprehend such events as the dawn of a new age. The merchants, government servants and those with some education did not mourn the passing of the European whites. For the peasants, absorbed by the demands of simply surviving, the passage of armies was of little consequence except in their pillage. Only the Chinese cowered in terror, and by the time others had experienced the full horrors of a Japanese occupation it was too late.

Geographically the environment was hostile to Europeans waging guerrilla warfare. No European could hope to survive undetected in any Asian city, yet for the guerrillas to be effective they had to attack targets near centres of population. So the Europeans skulked deep in the jungle, far away from the enemy, betrayal and worthwhile targets.

Another problem was the Japanese war ethic. Throughout the war the Japanese treated unsurrendered servicemen or soldiers caught operating behind their lines as outlaws rather than prisoners-of-war. Upon capture, these men almost without exception were executed summarily. Such actions were a further and brutal deterrent to the use of guerrillas in uniform, but were quite legal under the existing rules of land warfare.

The biggest obstacle of all was the jungle.

In the West, the perception persists that the jungle is filled with choice fruits, a tropical paradise where living is easy. In reality the opposite is the case, as Spencer Chapman discovered when he became a guerrilla in Japanese-occupied Malaya. Chapman's brilliant account of his experience is evocatively entitled *The Jungle is Neutral**, meaning that it is impartial in its hostility. The native survives with difficulty and for the European to do the same for any prolonged period absorbs so much of his time and effort that he has little energy left to fight the enemy – that is, unless he is first carefully prepared and acclimatized.

Travel in the jungle, especially on foot and over any distance, is a slow and laborious business filled with danger and risks from

---

*Spencer Chapman, *The Jungle is Neutral* (Chatto and Windus, London, 1963).

predators, two-legged and otherwise. In parts of Burma and Malaya, a journey of 50 miles through the jungle could take a small party anything up to two weeks. In the jungle, guerrillas had little tactical mobility. This was a lesson learned the hard way by the Chindits, years after by the Communists in Malaya, the French and later the Americans in Indo-China.

Once the British had been expelled from Malaya, the nearest friendly base for support and supplies lay thousands of miles west across the Indian Ocean in Ceylon. Until 1944 and the arrival of the Liberator bomber, only the slow and desperately vulnerable Catalina flying-boats possessed the endurance to make the round trip. It was 1,300 miles from Colombo to Penang and a further 400 miles to Singapore; with such distances involved, the use of surface shipping was quite out of the question. It would have required an ocean-going vessel to make the voyage and such a ship would easily be spotted amongst the coastal traffic – sampons and fishing boats – which sailed off shore.

Militarily, very little forethought was devoted to guerrilla warfare before the outbreak of hostilities, which is hardly surprising since it smacks of defeatism. While it is the task of the military profession to contemplate the worst possible scenario, that did not include defeat of the land armies. The Japanese threat was seen in strictly conventional terms and with the priorities resting on home defence, then the Western Desert and the Mediterranean, there was precious little to spare for the Far East – and none for the unconventional.

While it was true that conventional defences had crumbled before the German blitzkrieg, the Japanese were not considered in the same league, akin to the Italians, in capability. What was also pertinent to defence planners was precedent. The local resistance movements in Europe had yet to make their mark despite more than a year of occupation. Neither had the Commandos launched any significant raids across the English Channel into Occupied Europe, even though they enjoyed the Prime Minister's personal interest and patronage.

Thus when it came to the Far East it was hardly surprising that only a token effort was made in the unconventional field of warfare. It was to be a colonial responsibility. Just as the Middle East Command had formed its Commandos, so volunteers were called from the Australian and New Zealand Armies to raise their own independent companies.

A training team was despatched from England under the command of Colonel A. Mawhood. The instructors included Mike Calvert, a Sapper officer who was a specialist in demolitions, and Spencer Chapman, a schoolmaster in peacetime with an established reputation as a mountaineer and explorer. Both young officers had volunteered for the Scots Guards Ski Battalion, a force raised at the outbreak of war to fight on the side of Finland against Moscow's Bolshevik hordes.* Thereafter they had been posted to the newly created Commando Training School at Lockailort in Scotland, where they worked alongside those who were later to become the legends of Special Forces such as David Stirling, 'Mad Jack' Churchill and others.

In August 1940 even as invasion threatened Colonel Mawhood took his team – to be called No. 104 Military Mission – to Newport Docks in South Wales, where they boarded the SS *Rimutaka* for the long voyage to the Antibes. It was a lone voyage too, for their ship, a cargo-liner of the New Zealand Shipping Company, was considered to be fast enough to make an independent passage. Even so, her route was carefully plotted to avoid the U-Boat menace and threat from commerce raiders operating in disguise. They sailed high across the North Atlantic and to Bermuda, thence via the Panama Canal and across the Pacific to Pitcairn Island, Auckland, Sidney and finally Melbourne.

Neither in Australia nor in New Zealand could the military top brass agree on a set of objectives for the independent companies. It was accepted that the Japanese had for some considerable time been preparing for war in the greatest secrecy and doubtless with time and place in their favour they would seize territory, if only islands in the Pacific. So what role could most usefully be fulfilled by the independent companies? One school of thought favoured the creation of cadres, guerrilla leaders to direct the local resistance; another advocated stay-behind parties whose task would be to coordinate raiding operations. A third group believed the answer lay in sabotage parties along the lines of the infant SOE in London. From all these confusions jungle fighting, raiding and amphibious warfare seemed a common theme, and it was to teach these skills that Military Mission 104 established a training school.

Wilson's Promontory, a national park in Southern Victoria, was chosen because of the wide variety of terrain and conditions that were available. There was forest and mountains, swamps, rivers and sand-dunes behind long shelving beaches in the lagoons formed by offshore islands. Here men could be trained to fight for the desert of North Africa or the jungles of New Guinea. In the New Year of 1941, Colonel Mawhood and his team were hard at work establishing their Australian version of Lochailort.

Syllabus and training methods were very similar to those in Scotland. Changes would be made, but only in the light of experience,

---

*The author's own account of this bizarre formation is detailed in the first volume of this series, *Churchill's Private Armies* (Hutchinson, London, 1987)

and there had been precious little activity in that direction in the war to date. Australians and New Zealanders were put through their paces on a six-week course where officers and men were treated exactly the same and those who failed to make the grade were sent back to their units. Had the Middle East Commando received the benefits of a centralized training scheme in their early days, perhaps their story might have been different and the units subject to less misuse and abuse by the military hierarchy.

By the summer of 1941 the British instructors had achieved their objective. The school was established and running smoothly and both Calvert and Chapman had trained their replacements. Mike Calvert went to Burma, where he joined the recently formed Bush Warfare School outside Rangoon. Spencer Chapman was sent to Singapore and in September 1941 reported as the first Chief Instructor to the Special Training School there.

Pearl Harbor was just three months away.

CHAPTER TWENTY-FOUR

Defeat in the East

In 1926 the American War Plan code-named *Orange* envisaged that the Philippines would be the principal target for the Japanese. Washington's grand strategy, as simple as it was naïve, assumed that the Japanese would send their fleet against Lingayen Gulf, the most obvious bay for an amphibious invasion of the main island of Luzon and a descent on Manila. Thence the battleships of the US Pacific Fleet would sally forth from their sanctuary at Pearl Harbor to succour the Philippines and there would be a grand victory somewhere in the South China Sea. In the unlikely event that the fleet should be delayed, then the garrison would retreat into the mountains and island forts in Manila Bay until the Navy won through. America, after all, was an optimistic nation which had never known defeat.

In June 1941, after a series of high level and top secret conferences with senior British officers, the Americans reappraised their grand strategy. War Plan Five was agreed and adopted by Roosevelt's Joint Army-Navy Board. On the assumption of a world war, it was the Allied intention to pursue a 'Europe first strategy'. So far as the Philippines, Malaya and elsewhere in the Far East was concerned, the Allies would pursue a 'defensive strategy'. For the Americans at least, that was a rather polite way of saying that the Philippines would be abandoned to the enemy.

This was not because the planners believed that a Japanese strike on Pearl Harbor would cut the lifeline to the Philippines. Nobody in authority saw Pearl Harbor as even threatened. From the very outset the target was always perceived to be the Philippines, the capture of which would sever the American lines of communication and deny the United States a naval base in the Western Pacific.*

Against this threat the task of the American garrison was to hold the entrance to Manila Bay and deny its use to the enemy for as long as possible. The old Plan *Orange* optimistically called for the defence to hold out for six months, by which time the Pacific Fleet would have fought its way into Manila Bay to succour the fortress.

After June 1941 there was nobody in Washington privy to the debate who believed that such a rescue was possible. The Philippine Islands are strategically located in the very heart of the Far East; Manila is over 5,000 miles from Honolulu and less than 1,700 miles from Tokyo. The islands lie athwart the main trade routes from China and Japan through the South China Sea and thence into resource-rich South-East Asia and the Dutch East Indies. Japanese air bases on the island of Formosa were only 700 miles from Manila. In 1941 it took three days to fly by Pan American clipper the 7,000 miles to San Francisco. With these distances involved, the resources were simply not available to actively pursue a war on two fronts.

No evacuation plans for the Philippines or Malaya could be ordered. Instead, those select few in Washington and London privy to the contents of War Plan Five would have to live a lie. Naval experts anticipated that it would take the fleet at least two years to fight their way across the Pacific. War Plan Five said nothing, but the assumptions were clear: once the supplies were exhausted, the defenders would have to surrender.

The great American public might forgive a defeat in the Philippines after a spirited resistance, but the public outcry could destroy the administration if they thought their boys had been abandoned. Roosevelt and the Chief of Staff, General Marshall, knew the charade had to be played out to the end. Reinforcements, politically adequate and suitably packaged in a patriot fervour, were sent to the Philippines.

It was not until October that General MacArthur, the Commander-in-Chief in the Philippines, was informed of War Plan Five and its implications. In the meantime besides the reinforcements other means were sought to dissuade the Japanese. Squadrons of B17s, the new wonder bomber, were despatched to the Philippines as a physical deterrent to the threat of Japanese aggression.

The British had much the same thought about the need for a deterrent. Churchill despatched the capital ships *Prince of Wales* and *Repulse* to Singapore, but in other senses they placed a different

---

*For a more detailed account see the author's own account *Corregidor: The Nightmare in the Philippines* (Hutchinson, London, 1982).

interpretation on the regional implications of the Europe first strategy. They were confident of thwarting the Japanese even though playing second fiddle to the German War. After all there were the vast resources of India upon which to draw and the formidable seaward defences of Singapore upon which to rely. Nobody was under any illusions about the importance of Malaya and its desirability to the Japanese, given their own desperate need for raw materials; neither was the possibility of a seaborne invasion of the Malayan Peninsula followed by an advance overland disregarded.

Singapore was at the very centre of British grand strategy because it was seen as the key to a power which was essentially maritime. Everybody believed in the impregnability of the naval base to the extent that it had become an article of faith, held as much by Winston Churchill in Whitehall as the rickshaw boy on Orchard Drive in downtown Singapore. It was spacious enough to accommodate a good-sized battle squadron; the island was defended by massive fortifications to repel sea attack and the landward approach was protected by nature, impenetrable jungle.

Where the British High Command miscalculated so abysmally was in their perception of the jungle as a barrier, in the fighting ability of the Japanese and the quality of their own troops to see off the enemy in that jungle.

The British had convinced themselves that the jungle was impenetrable. Only one battalion, 2nd Argyll and Sutherland Highlanders, had specialized in jungle warfare, but their skills were an embarrassment since they demonstrated the jungle was anything but impenetrable.

Nobody in authority was prepared to face the truth, as Spencer Chapman found when he joined No. 101 Training School. Their task was to undertake all the training, civilian and military, Europeans and Asians, in irregular warfare and clandestine intelligence gathering. There was a substantial corps of instructors, 10 officers and 50 soldiers led by Lieut-Colonel J. H. L. Gavin R. E., another Lockailort graduate.

Officialdom's attitude to guerrilla warfare was made clear in October, when a detailed contingency plan prepared by Gavin and Chapman was forwarded to the Governor-General and the Commander-in-Chief for their consideration. Their premise was that initial Japanese impetus would enable them to secure a presence on the Malayan Peninsula, but then the defences would hold firm. Such a situation presented ample opportunity for guerrilla warfare behind enemy lines.

They did not have to wait long for a response. Rejection arrived abruptly and initially without any explanation. It was only by persistent questioning – of the kind that would have spelt doom to a regular officer's career – that any reasons were elicited. The concept was seen as defeatist and the plan, which depended upon the use of Chinese, trained and armed for the job, politically naïve.

Perhaps the government in Malaya could be forgiven for being reluctant to change its stance over the Chinese. At the time the two million Chinese made up to 40 per cent of the population of Malaya, by far the highest overseas Chinese proportion of any nation. Resistance to British rule found a coherent expression after 1930 when the Communist Party was established, interestingly not under the auspices of Mao Tse-Tung's Chinese party but rather as an offshoot of the Kremlin's Far Eastern Bureau based in Shanghai.

From the outset British Special Branch had been able to penetrate the movement, and at the highest level. The leader Lai Tek was at least a double agent – he worked both for Moscow and London – and when the Japanese came, a triple agent, since there is more than a suspicion that he was recruited by the Kempetai, Japan's military intelligence.

Chinese resistance to British rule had been persistent but low key and containable. The threat always appeared greater than the reality; but the community was one not to be trusted.

The first change came in July 1941 when Hitler invaded Russia. Britain and Russia were now allies, the Malayan Communist Party suspended operations and an uneasy truce reigned in the months before the outbreak of war in the Far East.

Some half-hearted talks were held between the General Staff and representatives of the Chinese community on the ways and means in which the latter might contribute. Little progress was made by the time the Japanese crippled the American Fleet at Pearl Harbor and then turned their full force and fury on to the Philippines, Hong Kong and Malaya.

The beaches at Kota Bharu, close to the Kra Isthmus and the northern border of Malaya with Siam, had long since been identified as a possible invasion point and were defended by battalions of the 8th Indian Infantry Brigade.

What caught the defenders by surprise was the speed and ferocity of assault by an enemy willing to accept higher casualties than they, and the surrender of their air cover to an enemy flying more and better machines than the Royal Air Force could muster. The loss of the *Prince of Wales* and *Repulse* on Wednesday 10 December was a terrible shock which, when combined with enemy success on land, caused morale to plummet among the fighting troops and the High Command to surrender initiative on the battlefield. Individual acts of bravery and heroism were overwhelmed by the relentless tide of the Japanese advance.

Partially trained and poorly led, the British and Imperial troops fell back in disarray as an orderly retreat took on the dimensions of a shameful rout. In the face of such failure General Percival, the Commander-in-Chief, and his staff had to re-think their strategy.

Gavin and Chapman were summoned to Headquarters and ordered to implement their contingency plan without delay. The Russians ordered Lai Tek to offer the British every assistance and, in the few weeks that remained, stay-behind parties were hurriedly organized and some even deployed into the field.

The problems were immense. While one element of No. 101 Special Training School assumed responsibility for the Chinese, Spencer Chapman concentrated on creating guerrilla groups to be run by the British. The Chinese operation had to be a separate affair because there were few Chinese-speaking British officers; such was the colonial conceit that it was inconceivable that the Chinese could be entrusted to run their own show.

Chapman planned to deploy a chain of parties, each comprised of officers with local knowledge, planters, mining engineers etc. and a demolition expert, together with Malays and Tamils. Sites had to be chosen, dumps stockpiled with supplies and the guerrillas hurriedly trained and in place before the enemy reached the area. The sites had to be chosen with the Europeans in mind; no white man could hope to survive in an Asian city, neither could he pass himself off as Hasaldene and others had been able to do when they moved among the Arabs in the Western Desert. So Chapman had to choose locations that were remote enough to serve as sanctuary but still close enough to the main centres of activity for the guerrillas to function effectively.

There were enormous obstacles to overcome, most of which could have been solved had there been more time and preparation. As it was, those very few teams of incredibly brave men took to the field inadequately prepared and without that special bond of trust essential between men operating as guerrillas behind enemy lines.

The guerrilla teams took to the jungle without adequate communications, for there were no decent radios available to the British anywhere in the Far East. Guerrilla warfare had belatedly assumed its rightful priority, but even then the only radio available was so heavy and cumbersome that with its generator, battery and fuel it required six men to manhandle it into battle.

Another unit of raiders was raised when those Royal Marines who had survived the sinking of the *Prince of Wales* and *Repulse* joined *Roseforce*. Major Rose, from the 2nd Argylls, was a keen sailor and he had gathered around him some like-minded individuals together with a few specialists in demolition. They used some motor-boats based at Perak and carried out one raid.

On 28 December *Roseforce* sailed north from their base 140 miles to Trong, where a party was landed to raid the rear areas of the Japanese 5th Infantry Division and its vulnerable lines of communication. The attackers shot up a couple of convoys, laid some mines and scuttled back to the waiting boats before returning unmolested to Perak.

Roseforce had no opportunity to repeat their success, as Japanese bombers destroyed their depot ship and most of the small craft. Robbed of their mobility, *Roseforce* became embroiled in the retreat, providing rearguard cover for demolition teams.*

On 5 January British defences along the Slim River were ruptured by an enemy inferior in numbers and largely dependent for supplies on the largesse of his opponent. The wealth of Central Malaya and Johore lay open to the Japanese. Kuala Lumpur, that city which has come to epitomize Imperialism, was hastily abandoned with its vast dumps of war material largely intact. The Allies made for the supposed sanctuary of Singapore in undignified haste.

Even though no plans had been prepared for an orderly withdrawal inland, for the stockpiling of supplies or for the island's defence in a prolonged siege, few could accept that it was only a matter of time before the British were to suffer their worst defeat in military history. Certainly Spencer Chapman had no such forebodings as at the head of a small party he prepared to stay behind enemy lines.

In two weeks Chapman inflicted a considerable amount of damage on the Japanese. In guerrilla actions of this sort it is impossible to keep an accurate tally, but Chapman believed they derailed 8 trains, blew 15 bridges, ambushed 40 vehicles and cut the railway in more than 60 places. The Japanese must have suffered heavy casualties from such deprivations and the tragedy is that there were not more guerrilla groups causing similar mayhem.

In these circumstances guerrillas seek to achieve two objectives. The first is to disrupt enemy communications so that the effects are felt in the front line. Success in this area opens the way to the second objective, for the enemy cannot allow this intolerable situation to continue, and so diverts precious resources from the front to destroy the guerrillas, thereby easing the pressure on the latter's own conventional forces.

---

* *Roseforce* stayed with the retreat all the way to Singapore, where the Royal Marines were incorporated into the Argylls. Those companies which had Marines were immediately dubbed 'Plymouth Argylls' – HMS *Prince of Wales* and *Repulse* had been Plymouth ships.

Whether more extensive guerrilla action would have materially altered the outcome is unlikely. Some maintain that the Allies were a beaten force by Christmas and that the High Command was singularly incapable of taking the initiative, let alone decisive action. However, had the Japanese been molested and delayed in their advance by the concerted action of numerous guerrilla bands, then the defending forces might have had the time to deploy properly for battle.

Almost without exception, British and Imperial soldiers in this campaign were most appallingly served by their senior officers. The decisions made by General Percival and his subordinate commanders directly contributed to their defeat. One of those fateful decisions was the point-blank refusal in October 1941 to countenance the training of guerrilla forces. Simply because guerrilla warfare required thinking about the unthinkable does not exonerate commanders from planning a strategy for a 'worst case' scenario.

The surrender of more than 80,000 troops in Singapore on Sunday 15 February 1942 condemned them to four years of the most terrible suffering as prisoners of the Japanese. For Chapman and his tiny group, by then out of supplies and on the run from a vengeful enemy, it became a matter of survival. The answer lay in linking up with one of the Chinese teams. About 200 stay-behind parties had been hurriedly prepared. Most infiltrated into the jungle, armed and supplied, but none was adequately trained in the techniques of guerrilla warfare.

Initially Chapman and his party hoped to get out of Malaya. They tried to make it across country to the east coast, there to beg, borrow or buy a boat to take them to one of the islands of the Dutch East Indies, and thence south until they rejoined the Allied lines, or even to Australia. Japanese vigilance and the absence of any remotely suitable craft forced Chapman to think again and approach the Chinese. A European on the run could not hope to survive without help. The Malay or even the Tamil might be willing to help, but ran the risk of retribution from the Japanese. The Chinese bands had already taken to the jungle but were poorly trained; they needed Chapman's skills to survive.

At first Chapman also came across a number of British soldiers who were separated from their units. Very few lasted more than a year, often simply because of attitude. Some saw the jungle as a primitive paradise. They quickly succumbed to one or other of the many hidden dangers which entrapped the unwary – disease, poisonous fruits or reptiles. Most saw the jungle as a green hell full of peril from snakes and other wild animals, leave alone an enemy who had proved the master of jungle warfare.

It was Chapman who appreciated that:

The truth is the jungle is neutral. It provides any amount of fresh water and unlimited cover for friend or foe: an armed neutrality, but neutrality nevertheless.

It is an attitude of mind that determines whether you go under or survive. There is nothing either good or bad but thinking makes it so. The jungle is neutral.*

Spencer Chapman was destined to spend the next three years and more behind Japanese lines putting that theory to daily test and eventually emerging as living proof of its validity.

---

*Spencer Chapman, *The Jungle is Neutral* (Chatto and Windus, London, 1963)

CHAPTER TWENTY-FIVE

On the Long March to India

In contrast to Malaya, no thought at all had been given to defending Burma. Nobody believed that a major campaign would be fought in this jungle-clad country – an extraordinary omission, for the country's strategic importance was never in doubt. Burma guarded the entrance into India and the back door to China. Burma's airfields serviced the route to Malaya, and the country was resource rich in those vital raw materials, not least oil, which the Allies needed to fuel the war effort.

Burma was also very difficult to defend, especially from a threat to the east. The long river valleys which dominate the country ran parallel to the equally long and very exposed border with Thailand. The major port and capital city of Rangoon was easily outflanked and the overland routes to India were poor and vulnerable to interdiction from any one of a hundred places across the Thai border.

The defence of Burma was the responsibility of the British in India, and in 1941 came under the remit of General Wavell as Commander-in-Chief. Sent back to command sepoys for failing against the Germans, Wavell had other problems with which to contend. In the first weeks of the war in the Far East he persisted with the notion that the Japanese fighting machine – its men and equipment – was inferior to that of his own Indian Army.

By the time he was disabused of such prejudices and ready to address himself to the defence of India, Wavell's attention was diverted elsewhere. Winston Churchill spent Christmas of 1941 in Washington, though little time was given to festivities. Instead there was a series of crisis meetings with President Roosevelt. Christmas afternoon was devoted to the War in Asia. General Marshall proposed that a number of theatres of operations should be established, each with a supreme commander. In the Far East the Allies created ABDACOM (American, British, Dutch and Australian Command) and Wavell was appointed in command. His responsibilities included all the Allied Forces in Burma, Malaya, the Dutch East Indies and the Philippines, though his orders effectively excluded him from directly exercising that high command. He had no power to dismiss a subordinate commander, which was just as well considering the American commander in the Philippines was the prima donna Douglas MacArthur; neither could he interfere in the command structure of the troops under his control. Wavell was specifically charged with the coordination of the defence of Malaya, Burma and Australia. Such a compromise suited the British, who had little faith in the Americans at this stage and believed that the Philippines and Dutch territories were disaster areas.

In January 1942, Wavell established ABDA Headquarters in Java, from whence he was tasked by his political masters to prepare an all-out offensive against the Japanese. In reality he devoted all his efforts to defending the Malay Barrier; this included the Malayan Peninsula, Sumatra, Java, Bali and the island chain that stretched to Timor in the east. The anchors of the barrier are Burma and Australia. In the case of Burma, Wavell could despatch men and supplies but was too remote to exercise any effective control even though he still retained his position as Commander-in-Chief in India.

ABDA disintegrated in February 1942 when the Japanese invaded Java and forced the Dutch to surrender. Wavell reverted to his previous job, but by the time he had returned to Delhi it was early March and the situation in Burma had already become desperate; the Japanese had captured much of the south and were only days away from entering Rangoon.

The Japanese Fifteenth Army had invaded Burma from Thailand. This was a grand title for a force led by Lieut-General Shojiro Iida, comprising two under-strength army divisions, but they proved more than adequate for the task in hand. The pattern was by now depressingly familiar. The Japanese won the air battle in the border area, invaded on 15 January and quickly captured the airfields in Tenasserim or southern Burma. These airfields were very quickly brought back into use by the enemy and used to bomb Rangoon.

Royal Air Force pilots in obsolescent Brewster Buffaloes and 'Flying Tigers', American volunteers, and mercenaries hitherto in Chinese pay, succeeded in inflicting heavy losses on the over-confident Japanese. Though collateral damage to the port was minimal and the enemy soon reverted to night raids, one important aim had been accomplished. The

Burmese and Indian labourers at the port fled the city and ships with vital supplies were left unloaded.

The British in the meantime deployed into the southern part of the country and across the formidable obstacle formed by the Sittang River, a natural defence barrier for Rangoon. Wavell had charged Lieut-General T. J. Hutton with the defence of Burma but it was a poor choice. Hutton had recently been appointed as Chief-of-Staff in India and most of his career had been spent in staff appointments. In Burma he was hopelessly out of his depth and the men under his command were to pay dearly for such inexperience.

The main fighting unit was the 17th Indian Division, on paper formidable, with 14 infantry battalions in 4 brigades. They were led by Major-General Jack Smyth V.C., a brave and honourable veteran of the Great War but in poor health. The Indian battalions had not been trained in jungle warfare and had all been milked of their best officers and NCOs, British and Indian, to meet the needs of the 4th and 5th Indian Divisions fighting in the Middle East.

The 2nd Burma Division – largely Burma Rifles, some Indian troops and a British battalion of Gloucesters for stiffening – were deployed to the defence of Rangoon itself. Smyth wanted to make use of the Salween River and dig in there to hold the Japanese, but Hutton would have none of it. He feared the political consequences on the already sullen and uncooperative Burmese of surrendering so much territory in the south.

In the ensuing weeks the 17th Indian Division – outnumbered and outgunned, though not out-fought – fell back across 100 miles of territory towards the Sittang River. There was one bridge over the 100-yard-wide river, and this had already been prepared and primed for demolition by the time the two brigades had crossed safely to the other side. The 48th Gurkha Infantry Brigade was charged with the defence of the bridge and its approaches, but hardly had they set about preparing the defences when disaster struck.

The order for withdrawal was radioed in clear language to the rearguard. This alerted the commander of the Japanese 33rd Division and he despatched a small force to seize the bridge. The attack failed, but the sudden and unexpected appearance of the enemy in unsuspected strength near to the bridge panicked the local commanders. The brigadier in command of the 48th Gurkha Infantry Brigade fought off the enemy attacks on the bridge but in the heat and the dust, the fatigue and confusion of an army in retreat, the threat was perceived to be much greater than it really was. At 0430 hours in the morning of 23 February, the brigadier told Smyth that he doubted whether his men could hold for another hour. There appeared only one solution. If the bridge could not be held, then it must not be allowed to fall into enemy hands. There was another answer, which would have required Smyth to return the short distance to the bridge and assess the situation for himself before he gave the order to abandon part of his division. But he did not, and an hour later, at 0530, the Sittang River bridge was totally and utterly destroyed in one of the few really efficient operations in the Burma campaign to date.

The Japanese wasted no time, and immediately moved off further north in search of another way across the river. A large number of the stranded soldiers, unmolested by the enemy, found various means to cross, but they left behind their wounded, their equipment, heavy weapons and stores. As a fighting formation the 17th Indian Division ceased to exist and there remained only the ill-trained and uncertain Burma Rifles to defend Rangoon.

General Smyth, already sick and now broken in spirit by the disaster, was dismissed. When Wavell returned, he brought Lieut-General Harold Alexander to take field command in Burma and Hutton was displaced to become his Chief-of-Staff. Alexander quickly decided that Rangoon was untenable. The city by this time was in a shambles; the police had deserted, the dockside workers had either stayed away or turned to looting, and fully-laden ships stood idle. Lawlessness was endemic; Burmese and Indians spent their days settling old scores. A Japanese 'fifth column' was particularly active and all the Europeans that could do so had long since fled the city. Rangoon was not worth any further sacrifice, so Alexander ordered his forces to retreat northwards. He planned a new defence line centred on Prome in the Irrawaddy Valley.

On 8 March 1942, Rangoon was abandoned to the enemy. General Iida now had a port through which he could receive supplies, while the British and Chinese had lost their only port of any consequence. In 1942 no road connected Burma with India, so any supplies from India could only reach the front by air and there were neither the air crews nor the machines available.

However, Alexander was determined to make a fight of it against the Japanese. He brought in Major-General Bill Slim to lead his land forces, now reorganized into the Burma Corps (Burcorp). These included the remnants of the 17th Indian Division and those of the 1st Burma Division which had not fled to join the units of the Japanese-sponsored and renegade Burma Independent Army. There were the tanks and armoured cars of the 7th Armoured Brigade, veterans from North Africa, and a couple of Chinese divisions of indifferent quality – despatched south by Generalissimo Chiang Kai-Shek – to cover the eastern flank in the Shan States, the Karen Hills and the Salween Valley.

Now that he had a major port, General Iida received ample

reinforcements. The missing regiment from the 33rd Division arrived, along with the 18th Division fresh from its victories in Malaya and the 56th Division from Java. There were regiments of tanks and enough front-line aircraft to ensure air superiority against the few RAF pilots and Flying Tigers that remained.

General Wavell, in confronting the problems of defending against a force superior enough to expel his own divisions from the field, continued to show as marked an antipathy to any notion of Special Forces or guerrilla units as he had displayed in the Western Desert. Alexander, however, saw things in a different light. The River Irrawaddy was now a vital highway for both Allies and enemy; it opened up all kinds of opportunities to the unconventional and the daring.

In the last days of January 100 Royal Marines, all volunteers from the 1st Royal Marine Coast Regiment, had been rushed in the cruiser *Enterprise* from their base in Ceylon to Rangoon. They were commanded by Major Duncan Johnson, who christened them *Viperforce* after the only British poisonous snake, for they were supposed to bite the enemy hard.

Viperforce (*V Force* for short) were joined by selected members of the Burmese Royal Naval Volunteer Reserve, as well as British engineers working in the oil-fields who in peacetime had been ardent yachtsmen. Together they fitted out four government requisitioned touring launches which became the nucleus of a guerrilla flotilla. The launch crews were natives of Chittagong, whose language the RNVR officers spoke, and the Marines shipped aboard as gunners and raiders. Mike Calvert joined as their expert on demolitions. Each launch had a Vickers .303 water-cooled machine gun mounted above the deckhouse, a Bren gun or two and a mortar.

V Force was ready before the end of February and had a handy shakedown cruise patrolling Rangoon docks to deter the worst of the looting. Offenders caught were taken to the main square and flogged by the Marines. This worked for a few days until some well-meaning soul opened Rangoon Jail in a last act before leaving the city. The inmates (they numbered over 2,000, and included the criminally insane) were released to fend for themselves. They instigated a reign of terror which the Marines were helpless to prevent.

In early March *V Force* abandoned Rangoon and took to the river. As they moved slowly northwards along the Irrawaddy, they destroyed all river traffic and shore facilities that had been left intact.

Over the succeeding weeks *V Force* engaged in a number of varied and hazardous tasks. The easy part was to guard the open river flanks of 17 Division as it retreated northwards. The more difficult operations occurred when they carried demolition teams, trained and frequently led by Mike Calvert, down river to raid enemy installations.

Calvert was seconded to *V Force* as their specialist in demolition. One morning he stripped off his uniform and was taking an early morning swim in the Irrawaddy when he encountered a Japanese officer who was also naked. Though neither was armed and both within shouting distance of their own men, they fought to the death.

> He knew his jujitsu and the water on his body made him as slippery as an eel, but I was bigger and stronger. We fought in silence except for the occasional grunt, and struggled and slipped and thrashed around until we were at times waist deep in the swirling water. It was an ungainly fight, almost in slow motion, for it is extraordinarily difficult to keep balance or move quickly and surely in two or three feet of water. Our breathing grew heavier and the Jap got more vicious as he jabbed his fingers at my face in an attempt to blind me. I think it was not until then that I fully realised this would have to be a fight to the death.
>
> I was a trained soldier, taught how to kill with a gun, or a bayonet, or even a knife in the thick of battle. Somehow this seemed different, more personal, as the two of us, naked as we were, fought in the water. Apart from anything else, I had come to admire this little Jap. He had all the guts in the world....
>
> ...I was thankful for one lesson I had learned: never to take my boots off in the jungle outside camp.... I managed to grab the Jap's right wrist and force his arm behind his back. And I buried my face in his chest to stop him clawing my eyes. Then as he lashed out with his left arm and both feet I forced him gradually under water. My boots gave me a firm grip and I shut my eyes and held him under the surface. His struggles grew weaker and weaker, flared up again in frantic despair and then he went limp. I held on for a few seconds longer before releasing my grip ... his body emerged on the surface a couple of yards away and floated gently off downstream.*

By the middle of March the river level had fallen considerably, which made navigation all the more difficult for these slow river boats which often appeared to make little headway against the swift currents.

V Force suffered casualties, which was bound to happen when conducting raids against an alert and numerous foe. There were occasions when the raiders themselves were ambushed; and small parties, finding their retreat to the river cut off, had little choice but to head inland to evade the enemy and link up with the British rearguard.

Early in April a number of volunteers for river commando work

* *Prisoners of Hope* Mike Calvert (Cape, 1952).

joined the flotilla from the Army's inland water transport companies and they helped to make good the losses which the force had suffered.

The retreat continued, moving jerkily northwards. The launches kept pace, burning boats along the bank, rescuing parties that had been cut off, and occasionally turning back downstream at night to carry another sabotage team as close to their objective as they dared.

On land there was but one outcome. General Slim's force had fought the Japanese in scorching temperatures and for a month denied the enemy the great oil-fields around Yenangyaung. But the Japanese were able at last to break through the Chinese forces in the east, into undefended country, and they moved on quickly to threaten Lashio, the southern terminal of the Burma road to China.

The Japanese had turned the Allied flank and threatened Mandalay. On 16 April 1942 the oil-fields were destroyed and Alexander ordered his forces to retreat overland into India, while some of the Chinese made their way through Lashio and on to the Burma Road before the town fell. There could be no reinforcements. Wavell had already appreciated the strategic importance of India rather than the tactical battle for Burma, which in any case had already been lost.

V Force still covered the river flanks of the retreat all the way to the junction of the Chindwin River at Sameckkon; very often the boats withdrew only when the enemy were in sight, and they still made an occasional night foray downstream. At Sameckkon the launches were used to help ferry the brigades of 1st Burma Division across the river so that they could continue their retreat along the Chindwin. Then all the bigger launches, with too deep a draught for the shallow Chindwin, were sunk to block the Irrawaddy Channel. Some of the force battled on in small motor-boats, armed only with Bren guns, and a number were to die fighting. The survivors of *Viper Force* eventually marched out of Burma along 200 miles of jungle trail in a race against the enemy and against time. Mandalay fell on 1 May and by the end of the month the bulk of the British forces, behind sensible rearguards, fought their way north-west to Kalewa and thence over appalling mountain tracks to the Manipur Plain and Assam in India.

PART FIVE

LONG-RANGE
PENETRATION

CHAPTER TWENTY-SIX

Wingate

The United States, Britain's new-found but already senior partner, was impatient for the recapture of Northern Burma. The American military establishment wanted a strong China to help defeat Japan, so the collapse or surrender of Chiang Kai-Shek's government would be a severe setback to American strategy. This was the reasoning that influenced the campaign to supply, invigorate and mobilize China, and to re-open the land link through Burma. In addition the Americans had bombers based in China which, with considerable success, raided Japanese positions on the mainland and sea routes to the Philippines.

President Roosevelt wished to expand that effort and send B29s, the new Superfortresses specially designed with the long range necessary to undertake a strategic bombing offensive against Japan. It was a time after all when the bomber barons still held sway and their promises had yet to be exposed for the empty boasts they were in reality.

The Japanese had cut the Burma Road and everything used in China was flown in from India. The Hump, that air-bridge over the southern spur of the Himalayas to China, could not sustain such an increase in effort as envisaged by the President. So the Americans planned to open a new road from the end of the existing road-head at Ledo – over 500 miles of jungle and mountains – in to China. Only when the road was open and the trucks moving, could supplies be transported in sufficient quantities to support a major bombing offensive.

Before the road could be built, however, the enemy had to be pushed back from much of northern Burma, preferably as far south as

Mandalay. In vain did the British appeal that the effort required to build and secure that road was not worth it in terms of manpower and resources. Churchill was of the view that by the time it was complete Allied strategic needs and priorities would have changed, but the Americans were adamant.

Washington planned to begin their offensive at the end of 1943. By this time, the acerbic American general, 'Vinegar Joe' Stilwell, reckoned that his two Chinese divisions, which were being reformed and re-equipped in India after the retreat from Burma, would be ready to return to the fray.

In the meantime, Washington looked to the British to get things moving.

The cautious and conservative Wavell was equally determined to return to the offensive, but not yet and not in Northern Burma. As Commander-in-Chief of the Indian Army, he did not need to be reminded how potentially catastrophic the loss of Burma could be for the British in India. Independence had been promised but at a time of Britain's own choosing, and already upwards of a division's-worth of troops were tied down on internal security duties against Indian nationalists.

The threat of invasion and the surge of nationalism was a potent combination and reached the bewildering, bloodthirsty proportions of mob action in the cities. In the summer of 1942 they were whipped into mob frenzy by Chandra Bose, the renegade Indian nationalist who was now collaborating with the Japanese in Burma.

Wavell was a Sepoy general of the old school imbued with the conviction that the Indian Army was infinitely superior to anything the Japanese – or anyone else for that matter – cared to put in the field against them. The trouble was that other theatres had taken priority. In North Africa Rommel still seemed unstoppable, while the rapid German advance across the southern steppes to the Don threatened Iraq and Persia. These threats were far more important than a campaign in Northern Burma and all the resources that were available in India were sent to the Middle East. Wavell also appreciated that a campaign in Burma presented other problems for the few troops which remained. Morale among the Sepoys was very low; it could not be otherwise after the humiliation of that retreat through Burma and the loss of so many fine regiments in Singapore. So Wavell planned an offensive in the Arakan, the name given to that narrow coastal strip of Burma running down from Chittagong almost to Rangoon.

Wavell's instructions to what was then called the Eastern Army were much less ambitious than those sought by the Americans. He ordered an advance to take the Mayu Peninsula and the airfields at

Akyab, from which the Japanese could threaten Chittagong and even Calcutta.

So what became known as the First Arakan Campaign began in September 1942, when the 14th Indian Division set out cautiously from Chittagong on the road southwards. The Arakan, however, was not where the Americans wanted an offensive, but Northern Burma was a different proposition altogether – nobody in their right mind relished the prospect of wresting it from the Japanese; the jungle not only favoured the defence, but was a terrain in which the Japanese proved the masters.

It was not just a question of morale. Logistics presented well-nigh insuperable problems. Most of the main supply depots for the front in the Chindwin were around Calcutta – like having supplies in London for a campaign the front line for which is in Vienna or Rome, except that the roads were practically non-existent.

To the pundits the situation was tailor-made for guerrilla or irregular warfare. The field army was unready to return to the fray, but there was a need for some form of offensive action. The local populations, even within these few short months, were beginning to experience the full horrors of Japanese occupation. Many who had collaborated in a pan-Asian alliance against European imperialism were fast learning the error of their ways and there was a new sympathy for the British from the native population.

Wavell had not shown any preference for irregular warfare whilst in command in Cairo and had, as we have seen, cold-shouldered the Commandos, but even before the retreat in Burma had run its full and bloody course he sent for Wingate once again. No matter that the latter's contribution to the war in Abyssinia was, at the most charitable, marginal; Wingate was Wavell's man. He was a soldier with fire in his belly, a man of zeal and boundless energy – rare commodities in the enervating atmosphere of Eastern Army Headquarters where the taint of defeat and failure lingered. Wingate, still a major, was at home on convalescent leave, command of Gideon Force having brought about a nervous breakdown and a botched attempt at suicide. On 4 July 1941 in a sticky Cairo hotel room Wingate, suffering from a drug overdose, plunged a hunting knife into his neck. An officer in the next room heard him fall and broke down the door.

Now Orde Wingate answered his patron's summons and flew out to India at the first opportunity. Deciding to give the unorthodox a try, Wavell asked Wingate to examine the situation and propose some solutions for a speedy return to some kind of offensive in Northern Burma. Wingate made a close study of the First Burma Campaign and spotted what he believed was the counter to Japanese tactics in the jungle. Japanese encirclement tactics were normally directed against their opponent's lines of communications, and relied on road-blocks. The answer lay in troops which were not road-bound and were prepared to take the battle to the enemy. He proposed a force trained in the techniques of long-range penetration, raiding and guerrilla warfare, operating deep behind enemy lines. Carrying supplies on their backs and using animal rather than motor transport, the raiders could take to the jungle and thereby be immune from the threat of road-blocks.

This was nothing new. Such raiding groups have been the mainstay of irregular warfare since the dawn of recorded time. What was new was the use of air support to give his raiders strategic mobility. Regular re-supply, Wingate maintained, reduced the weight of equipment they had to carry and would thus allow them to operate behind the lines almost indefinitely.

The primary mission of such units, Wingate suggested, should be to precipitate disorganization behind Japanese lines, which could then be exploited by pressure from conventional formations. Wavell saw this as the opportunity to contribute to Stilwell's forthcoming campaign. Wingate could move ahead and prepare the way for the Chinese divisions. Thereby the British would be seen to be cooperating and contributing to American strategic directives, without under-mining the security needs of the Middle East.

In September 1942, Wavell gave Wingate the 77th Infantry Brigade and the rank to go with the job, and told him to prepare for operations as quickly as possible. Enquiries from the Prime Minister as to when he might look forward to active campaigning in Burma were becoming annoyingly persistent.

There was another fear troubling the Commander-in-Chief. Intel-ligence branch at Army HQ believed the Japanese intended to continue with their advance, cross into Assam and possibly invade India. It was essential that the Allies attack first, even if it was only a spoiling raid which disrupted the enemy in his preparations and knocked him off his stride.

Wingate took the 77th Infantry Brigade into the jungle regions of India's Central Provinces for six months' arduous training. At first sight the raw material was hardly the stuff of an elite special force of jungle fighters. The British element was a battalion of the King's Liverpool Regiment, plus the odds and ends from a score of other regiments. The King's were Territorials whose average age was 30–35 years of age, despatched to India for guard and internal security duties. It was a 'cushy number' which many must have thought would see their war out nicely, but now they were in for a very rude awakening. There was also a battalion of Gurkhas and another of

Burma Rifles to complete the brigade. In addition Wavell made available some Commandos and a Company of Muleteers for transport.

Orde Wingate is one of the most controversial generals in the Second World War, but he was undoubtedly a brilliant trainer of men. He introduced a regime which aimed not only to weed out the weaker brethren, but to instil the remainder with a feeling of confidence in their own skills and abilities. The soldiers of 77 Brigade were not volunteers but were nevertheless subjected to a training cycle as tough as any for the Special Forces – one in which rigour, privation and physical endurance were the foundation upon which jungle skills were taught. Every man became a specialist; scouting and reconnaissance, medics, signals or demolition and sabotage were the chosen tools of the new guerrillas' trade. Junior commanders came under his spell and some lost the ability to distinguish between the feeble and the fantastic.

By the year's end when Wingate pronounced the brigade ready for war, it was unrecognizable to the conventional military establishment. Gone were the battalion, company and platoon structures. In their place, the numbered column became the base unit of organization. There were seven columns in the brigade, the column being built around the firepower of a company of infantry to which were added the support troops, signallers and heavy weapons etc. and pack train. A column numbered between 400 and 500 men, had over 100 animals and in single file was a mile long. In tactical terms, Wingate saw the column as big enough to inflict damage and small enough to evade pursuit.

Tactical mobility was also a measure of a soldier's encumbrance. The Chindits carried about 60 pounds weight; besides their bedding, a waterproof ground-sheet 6 ft × 2½ ft and a light cashmere wool blanket, each man carried a change of clothing and six days' hard rations. The latter, known as paratroop rations, consisted of high calorie concentrates of chocolate, nuts, raisins, cheese, hard-tack biscuits etc., together with the inevitable tea, powdered milk, sugar and tins of bully beef.

These rations were prepared in India and were not of the highest quality. The wrappings were soggy. Tea and sugar came in twists of paper and were mouldy. Moreover, the greatest drawback was their calorific value. The rations supplied a daily intake which was at least 1,500 calories short of that deemed necessary for soldiers in combat conditions; neither did the latter calculations make any allowance for special operations. And since the men were to begin their operation on two-thirds rations, nourishment and thus efficiency was to prove a problem from the outset.

However, since the pack train included elephants carrying mortars and Vickers heavy machine guns, buffaloes and oxen dragging carts, the guerrillas could hardly have been nimble or fleet of foot.

Salt formed an important part of the diet. The soldiers had already come to realize its importance, when in the jungles of Central India they had sweated continuously day after day. In these conditions, heat exhaustion was at best unpleasant and for some fatal. They needed no urging to take plenty of salt and soon learned how to gauge their daily need on the march. One method was simply to look at their shirts; if these were caked with a white crust then everything was fine, alternatively it was enough to taste their own sweat.

By the time that Wingate was ready, the Chinese had found many reasons for postponing their part in the reconquest of Burma. It was the old story. A Special Force had been raised, precious resources diverted to meet its special needs – and by the time it was ready, the war was not.

Nothing daunted, Wingate asked permission to test his theories against the Japanese in what was now to be a guerrilla campaign which could not achieve very much since it would not be supported by conventional troops to reinforce success.

To use men and lives simply to test the validity of a theory is criminal and it simply showed how dangerously unbalanced Wingate had become in pursuit of his own beliefs. But the old story also shows that Special Forces are always abused, and 77 Brigade was to be no exception. It would be deployed and good reasons found to support the decision.

Wavell did not have to look very far. In January 1943 the campaign in the Arakan had already gone sour, and unless the British could show some success against the Japanese there was bound to be further unrest in India and even greater risk of invasion.

Suddenly everything – politically and militarily – was riding on Wingate's columns as they moved slowly down to the Chindwin.

CHAPTER TWENTY-SEVEN

'Clive of Burma'

Wingate had chosen Chinthe, the iron-handed dragon which is the guardian of Burmese pagodas, as 77 Brigade's insignia. The soldiers he called Chindits.

On St Valentine's night, 14 February 1943, seven columns in two groups crossed the unguarded Chindwin River and moved into enemy territory. The northern group, led by Wingate, consisted of five columns, 2,200 men and 850 mules; this main force crossed the Chindwin some 30 miles to the north of Sittaung. By all accounts it was as well there were no enemy in the area, for it proved to be a shambolic business. They used the local villagers to ferry soldiers across in their dugouts, while the animals had to swim. The mules proved particularly troublesome; they are good swimmers, but only as far as the nearest dry land. Time after time, having been coaxed into the water, one mule would head back for the near shore and all would follow. Their loads were ferried across on the few sampans available, or by dugouts lashed together.

The southern group had two columns, 1,000 men and 250 mules.

There was no coherent objective and the ensuing campaign was a confused affair. The first target was the railway which lay about 100 miles distant, but allowing for terrain it was more like twice the distance in terms of the march. Wingate planned to hit the railway along some distance of track, causing maximum damage not just to the permanent way but to supply points, stations and bridges.

At first all went reasonably well and by 1 March, Wingate's group had reached Pinbou. The Japanese were not slow to react and quickly

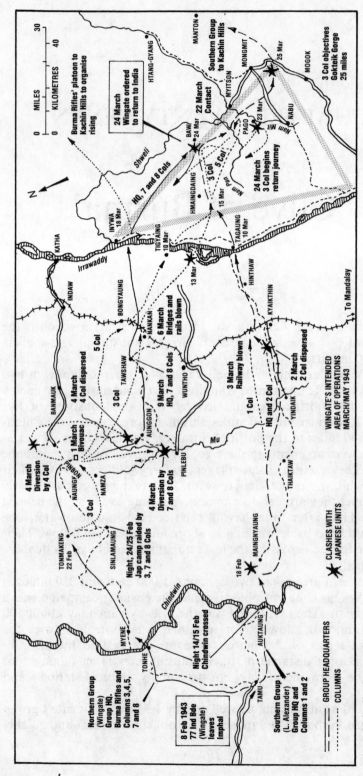

First Chindit Operation

appreciated that a sizeable force had penetrated behind their lines. A battalion on frontier duty was quickly deployed and a division further south loaded up its elephants, bullocks and mules and prepared to take to the trail. Within days Wingate's force was outnumbered 5:1, but in true guerrilla style managed at first to retain the initiative. Outposts were obliterated before they could report to their headquarters, the railway was cut, motor vehicles ambushed and bridges blown. Major Mike Calvert, leading No. 3 Column, was particularly successful. As befitting his background, he was assigned the destruction of steel girder bridges and culverts between Indaw and Wunthow, where the Japanese had garrisons. One night he attempted to blow up a railway embankment when the enemy were close by and sentries within earshot. The charges misfired, faulty detonators being a perennial problem, and Calvert needed a light by which to prime fresh detonators, but the enemy were ominously close and the embankment was bare of any cover.

He turned to Geoffrey Lockett, a Highlander, and had him kneel on the ground and raise the folds of his kilt. Calvert disappeared beneath this makeshift blackout with matches, hunting-knife and detonator while Lockett tried to keep his mind on other things.

The ruse worked for the pair of them. The detonators were correctly primed and as they scurried away Lockett relaxed. His pride might have been dented, but the 'family jewels' were intact.

Bernard Ferguson, the monocled son of a former Governor-General of New Zealand and now a Black Watch Major commanding No. 5 Column, had a number of bloody encounters with the Japanese. He managed to dynamite the strategically important railway bridge over the Bongyaung Gorge. This was a particular loss to the enemy. It had been a 300-mile journey to that bridge and was a brilliant piece of jungle navigation.

Wingate planned and directed the actions of his widely separated columns by means of radio or, on occasion, courier dogs. Air drops were arranged and in the first month these worked very successfully. Dakotas and Hudsons flew 4,500 thousand pounds of supplies in a mission; the crews called themselves aerial coolies. Manhandling those bulky loads out of the door of a plane bucking through the turbulence was a backbreaking and often dangerous job. On each occasion the men received their mail, newspapers and magazines. Personal needs were also catered for: false teeth and spectacles were frequently supplied.

Gradually, however, the Japanese – stronger on the ground and with local knowledge in their favour – began to gain the upper hand. One of Wingate's columns ran into a bigger force than they had reckoned and were scattered. Some of the men made their individual and precarious way back across the Chindwin, but most perished in the jungle.

The Southern task force had fared badly. The headquarters group and No. 2 Column led by Major Emmett were both ambushed and forced to scatter. Very few made it back to friendly territory. Emmett was caught laying demolition charges on the railway track some forty miles south of Nankan. Outnumbered and outgunned the soldiers dispersed, the mules stampeded and their loads (including the precious radio) were lost. Emmett gathered a group and headed back to the Chindwin with what few supplies they had been able to salvage. Some raiders managed to link up with other columns, but a sizeable group had been knocked out of the battle.

For the columns that remained operational, there were other problems to overcome. The physically weak had been weeded out, but not necessarily those who had character or other defects. Misdemeanours had to be dealt with on the spot and some columns had men who continued to soldier on even though they knew a court-martial waited them if they survived and returned to civilization. Some crimes Wingate insisted on being dealt with immediately. If a sentry was found asleep, at the first convenient opportunity he was stripped, tied to a tree and flogged by a senior Warrant Officer or Sergeant – as much a deterrent as a punishment to fit the crime.

In his excellent account* Charles Rollo describes Wingate at this time:

> Wingate already seemed to be taking on the characteristics of the wild beasts that prowl the jungle. He marched with his head sunk forward like a panther and the tense stoop of a hyena in his shoulders. His eyes had a wolfish glint, his beard was shaggy as a lion's mane.

In mid-March, Wingate ordered the columns to push deeper into enemy territory and cross the Irrawaddy. This was well beyond the planned limits of the operation and was a serious error of judgement. The men were already exhausted and, despite the fact that they were still in receipt of regular and accurately delivered air drops, the strain of operating behind enemy lines was beginning to exact its toll. The elephants, buffaloes and oxen were the early casualties in the pack train and some columns had lost all their mules too, which meant that everything had to be man-carried. The Japanese were by now aware of the size and disposition of the raiders and had some 20,000 troops deployed. The situation would have been ideal had there been a

---

*Charles Rollo, *Wingate's Raiders* (Harrap, 1945).

conventional battle and the enemy forced to denude the front to handle the threat in his rear, but such was not the case.

The ground into which the columns advanced was most unsuitable. They were hemmed in to a triangle of land formed by the Irrawaddy and its tributaries, the Shweli and the Nam-mit rivers. At this point the expedition was just about equidistant from Assam, Tibet and China in country where the jungle had given way to dry scrub, a near waterless wasteland. The known watering places had to be avoided for the Japanese, aware of the raiders' predicament, set ambushes. Neither in their preparations had it been considered necessary to practice dropping water supplies for operations, which after all were meant to be in tropical jungles.

Burma is a land of stark contrasts and now their most urgent need was water. The animals that remained were the first to die and the manner of their going caused these gaunt, haggard men even more distress. With the enemy all around, it was not possible to shoot a mule. Instead the soldiers could only slit their throats and sit on the creatures' faces to stifle the death scream.

It was hopeless, and Wingate was soon forced to concede defeat. Air drops were no longer possible and the little food that remained was strictly rationed. On 24 March, with the enemy closing in, he ordered the columns to break north and head for home.

The march out was as bad as anything experienced in that first retreat from Burma. Most of the mules had gone, run off, were dead or eaten. The soldiers carried what they could and trekked to the Chindwin, hounded all the way by the enemy. The seriously wounded, those ravaged by disease and unable to keep up were left behind. Some survived for a time, sheltered by the hill tribes. But those taken by the Japanese were killed out of hand; if they were fortunate, their end was swift, but captured officers were routinely tortured for information before they were despatched. Late in the campaign Charles Rollo recounts the experience of one group entering a village only to find an officer who had been stripped, bound hand and foot and bayoneted to the wall of a hut. His entrails hung from a ghastly wound in his belly. When he saw his comrades he said quietly: 'For Christ's sake shoot me.'

The returning columns encountered hardening Japanese resistance, for it was not enough that the British were in full retreat. Only the fittest could survive, officers set a punishing pace to escape the enemy and men began to fall out in increasing numbers. Soldiers were starving. They shed all equipment except weapons and ammunition, for it was all they could carry. On average they lost over 30 per cent of their body weight and they had been very fit before the campaign. In some instances all march discipline broke down when the columns broke into smaller groups to evade detection and junior officers failed to keep control. In contrast others emerged as amazingly disciplined bodies of men. Major Gilkes brought his column out by way of China. They crossed 10,000-foot-high mountains and made contact with Chinese guerrillas, most of whom were in no better condition than the British soldiers. The guerrillas in turn passed them on to the regular Chinese Nationalist forces, but their ordeal was far from over. They bypassed a major set-piece battle between the Chinese and Japanese troops in the Salween Valley, and headed by way of the Mekong river to the main Chinese base at Kunming. Of the raiders who had set out from Imphal, Gilkes' group had marched 1,500 miles in their campaign.

Wingate, Ferguson, Calvert and others kept their men together and brought out as many as they could. One young Royal Signals lieutenant, worn out by dysentery, could not march another step and dropped to the side of the track muttering, 'Well, I've had it, chaps.' Wingate came by, halted and talked to him gently for a few moments. When the brigadier turned to go, the young officer rose and saluted before collapsing in a heap.

Wingate kept his column together by shear force of personality. He gave orders that no one should drop out, or even stop to empty their bowels. 'Don't mind messing your trousers – just keep marching,' he instructed. And march they did, even though their condition was pitiable. Many were barefoot. The jungle and 1,300 miles of trekking had rotted the boots off their feet.

Most of those who survived crossed the Chindwin in mid-April. Other groups and individuals came out weeks later. A thousand men failed to make it back; of those emaciated scarecrows who did, there were very few ever fit enough to soldier in the front line again. Figures vary but, as is so often the case after a traumatic experience, many soldiers died in the weeks following their return to India and to safety. Of those who did 'recover', fewer than 600 were fit for further military service.

Was it worth it? Not in the simple military sense of harm inflicted on the enemy who took less than 1,000 casualties, and suffered damage to a few miles of railway track and the odd bridge – all of which could be repaired. This does not detract in any way from the enormous courage and bravery shown by the men of 77 Brigade. It was claimed at the time, and on numerous occasions since, that the real success was in laying the myth of Japanese military superiority. Wingate showed that ordinary infantry with the proper training could take on the Japanese in the jungle and beat them. Such a revelation is supposed to have done wonders to the morale of the British and Indian troops.

Those who were defending the Chindwin or stationed in Assam would have seen for themselves the pitiable physical state of the survivors of 77 Brigade. They could not have been anything other than depressed by such appalling suffering and recognized that if this was the only way to take on the Japanese then perhaps the price was too high.

Wingate entertained no doubts at all. The operation proved that long penetration worked and indeed this was the only way to defeat the Japanese. That was good enough for the generals in command and the politicians at home.

In despatches Wavell, the patron, made his own assessment of the campaign:

> The enterprise had no strategic value and about one third of the force which entered Burma was lost – but the experience gained was invaluable. The enemy was obviously surprised and at a loss ... in general Brigadier Wingate's theories of leadership were fully vindicated.

Even before Wingate had returned to Assam, Wavell ordered the foundation of a second Long Range Penetration Group. The 111 Indian Brigade comprised two battalions. The 1st Cameronians was a regular battalion which had fought its way out of Burma and in any case enjoyed a reputation as one of the toughest in the British Army. Men taken from the slums of Glasgow carried razor-blades sown into the peaks of their caps and none but their own officers could handle them. They waged street fights with secreted bayonets, broken bottles and potatoes with razors stuck in them. On at least one occasion since coming out to Burma, they had fought against another battalion with rifles and ball ammunition. Calcutta, where they were bar-racked, had had enough of their presence. None of the military in the District HQ could think of a more appropriate fate for the Cameron-ians than that they should be despatched into the deepest jungle as guerrillas.

In contrast the 4/9th Gurkhas was a war-raised battalion. The 9th recruited high-caste Gurkhas, noticeably taller and thinner than most Nepalese but with the same martial qualities.

The new brigade assembled at Ghatera, Central Provinces, where it was to be organized into four columns. In overall command was Brigadier Joe Lentaigne, who had led his battalion of Gurkhas through the retreat in Burma and had close, personal experience of the Japanese. On a number of occasions when part of the desperate rearguard, this six-foot Irishman had led bayonet charges against enemy road-blocks. Now Lentaigne chose John Masters from the same regiment to be his brigade major.

By the time Wingate was out of Burma, Lentaigne and Masters had already experimented with the column formation. Finding Wingate's model to be unwieldy and inflexible, they introduced a looser, easier structure.

The brigade was ordered to be ready for operations by mid-November. While 77 Brigade was rested and refitted, Lentaigne's command would take the field in a raid planned in conjunction with main force operations. This appeared to be a wise and sensible use of resources – guerrilla warfare in the classic sense of the cavalry-type raid, used when the enemy has the advantage strategically.

Lentaigne chose the device of a snarling leopard's head as the Brigade emblem. There were now the Leopards and the Chindits. But the Leopards, proclaimed Lentaigne to his staff, were 'going to wipe the eye of the Chindits.'*

The raising of Lentaigne's brigade passed unnoticed in contrast to the Chindits, where Wingate remained the flavour of the month.

Army public relations dubbed Wingate the 'Clive of Burma' and the press eagerly took up the cry. Overnight he became a folk hero. In England it was a time of heroes. In the long middle years, before the Second Front and with no end to the war even remotely in sight, the national morale was in part sustained on a diet of heroes. Wing Commander Guy Gibson has become famous as the Dambusters' leader. In May 1943 his squadron breached the Möhne and Eider dams in an operation marked by great valour and questionable military worth.

How did the civilians in Burma react to the raid? Nobody could of course canvas their views, but they are not difficult to guess. Those villagers who sheltered, aided or were even suspected of helping the British suffered savage reprisals on the part of an enemy who didn't even need that excuse to kill, rape or plunder the local population.

The Burmese who lived in Upper Burma suffered grievously and those who lived further afield, in the towns and cities further south, didn't even know.

How did the enemy react to Wingate's raiders?

General Mataguchi, who commanded the Fifteenth Japanese Army in Burma, learned some lessons. No longer could he regard the Chindwin as the Hadrian's Wall of the Japanese empire, a secure barrier to invaders. Mataguchi was under no illusions that the British would return to Burma, and in much larger numbers. He determined therefore to pre-empt, and invade Assam, destroy the depots and supply

---

*John Masters *The Road Past Mandalay*, p. 135 (Michael Joseph, London, 1961).

dumps, restore Japanese moral superiority and unleash the quisling Indian National Army on a turbulent sub-continent.

Wingate's first Chindit operation had all the hallmarks of a self-fulfilling prophecy.

CHAPTER TWENTY-EIGHT

The Mantle of Lawrence

In March General Nye, the Vice-Chief of the General Staff, who had been to India on a fact-finding mission, told the Prime Minister of Wingate's exploits. The previous year, Churchill had been badly frightened by the incompetence of the High Command in the Western Desert, when the fall of Tobruk after a single day's battle and the surrender of 30,000 soldiers had resulted in a House of Commons motion of censure. He was not about to be dragged down by the failure in India. In the Middle East he had sacked Auchinleck and brought in the new team of Alexander and Montgomery, which had proved a winning formula. For the Far East, he had a similar remedy in mind.

Still raging at the military feebleness of his generals, he proposed Wingate as the new commander for the Army against Burma. He minuted his Chiefs of Staff on Wingate:

> He is a man of genius and audacity and has rightly been discerned by all eyes as a figure quite above the ordinary level. The expression, 'The Clive of Burma' has already gained currency. There is no doubt that in the welter of inefficiency and lassitude which has characterized our operations on the Indian front, this man, his force and his achievements stand out; and no mere question of seniority must obstruct the advance of real personalities to their proper stations in War.*

---

*Prime Minister's Personal Minutes, D/140/3, *Most Secret*; 24 July 1943: Churchill papers 20/104 as quoted in Mark Gilbert, *Road to Victory*, p. 451 (Guild Publishing, London, 1986).

New Delhi was too far to travel and in any case Churchill was due to
sail for Canada early in August for another round of meetings with
the Americans. The Allies had landed in Sicily and the vexed question
of the Second Front was bound to be prominent, but even more
pertinent was the war in the Far East.

Churchill decided to make up his own mind and so he ordered
Wingate home. A general who was not afraid to take on the Japanese
was a rare enough breed to warrant a closer look.

On the evening of 24 August, Winston Churchill was about to sit
down to dinner at Number 10 Downing Street. It was to be a quiet
family affair. For a change, the Prime Minister was to dine with his
wife and daughter Mary. Later that evening they were taking a special
train to Greenock, there to board the *Queen Mary* and sail to Canada.
The next round of bilateral summits with the Americans, code-named
Quadrant, were to be held in Quebec.

General Ismay entered the sitting room and announced that Brigadier Wingate had arrived. It had taken him three days to fly from
India. When the plane landed at RAF Northolt, an airfield on the
northern outskirts of London, he delayed only long enough to telephone Lorna, his wife, who was in Edinburgh and who arranged to
catch a morning train to London. Then a staff car took him straight
to Downing Street.

Churchill ordered Wingate to be ushered in without delay. The
gaunt, bearded brigadier entered the private chambers still dressed in
the threadbare Khaki drills in which he had spent the last three days.
Pleasantries quickly over, the Prime Minister got straight down to
business and quizzed Wingate on the problems of defeating the
Japanese. Wingate outlined his views on how to fight an offensive in
Burma, long range penetration groups landed by air behind enemy
lines. Within half an hour, Churchill felt himself in the presence of a
man of the highest quality.*

Wingate stayed for dinner and entranced his host with tales of
jungle warfare. Churchill decided on the spur of the moment to take
him to Canada, there to join the other carefully selected heroes in the
entourage† to meet the President.

'You must come with me and tell the President,' ordered Churchill.

Wingate for once was completely taken back and protested that he
had no clothes other than those he wore. An ATS driver on duty who
was despatched to Wingate's London flat to collect his uniforms
returned with the news that they had been eaten by moths, and held

---

*Winston Churchill, *The Second World War* Volume V, *Closing the Ring*.
†Guy Gibson was in the party.

up one battledress for everyone to see. Wingate thought he knew of a gunner officer on the staff in Whitehall who might lend him a battledress for a couple of weeks.

'Nonsense,' intoned the Prime Minister. 'You can borrow some of mine.' Mrs Churchill tactfully intervened; after all none of her husband's voluminous garments, though of the finest quality, would help the gallant brigadier to look the part. General Ismay was called back and he despatched an aide to borrow a battledress complete with brigadier's insignias and a cap to match.

Suddenly Wingate remembered Lorna and explained the situation.

'She will come too,' the Prime Minister ordered and another aide went to telephone Mrs Wingate. She was ordered to be in Waverley Station, Edinburgh, at six o'clock the next morning; a staff car would collect her from home in plenty of time. No reasons or explanation were given, despite her protestations.

Shortly before midnight Wingate joined the 200 members of staff and 50 Royal Marine orderlies who were already on board the train waiting for the Prime Minister's party at Addison Road Station, in West London. This station was used because being so far out of the centre of London it was not likely to receive any unwelcome attention from the Luftwaffe. Even this far into the war, the capital was still subjected to frequent night raids and security was very tight. Although enemy espionage to date had proved singularly unsuccessful, there was always the fear that a leak in security to some hitherto unidentified member of a 'Fifth Column' could easily result in a bombing attack on the train.

The Prime Minister aboard, the train steamed out of the station and headed north for Scotland. Given highest priority, it sped through the night and early the next morning the Wingates were reunited on the platform at Waverley Station. The train made a brief stop to collect newspapers before continuing the short journey to Greenock.

The *Queen Mary* sailed that day for Halifax, Nova Scotia. Painted in drab battleship grey and escorted by a bevy of fast cruisers, she appeared the very epitome of warlike efficiency as she steamed out into the Atlantic at full speed. Appearances can be deceptive, for all on board enjoyed a cuisine and standard of luxury which had made the ship renowned in peacetime.

However, it was not all play. During the sea voyage the Chiefs of Staff Committee spent long hours agreeing a joint position – one to be defended by all services – over future strategy in S.E. Asia. Wingate was called to brief them on his ideas which were well received by the Chiefs, none of whom had any experience of jungle warfare. They agreed that his concept of long range penetration forces seemed to provide the answer to the Sino-American needs in Northern or Upper Burma, but at the same time these astute strategists recognized the immediate and longer-term consequences. Wingate's forces could not conquer, so there would have to be a conventional style advance to make good what he had gained. Secondly, in the longer term – i.e. the following year – there would have to be an offensive to complete the conquest of Burma, and this in turn would require forces and resources that might otherwise have been used elsewhere. There were those who favoured an amphibious campaign, island-hopping straight to Singapore, and regarded Burma as a strategic cul-de-sac; another school realistically accepted that the Second Front in Europe would take priority for landing craft and thence the American strikes in the Pacific would swallow up everything else. There might just be sufficient resources made available, provided the case was adroitly handled through committee for one major operation in the Indian theatre.

What does seem to have been totally accepted up to this time was that in the re-conquest of Burma, the preferred route was from the south. The Allied invasion force would begin with a landing in Rangoon, march northwards and then link up with the advance from Arakan. Like the Japanese, none could contemplate a campaign in Burma without recourse to a port. Now it was all change, it was to be an advance from the north southwards. A guerrilla campaign was about to dictate the grand strategy of the main or conventional offensive, and that made no sense at all.

Wingate was plausible, and there were even those on the Chiefs of Staff Committee who were magnanimous enough to overlook his crude manners and habit of eating raw onions as if they were apples. Nevertheless on one issue there was unanimity. Bearded prophet he might be, and even worthy to inherit the mantle of Lawrence as the guerrilla guru, but they would not sanction such a promotion as giving him command of an Army.

In this the Prime Minister acquiesced. On Sunday 8 August, as the *Queen Mary* and her escorts neared the Canadian shores, he summoned Wingate again and they spent an hour closeted together. Churchill confirmed his appointment to a Special Long Range Penetration Group, a division-size force over which Wingate would have carte blanche in all matters relating to selection and training of the men and their equipment.

On Wednesday 11 August, Churchill cabled Deputy Prime Minister Attlee and Foreign Secretary Anthony Eden in London:

> Brigadier Wingate is a remarkable man, and he also in his jungle sphere would fit in with my ideas of vigour and inventiveness in this decayed Indian scene.

Lord Louis Mountbatten, as Director of Combined Operations, was a member of the Chiefs of Staff Committee, and listened with great interest to what Wingate had to say. He was not repelled as were others by such arrogance and eccentricity. Mountbatten asked Wingate during the voyage to address his own specialists and staff in Combined Operations, and this gave him another opportunity to study the man closely. By all accounts, he was not fooled; in later life Mountbatten described Wingate as a mixture, a heady cocktail of courage and imagination, messianic zeal and braggadocio.

Mountbatten too came under the microscope. Churchill intended to reorganize the High Command in the British Far East and he wanted 'a young competent soldier, well trained in war, to become Supreme Commander and to re-examine the whole problem of the war on this front so as to infuse vigour and authority into the operation'.*

The old guard – Wavell as Viceroy and Auchinleck as Commander-in-Chief – were discredited. Leo Amery, Secretary of State for India, had already reported to Churchill that he considered Wavell was a spent force. Churchill had never liked the austere Auchinleck and regarded with scant respect his gloomy prognosis that the Army in India was barely able to defend, let alone contemplate any offensive. What the Prime Minister refused to accept were the facts of the situation. The fault did not lie with Auchinleck or with Wavell, both commanders of great wisdom and military insight, who had been made scapegoats for the failures of the politicians. The truth was that the Far Eastern theatre was so low a priority that Auchinleck was starved of trained troops and modern equipment, while Wavell was plagued by the need to maintain security in India itself.

The Prime Minister decided that it was time to separate the function of C.-in-C. India from that of prosecuting the war. He planned to lobby the Americans to agree to the establishment of a Supreme Allied Commander for S.E. Asia, who was to be British. C.-in-C. India would remain with Auchinleck, but as a training and administrative command – one ideally suited to this dour Sepoy general.

Mountbatten was not the first choice for the new top job of Supremo, nor the second or even third. The short list included Air Marshals Sholto Douglas – whom the Americans detested – and Tedder, who was too valuable as Eisenhower's deputy. On the naval side there were Admirals Cunningham and Sir James Somerville, but neither was popular with the Americans nor were they interested in what was essentially a land appointment.

The 'second eleven' numbered Generals Sir Henry Maitland-Wilson

---

*Churchill to Ismay, 26 July 1943.

and Sir George Giffard, Lieutenant-Generals Sir Henry Pawnall and Sir Oliver Leese and Air Marshal Slessor. All were men of very ordinary talent in the judgement of General Ismay.

The Quadrant Conference met at the Citadel in Quebec. Wingate's presence remained a closely guarded secret, though a bearded Army officer in an ill-fitting uniform could hardly have been inconspicuous. The attendant press corps were forbidden to reveal his identity, and every effort was made to ensure that he was well out of the way whenever photographers were on the scene.

When discussion turned to the Far East, major differences quickly surfaced and the debate became heated and frequently acrimonious. The Americans wanted the British to commit the resources of India and deploy large field forces to Northern Burma, but this was not reciprocated. The British Chiefs countered with their own proposal – an amphibious operation to seize the northern tip of Sumatra and then drive for Singapore. This stratagem, they believed, would at one stroke outflank the Japanese and make their whole position in S.E. Asia, Burma and Thailand untenable. The Americans, rightly, dismissed this as hare-brained.

The British had in mind operations in Northern Burma which, because of the desperate shortage of resources, however, could only be on a limited scale. Brought in to address the conference, Wingate proposed a strong, long-range penetration group of specially trained and properly equipped jungle guerrillas. Under his command, this Special Force would establish a centre of operations in the enemy heartland of Northern Burma. They were to operate out of sanctuaries, strongly defended fortresses, from which they would sally forth to attack enemy communications and supply dumps. This stratagem, Wingate explained, would have two results. First, the Japanese would be forced to divert men and resources to combat such a menace. Second, the enemy, starved of supplies, would become less effective.

Wingate's proposals had merit and some of the initial tension was dispelled. With Northern Burma so isolated, the pressure would be off Stilwell, who could in turn complete the Ledo Road unhindered. At the same time, the Chinese forces on the Salween River front should be able to attack the then weakened Japanese, thrust them aside and link up with Stilwell. The road from India to China would be open and the Americans could exploit all the opportunities from a more viable theatre of war.

At Quebec, Roosevelt and General Marshall came under Wingate's spell. Full of enthusiasm, Marshall committed an American Regimental Combat Team. He offered to send volunteers from army units with combat experience against the Japanese to India for training under Wingate.

In this new spirit of cooperation and goodwill, Wingate expanded on his theme and outlined the kind of resources he needed to ensure success. The key was air power. The jungle guerrillas, more than a division in number, were to be supplied totally by air. All their food and ammunition were to be air delivered, both to the fortress and to columns on the march. Equally important, the wounded and sick were to be evacuated, airlifted out to hospitals in India. Wingate conceded that abandoning casualties on the previous operation had proved counterproductive for morale.

It was more than just a question of air support or the number of aircraft to be devoted to the operation. In Wingate's opinion the air arm had to be completely integrated with the ground forces so that a level of cooperation, mutual trust and complementary skills could be achieved which had been hitherto unattainable. Here he struck a particularly sensitive issue. A month before during Operation *Husky*, the amphibious landings in Sicily, there had been most appalling disasters when British and American paratroopers were shot out of the sky by mistaken Allied anti-aircraft fire from the fleet.

It was Admiral Mountbatten who suggested that the only way to ensure the level of cooperation needed was to integrate the air arm under Wingate's command. Hap Arnold, the Commanding General of the US Army Air Force – though a keen advocate of a US Air Force which was independent of the Army – enthusiastically endorsed the proposal. Arnold was a four star general but one intimately involved in even the smallest details of the air effort.

The Americans accepted Wingate's plans and offered to provide the bulk of the air component. Hap Arnold hurried back to Washington and sent for two young fighter pilot aces: Colonels Philip Cochran and John R. Allison. Though barely into their thirties they were home after making their name in the Tunisian campaign. Cochran, 34 years of age, had commanded a fighter squadron and won five decorations. He became the role model for Colonel Flip Corkin, a character in Milton Caniff's comic strip 'Terry and the Pirates'.

Arnold gave Cochran command of the 5318th Air Unit, with Allison as his deputy. Allison had the experience. This 31-year-old, much decorated officer had flown with the Flying Tigers, but he was also an accomplished diplomat having spent time in Moscow as an Assistant Military Attaché.

Initially there were neither men nor machines in the 5318th, for it had no establishment. Instead, the young officers had Arnold's brief to ensure that: The United States Army Air Force spearheads Wingate's Campaign.

Arnold was playing power politics and aimed to ensure that Wingate's success was seen by all to have been made possible only by the skill and the resources of American air power. He also liked Mountbatten, whose appointment as Supreme Allied Commander in South-East Asia had now been confirmed. Arnold dubbed the 5318th the Air Commando Force. The title had a good PR image and it was a compliment to Mountbatten's previous appointment as Chief of Combined Operations.

'To hell with the paperwork,' was Arnold's parting remark as Cochran and Allison prepared to meet with Wingate. So, rather like Topsy, the Air Commando grew and grew to include everything from light liaison to medium bombers. There were fighters to ensure their own air superiority and the first combat use of the helicopter.

While Cochran and Allison gathered the men, the machines and the organization, Wingate returned to India with a Prime Ministerial carte blanche to create the Long Range Penetration Force; this was now referred to as Special Force, a name chosen to disguise its intentions. The Americans would join him later to establish bases and rehearse the skills needed to ensure success.

Wingate left Quebec with the press still none the wiser. A cloak of secrecy still hung over every aspect of the doctrine of Long Range Penetration, this revolutionary and hopefully war-winning formula to defeat the Japanese in the jungles of Burma.

CHAPTER TWENTY-NINE

Wingate's Private Army

Secrecy followed Wingate back to India where a new division, the 3rd Indian, was chosen to form the nucleus of Special Force. Wingate's promotion to Major-General and his command of the division was kept secret; the enemy was to have no inkling that he was even back in the theatre, let alone preparing to lead another raid behind enemy lines.

Early in October 1943, Mountbatten arrived in Delhi to take up his appointment as Supreme Commander in S.E. Asia. All the senior officers were lined up to greet him, including Wingate, but the censor forbade any mention of his name. Mountbatten did confirm that Wingate was to be given top priority, with the very best in equipment and resources that the theatre had available. With the exception of Joe Lentaigne and 111 Brigade – who lost their independence and were absorbed into the new organization (but as a three battalion brigade) – the nucleus of the division, brigade commanders and senior staff were provided by officers who had survived the first expedition. Those who chose to stay with Wingate were well rewarded. Fergusson and Calvert, zealous devotees, became brigadiers and many others rose two or three ranks in promotion.

The Chindits came from the 70th British Infantry Division, probably the best troops in India at the time. There was no question of training garrison troops for a fighting role; the men of 70th Division were veterans, and had already seen more than their fair share of battle. Having begun life in 1940 as the 6th Infantry Division, raised in Palestine from regular battalions, since that time they had fought in Crete and the Western Desert, and had been Desert Rats in the first and successful siege of Tobruk.

In Tobruk the Division was redesignated the 70th, a device to confuse enemy intelligence when it relieved the original garrison. Subsequently it fought the Vichy French in Syria before being shipped east to Ceylon where it formed part of the garrison to defend the island against a possible Japanese invasion. In Ceylon the 70th trained as the first to specialize in jungle warfare.

Special Forces at home and in the Middle East had been raised by attracting the best men from ordinary units with offers of better conditions, promises of excitement and not a little propaganda. The veterans of the 70th Division did not volunteer to become Chindits. They were drafted!

However, as raw material for Wingate's grand design there was none better. A division of regular infantry who were veterans and now specialists in jungle warfare was about to be reorganized and restructured to meet the needs of Special Forces. The plunder of such a formation, and the destruction of such an esprit de corps was a wanton act of military vandalism. The loss of that division, with a proven record as a cohesive, well-knit fighting unit, and its absence from the critical battles at Imphal and Kohima, were in no way compensated for by anything which it was able to achieve as Chindits.

Wingate was not impressed with the quality of the infantry. He demanded and received more units from which to select and train his force, which meant that Auchinleck had to disband a second infantry division to meet these needs. Wingate held Indian infantry – with the exception of Gurkhas – in very low esteem and refused to countenance their inclusion as Chindits. Such a position flew in the face of his favourite and oft-quoted dictum that there were 'no such things as bad soldiers, just bad officers', but none in authority dared challenge these blatant contradictions.

The result was that British units comprised about two-thirds of his command. The remainder were five battalions drawn from the 4th, 6th and 9th Gurkhas, Burma Rifles and three battalions of West Africans. The British contingents read like a *Who's Who* of the Regular Army:

    The Black Watch
    The Bedfordshire and Hertfordshire Regiment
    The Essex Regiment
    The Border Regiment
    The Duke of Wellington's Regiment
    The York and Lancaster Regiment
    The Royal Leicestershire Regiment

215

> The Lancashire Fusiliers
> The Cameronians
> The Queen's Regiment
> The King's Own Royal Regiment (Lancaster)
> The King's Regiment (Liverpool)
> The South Staffordshire Regiment

The 3rd Indian Division also had reconnaissance corps and gunners who were to serve as specialized infantry. Wingate was a gunner and insisted on the inclusion of the latter since, 'We need brains,' he declared.

Specialists in other fields were also asked to volunteer – Signals, Medics, Engineers and Supply, so eight more major units had to be disbanded to meet the needs of the Special Force.

Wingate had the equivalent of two and a half divisions under his command when he went to Slim to ask for more. He had his eye on British battalions in the 26th Indian Division, which had recently come out of the line after being bloodied in the vicious fighting in the Arakan.

The 26th Indian Division was the only reserve that Slim had in Fourteenth Army and he rightly refused to accede to Wingate's request. However, the latter was nothing if not persistent and demanded a meeting.

It was by all accounts a frosty affair.* Wingate began by saying that while he held a personal loyalty to Slim as the Army Commander, there was a higher loyalty. Slim knew what was coming, but nevertheless put the question.

'To the Prime Minister of England and the President of the United States,' replied Wingate. 'I am required to report directly to London and name those who in my judgement obstruct the preparations for this operation.' He paused to let his words take effect. 'This is such an occasion,' he continued. 'I'm sorry, General, but your refusal to release the 26th Division to my command must be reported to the Prime Minister, whatever the consequences to you personally.'

Slim simply pushed a blank signal pad and pencil across his desk and told Wingate to send his message. Wingate looked at him, the red flush of anger showing through his beard, grabbed his cane and battered topee and left the room without another word.

Maybe Slim was robust enough to call Wingate's bluff, for no mention was ever again made of the 26th Indian Division becoming Chindits. Others were not so fortunate and the demands for equipment and extra resources were accompanied by increasing tensions and

---

* For Slim's account see *Defeat into Victory* (Cassell, London, 1956).

acrimony between Wingate and the senior staff in South-East Asia Command. There could be little doubt that in a theatre starved of resources, his methods were already proving just about the most expensive way imaginable of waging war against the Japanese. If they should fail, then retribution would fall not just on Wingate, but upon the heads of all those who were associated with him. Joe Lentaigne summed up the situation succinctly:*

> Well, if we are going to be part of Wingate's Private Army, let's relax and enjoy it. We're Chindits now, and by God, we had better all stick together, because the rest of the Army's going to be out for our blood.

Such matters were not the concern of the more junior officers and men who for various reasons suddenly found themselves part of this new private army. Few indeed had even heard of Wingate or knew of his reputation.

John Campbell was a man of Kent who, until he arrived in India late in 1943 with a reinforcement draft for the 1st Kings, had enjoyed a particularly good war. Reading law at Oxford when hostilities broke out, he was called up the following year into the Buffs. He had his own pack of beagles, enjoyed fox-hunting and persuaded his first commanding officer to take the beagles on to battalion strength as a way of helping to train the men for war.

Campbell joined the 1st Battalion on anti-invasion duties at St Margaret's Bay in Kent, was promoted Lance-Corporal by virtue of his office as Master of Beagles and there spent two happy seasons on the cliffs of Dover hunting. Eventually he was sent to an OCTU at Sandhurst and subsequently commissioned into the King's Own Scottish Borderers – a regiment he chose because of its links with hunting. The soldiers came from the borders, John Peel country, and officers even in the third year of war were still expected to ride to hounds.

Second-Lieutenant Campbell was posted to the 5th Battalion. It was stationed in the north of Scotland as part of the 52nd Lowland Division, which was preparing for its specialist role as a Mountain Division.

Training in the bleak fastness of the northern Grampians was not to John Campbell's taste, and when a directive came from the War Office asking for officers to serve in the Far East he volunteered. He had been in India before the war.

A few weeks later he was summoned by the CO.

---

*John Masters, *Road Past Mandalay*, p. 140.

'There's a posting for you in India, but I've sent it back, John. We don't want you to go.'

'That's very kind of you, sir. In fact, I would like to go very much.'

Campbell put his foot down as firmly as he dared and soon found himself on his way to London; the convoy sailed via South Africa, where he spent two months playing polo. In India his knowledge and love of horses was soon put to good use. By the time he arrived, the 1st Battalion King's (Liverpool) Regiment was busy converting to the role of Chindits and 'Scouse' soldiers were learning to live with pack-mules and horses. In India, regiments of mountain artillery were stripped of their mules to meet the needs of the Chindits who named them after their girls back home, their wives or their favourite film star. Proud Indian Cavalry regiments in the process of mechanization saw their horse lines disappear and realized that the change to machine-age warfare was permanent. Wingate wanted his officers mounted, but this was not very practicable, and since bullocks and elephants did not form part of the new Chindit establishment cavalry chargers became beasts of burden.

Tim Biron had already seen plenty of action with the Royal Leicesters. As one of the original battalions of the 16th Independent Infantry Brigade, they had fought in Syria and Tobruk. The move to Ceylon was a return home, for Biron's war had begun on the island where he had worked on a tea plantation.

In India the battalion were dispersed into various camps throughout Central Provinces, training for their new role in long range penetration. For the hard-bitten veterans there was not much of a selection test; the real criterion was physical fitness and anyone who had had malaria more than twice was out and posted to another unit. Men who failed to keep pace on exercises or officers who did not measure up were also weeded out. Wingate sacked one battalion commander on the spot for daring to challenge 'the party line'. This meant that the selection process went into reverse, for those who failed to make the grade as Chindits were cast off into normal units where they arrived with the feeling of being second best.

General Slim was already striving to overcome the problem of morale. Upon his appointment to command the newly created Four-teenth Army, he had rightly identified the feeling of inferiority as his single biggest obstacle. He had to create a new esprit de corps, and to convince the men under his command that they were better than the Japanese. Slim was not well served by Wingate's antics of passing down his cast-offs for re-employment.

It was a period of painful transition, especially for those Chindit battalions which had served in the Western Desert and were used to motorized war. Even the jungle training in Ceylon had involved route marches and exercises from vehicles which were parked on tracks and roads. Suddenly everything had to be carried, on either the backs of men or animals, and this caused all kinds of problems in deciding what was essential and what was not.

In the battalions, regular officers included the CO and most company commanders – men whose service predated the war. Many of these officers had been around horses all their lives and this knowledge was invaluable. The same could not be said for the soldiers, therefore the selection of those who were to become muleteers was quite arbitrary. In most battalions everyone who was a driver and accustomed to looking after a vehicle now became accustomed to looking after an animal.

The biggest upheaval of all, however, was in the battalion's structure and organization. In conventional formations a battalion had a Headquarters company which comprised the command element and support weapons, and four rifle companies. As a Chindit battalion, Headquarters was slimmed down to the CO, second-in-command, Intelligence and Signals officers, Adjutant, RSM and RAF Liaison Officer. Two Chindit columns replaced the four rifle companies. Each column had two rifle and one reconnaissance platoons; everybody else was a muleteer.

When marching in single file the extreme length of a Chindit column, was to prove one of their major weaknesses. A Chindit brigade had four battalions which meant there were eight, possibly nine columns. Even on good ground where the going was easy, it took a brigade the best part of three hours to pass a given spot. In jungle-covered mountains it would take a day.

Tactical immobility went hand in hand with a lack of firepower. The Chindit column was fatally inhibited by the number of riflemen employed as muleteers and by the absence of heavy support – artillery, tanks and engineers, which are normally available to an infantry division.

Firepower was intended to be supplied by Cochran's No. 1 Air Commando and by October 1943, the first squadrons were beginning to arrive in India. They consisted of a number of C-47s specially fitted with apparatus which allowed them to make a low pass and snatch a glider from the ground into the air. The latter were the WACO CG 4A Gliders. Constructed of welded steel tube with a fabric covering, these robust machines had a hinged nose section for loading or unloading vehicles up to a jeep, or alternatively there were benches for 15 fully-armed troops. Cochran had a squadron of P51 Mustangs and another of B-25H Mitchell bombers – this was the model with 14 .50 calibre machine guns, a 75 mm tank cannon under the pilot's feet and 3,200 lbs of bombs. There were many light aircraft for liaison, spotting and light casualty evacuation. They were all marked with five diagonal white stripes at the tail end of the fuselage, which signified No. 1 Air Commando. To the British soldiers they became 'Cochran's Glamour Girls'. (The allusion was to the famous C. B. Cochran, the London impresario whose shows always had lines of long-legged, shapely chorus girls.)

Glamorous they might have been, but Cochran's Air Commando was no substitute for artillery. It is a lesson which armies never seem to learn, that aircraft are not so accurate, reliable or flexible as guns. Throughout the Second World War and subsequently in Korea, Vietnam, the Middle East, Gulf and Falklands, air-delivered ordnance has been seen as a substitute for artillery bombardment and has failed on every occasion to fulfil that function. The pilot delivers his bombardment, misses the target and speeds off on his way home for tea. The gunner opens fire, misses the target, corrects his aim and delivers the goods. Together, well delivered air strikes and artillery bombardment are a lethal combination, but the Chindits – who were in any case deficient in firepower – were to be dependent on air power alone; and they were to pay the price for such military recklessness.

CHAPTER THIRTY

A Jungle Corps d'Elite

As the year 1943 faded, the preparation and training for the coming campaign intensified. The columns marched deep into the Indian jungle to master tactics and techniques developed by Wingate and passed down to the local commanders by means of pamphlets and lectures. They learned how to come to terms with the jungle, an implacable environment where everything combined to make life an absolute misery. They struggled with heat, humidity and altitude, with stubborn mules and the bulky loads they were expected to carry.

The Chindits learned how to get their mules up a mountainside with the minimum of fuss and delay. Once a gradient gets beyond a certain point, the mule doesn't walk up but jumps up; and as soon as it starts jumping, it sheds its load. The Chindits placed two men at the bottom and two men every few paces to the top of the slope. At the bottom the mule was unloaded and then allowed to find its own way up while the men formed a chain-gang to manhandle the load – a charging engine, radio communication or whatever – to the top.

The Chindits practised Wingate's method for a night bivouac. The order would be given to halt on the trail; then a left or right turn, and the whole column moved individually into the jungle, perhaps a couple of hundred yards or more and at ninety degrees to the path. It was generally impossible to tell where the column had gone as the thick, well-nigh impenetrable jungle closed back over each man's passing.

The column re-formed and bivouaced by platoons, the platoon commander choosing a prominent tree in the immediate vicinity to act as focal point and HQ. A rendezvous was agreed, usually some easily remembered feature on the track which had been passed in the last hour of the march. It was to be used in case of an emergency, such as a surprise attack on the bivouac, which might force the Chindits to disperse. After the experiences of the first expedition, the emergency procedure was frequently put to the test on exercise.

Once the platoon commander had completed his orders, the sections fanned out around the tree and disappeared into the jungle. Lighting fires was another skill to be acquired. Bamboo was ideal as it could be coaxed to burn however damp, but once alight it burnt so furiously that it took two men a good half hour to cut enough bamboo to keep a fire blazing for a couple of hours. Some tried to burn bamboo logs, but quickly learned the error of their ways. Air pockets in the bamboo heated up and then burst with the retort of a 25-pounder shell, propelling blazing splinters in every direction.

The answer lay in burning only finely shaved shivers of bamboo. Fed in this fashion the fire would last for hours, but strangely this was not widely known among the columns.

Leeches were another unpleasant initiation for those who were new to the jungle. With the rains they came in sizes which varied from pin-length to a couple of inches. Thin enough to pass through the eye of a boot or the gap between fly-buttons, they could gorge until bloated to the size of a man's finger. The initial painlessness of the assault was unnerving and leeches could only be removed by burning them off with a cigarette. The pain of the attack, the itching sensation came later.

Likewise the discovery of lice caused a violent feeling of revulsion, but this the men found easier to accept than leeches. Lice were taken for granted, and in bivouac the Chindits sometimes held lice-picking contests – the winner being the man who had collected the most out of his clothing. Ticks were also unpleasant, especially at night when they could make sleep impossible. The only way to make a tick pull its head out of one's skin is to touch its backside with a red-hot needle. Such refinements were not available to the Chindits, who just pulled the ticks out with their fingers leaving the heads embedded.

Pill-taking went hand in hand with the exercises. Chindits were given daily doses of shark liver oil, cheaper and easier to extract than cod liver oil and twice as foul. They took their mepacrine, the Army's antidote to malaria, and their faces turned a dark unhealthy, jaundiced yellow, as did their urine. Rumours were rife about mepacrine: it made a man impotent, caused his hair to fall out and his teeth to rot. Soldiers tried every dodge in the book to avoid their dose until food rations were withheld and men had to down their dose under the eye of an officer. Mepacrine reduced the incidence of malaria and that was all that mattered; a malarial rate above a certain percentage meant instant dismissal for the unit commander.

The High Command had every reason to impose such draconian measures. Throughout 1943 on the Assam and Arakan fronts, an average of 623 out of every 1,000 soldiers were hospitalized with malaria. Not only was that about 45 times the number of battle casualties, it also meant enforced absence from the front for anything up to six weeks.

The boffins invented anti-malarial creams which were sent up to be tested under field conditions. None passed beyond the rear areas where they were tried by the staff, who always seemed to get the first bite of the cherry and live better than fighting men. On this occasion, the pungent odours given off by the creams would have been a dead give-away to the enemy had they been used at the front.

The MO in the Leicesters was against the use of mepacrine because nobody knew anything about the drug's long-term side effects. So in the Leicesters they concentrated on precautionary measures; all the men had head veils weighted with bamboo rings which they wore at night, along with long-sleeved shirts and canvas gloves. At bivouac the Leicesters looked like a convention of bee-keepers.

In December 1943 the pressure and pace of preparation was increased. They marched twenty miles a day with a 66-pound pack, swam rivers and lakes and slept among long-forgotten temple ruins. Ingenuity and improvisation played an important part in their preparation. Instructors who had experience of fighting the Japanese by night in the jungle passed on invaluable, often life-saving, hints. Silence became the golden rule and Chindits learned to sleep with string tied around their socked toes, ready to be jerked awake by the squad's sentry. Radio operators practised a new form of call signs. Blowing gently into the mouthpieces of their sets – one for the CO, two for the second-in-command, three for the mortars etc. – they gave a whole new meaning to heavy breathing! The Army Veterinary Corps cut the vocal chords of the horses and mules so that they could not bray, and those of the Alsatians which had been trained to carry messages from one column to another.

No expense was spared Wingate's jungle elite, and the demands he placed upon the theatre's supply dumps led his name to be reviled in many quarters as a maniacal publicity seeker. This he never was. Wingate believed passionately, with the force of a zealot, in the rightness of his action. The pity was, and remains, that what was achieved was besmirched because Wingate lived in a perpetual state of turmoil and conflict with his fellow men. He had a persecution complex that was so intense that had it occurred today, Medical Officers would have had him removed – forcibly if necessary – to hospital for psychiatric treatment.

None of this was common knowledge as the Chindits saw very little of their commander and cared even less about his reputation. Personal survival was uppermost in their minds. In 1943 Parliament decreed that servicemen who had been abroad for five years were to be brought home on long leave, no matter the theatre of war. Amongst the Chindits, most of the long-service regulars were due to be granted home leave. They had all been overseas for five years, and even longer in some cases. Their horizons were limited by the prevailing need to physically survive the next little push and make sure of their berth on a troopship home before the Army changed the rules.

Wingate did make sure that he addressed each of the British battalions in his command, but such a pep-talk had little impact on hard-bitten regulars, all well versed in the exercise of Army cynicism. John Campbell watched Wingate address his battalion. Wingate looked the part and was impressive, but Campbell came away with the distinct impression that here was a man who had the greatest contempt for his fellow mortals.

John Masters was Brigade Major to Joe Lentaigne's III Brigade. Neither officer was a Wingate fan. Along with many other professional soldiers, they felt that the Special Force had become too big, too cumbersome, with little tactical mobility and nothing to recommend either its structure or its fire power. Nevertheless, as professional soldiers they were required not only to obey orders but to carry them out in a manner which ensured success. It did not help that in Wingate they were dealing with a general who was not open to debate or persuasion.

John Masters also watched Wingate address the battalions. He spoke with a harsh flat voice and mixed obscenities and profanities with biblical quotations. Much of the latter was lost on the soldiers, but the force of his personality transcended indifferent diction. Some officers were so inspired by the sheer charisma of the man that his actual words escaped scrutiny. For those who wanted pep, they were pepped; but the more thoughtful, who looked for reasoned analysis and exposition on tactics, were depressed by what they heard. Wingate made little impression on the Jocks. He was just another general whose existence threatened theirs and they were canny enough to recognize the absence of either respect or affection in his manner. Bill Slim, in contrast, with his warm, gruff no-nonsense approach, inspired trust from even the most cynical of soldiery.

John Masters accompanied Wingate to each British battalion in the brigade. He thought the general looked ill and fanatical; but very impressive with the ribbon of a DSO and two bars on his chest.

Equipment scales were lavish, but this was the forgotten theatre of the war and the Chindits, like everybody else, had to make do as best they could. The men were told that they would be operating behind the enemy lines for up to 90 days, but they lacked a decent large rucksack which was suitable for their needs. So the Chindits turned to and adapted their ordinary service equipment. Magazine carriers, anti-tank pouches, Bren-gun pouches and anything else were cannibalized and sewn on to the Army issue large pack.

Boots were a problem, but every Chindit made sure that he was well shod and that quartermasters back at base had a spare pair with each name clearly marked. Their preparation could not have been more thorough. Details of prescriptions for spectacles and monocles, moulds and plaster casts for dentures were carefully recorded and filed.

Tim Biron had a problem because of his feet. He wore a size 12 and so he had a pair of boots specially made for him in India with an extra sole studded on to the bottom. Convinced that the Army would never be able to replace his boots, Biron equipped himself with a bradawl, wax and thread and learned how to make running repairs.

The equipment carried by officers and men was substantially the same. They were self contained. Each man had a large pack, ammunition for automatics, Brens or rifles, mess-tins and five days' rations – American Ks. To an Army which had hitherto fought the war on a diet of bully beef and spuds, the American rations were at first a tremendous novelty and a real pleasure. There were three kinds: one labelled breakfast, another lunch and the third supper. The breakfast ration was a tin of bacon roll or scrambled egg, or chopped bacon and egg; there were two packets of biscuits, one a very hard, floury one and the other more wheaty, both highly compressed; also a packet of coffee powder, a packet of dried fruit and a bar of dried fruit, five cigarettes and chewing-gum. The lunch pack was a tin of cheese, luncheon sausage or Spam, two packets of biscuits, a sachet of lemonade, a packet of glucose sweets, five cigarettes and chewing-gum. Supper was a tin of meat stew and another of mixed vegetables with all the extras. For all meals there were packets of matches, toilet paper, dried milk, sugar, coffee and salt.

The diet palled after a while and imagination had run dry on variations. One problem was the chewing-gum, the smell of which permeated every other item in the food packs. The K-rations were issued in five-day cycles, the cardboard was useful for lighting the bivouac fire and the cigarettes were a godsend. What seems to have escaped notice at the time, however, was that K-rations were scientifically developed for a specific purpose; they were combat rations, high energy foods designed for assault troops on a five-day emergency cycle. The K-ration was never intended to be a soldier's sole diet for months at a time.

Everybody carried a machete, and officers a small satchel and a map case. None had pistols, neither were badges of rank worn in most columns. At one stage later in the campaign, Tim Biron stood and watched a column of another regiment in the brigade go past. He couldn't even tell the officers, though he knew some of them. But the Chindits knew their own officers and it was all that mattered.

Some of the training was rudimentary. Gliders were a precious and fragile commodity, so very few had a chance to practise, let alone experience a flight. A number of mock-ups were made and on these the Chindits practised enplaning and debussing, in very much the same way that other soldiers in England practised what was known as dryshod landings.

One manoeuvre which was frequently practised and refined was that of glider snatching. Rather like the space shuttle of today, the gliders were intended to be used more than once and this meant recovery from an advanced, often very temporary landing-strip. As part of its equipment a glider carried two long poles, on top of each of which was a self-contained, battery-powered blue light. A third blue light was on the glider cockpit, to help the tug aircraft line up properly as it approached to make the snatch. The two poles were stuck in the ground some 200 feet in front of the glider and about 50 feet apart. The tow-rope, made of highly elasticated nylon, formed a triangle with the glider at the apex. Like all the best ideas it was simplicity itself. From the hook on the glider's nose, the tow-rope was threaded through the top of the left-hand pole, across to the right and back to the glider's hook.

The poles were then raised in the air and the glider manhandled into position with the tow-rope taut. The pilot sat with the brakes off and the flaps set for take-off. The tug, a C47 with a long boom and automatic catch lowered from the tail, came in at about 30 feet with engines throttled back, flaps down, propellers set at full pitch ready to take the strain. The sudden jerk as the tug's hook locked home pulled the rope taut, and the tension was absorbed by the nylon as the Dakota pilot pushed his throttles through the gate and lifted the nose. The glider, at a rate of acceleration aspired to but never emulated by Formula One racing drivers – 0–80 mph in a second and a half – rose immediately into the air and was swept away into the night.

Mountbatten and the top brass – Slim, Wingate et al – came to see a demonstration. After numerous hair-raising accidents the technique was considered sufficiently safe to be set before the Commander-in-Chief. Cochran and Allison between them provided a commentary for the assembled dignitaries.

On the second pass the Dakota locked on to its tow and the glider rose abruptly into the air. The assembled Americans gave vent to their natural exuberance and then all turned to see their chief's reaction.

'Jesus Christ All Bloody Mighty,' incanted Mountbatten.

As training progressed, the jungle hardly became the Chindits' friend as Wingate wished, but it was seen by most of them as neutral. At night, however, the jungle became a frightening place, full of strange noises, and the Chindits had to overcome their own private fears. In the desert, an evening stroll with the shovel had become an agreeable ritual. Bowel movement in the jungle was something to be completed as quickly as possible. It was a time when everyone felt particularly vulnerable. They had every reason to be afraid of snakes and king cobras in particular had a fearsome reputation; yet there were only three recorded deaths from snakebite in the whole of the Burma War.

Then there was the enemy. The Japanese not only fought by standards of ethics which were quite alien to the Allies, but they were also more at home in the jungle. Wingate warned his men to expect the enemy to use tactics deliberately designed to play upon their sense of uncertainty and fearfulness.

The Royal Army Medical Corps learned that the jungle was a place inimical to first-class medicine. There were sufficient casualties in the large-scale exercises for the doctors and surgeons to have a foretaste of what was to come. By this stage combat medicine had made considerable progress – in remedies, surgical techniques and drugs – but little of this had permeated to the Far East. While Wingate had recognized the need for casualty evacuation, what he failed to appreciate were the finite limits set by air mobility. Cochran's Air Commando gave the Chindits strategic mobility. They could be airlifted enormous distances in hours. But they were no more able to cover relatively short, even battlefield distances at speed than any other troops because of the topography and the climate. Speed was conditioned by the pace of a man leading a mule, and tactical immobility is a fatal weakness in any guerrilla force.

Most columns did not have a doctor. Neither were there the multi-skilled surgical teams that were part of the conventional division, infantry armour or indeed airborne. Everything depended upon speedy casualty evacuation.

Wingate had noted the dire consequences of leaving the wounded to die in his previous campaign and had rightly emphasized 'casevac' as a major priority. For a man to be evacuated he needed to be taken to the landing strip, and the impenetrability of the terrain meant that short journeys took many exhausting hours. Belly wounds, for example, were no longer fatal so often as they had been at the time of Dunkirk. But in Burma the statistics show that about 30 per cent proved fatal, except in the case of the Chindits, for if a man could not be evacuated he was unlikely to survive.

Penicillin was first used in significant quantities in Sicily in 1943, then in the Pacific and later in North-West Europe. In time it became common enough as a currency to be traded in the black markets but in Burma there was none to spare, at least in any appreciable amounts, until the end of 1944.

In Europe and the Pacific Campaigns, blood transfusions to wounded men were made possible because blood could be donated and stored, but not in the jungles of Burma by a guerrilla force dependent upon re-supply by air.

In the jungle there was always the risk of infection, and also a whole array of exotic illnesses lay in ambush. Apart from scrub typhus, dengue fever and malaria, a complaint called Naga sores was particularly painful. This was caused when a leech's head was left embedded in the flesh; within days a sore with putrified flesh the dimension of a saucer would erupt.

In Burma the disparity between battle casualties and sickness was in the ratio 1:129, and this remained fairly constant until the titanic struggles for Imphal and Kohima.

In January 1944 the Chindit Brigades entered the war zone of Assam, a swirling mass of humanity – a mini-United Nations of races and creeds where British, Americans, Canadians, Australians and New Zealanders rubbed shoulders with Negroes from the regiments of both East and West Africa. There were the Gurkhas; there were Chins, Kachins, Karens and Burmese whose families were held in thrall by the enemy. All had to be supplied and fed, in their base camps and later by air. There were companies which averaged 5' in height and took a size 6 boot, and black battalions where except for the white officers and senior NCOs there was not a man under 6'5" and size 10 boots. There were men who ate only meat, and others who were vegetarians; there were those who ate no pork and others who lived on rice. Some soldiers had four wives and others shared their wife with three brothers or more. Most had one wife and others openly practised sodomy.

The logistical effort required to equip, arm, clothe and feed this force was breath-taking. The aerial supply effort had already been recognized as beyond the capacity of Cochran's Air Commando. Wingate used the direct line, and as a result squadrons of C47 Dakotas from Brigadier-General Old's Troop Carrier Command were diverted to Burma. Americans had established their Troop Carrier Command in June 1942 to carry airborne infantry and parachute troops, to tow and fly gliders and to move men and cargo within a particular theatre of war.

In many critical aspects the situation had got out of hand, but none of the High Command seemed able or willing to curb Wingate's excesses. The result was that a very sizeable portion of the theatre's air strength was now committed to a secondary or subsidiary operation. In this constant battle for resources, Wingate would share with nobody. Some were already questioning whether a force raised for guerrilla operations should assume a higher priority than the main force. To this Wingate had his own answer. He regarded the Chindits as the main force, the arm of decision, while the task of other 'normal' divisions comprised of lesser mortals was to occupy the enemy in the perimeter, as peripheral forces.

CHAPTER THIRTY-ONE

'A fool lies here, who tried to hustle the East.'

Kipling

Wingate, with his energy, drive and uncompromising determination saw his dream turning into reality. Distrustful of superiors and subordinates alike and incapable of delegation, he presided in solitary splendour over his rapidly expanding empire. Lentaigne's brigade lost the last vestige of independence; the Chindits had swallowed the leopard whole.

What was to be the role of this Special Force? Even during these short months the strategic picture had changed enormously and the role envisaged and agreed in Quebec no longer seemed so important.

The Allied chiefs were now more optimistic about the war. The Anglo-Americans were on the Italian mainland and it seemed the European War could terminate as early as October 1944, while the Japanese might be defeated twelve months later. Operations in Burma and China were lagging. But the tempo of the Pacific had increased with the dual thrusts of MacArthur and Nimitz beginning to gather momentum. Viewed dispassionately in London and Washington, Japan could easily be conquered before the British had liberated Burma or the Chinese brought the enemy to battle.

In November 1943, Churchill had hosted a War Summit, code-named *Sextant*, in Cairo. President Roosevelt and Generalissmo Chiang Kai-Shek were there. Amongst other things, the scale of future operations in Upper Burma was finally agreed. The plan was to launch limited offensives by British and Sino-American forces to allow the

Ledo Road to be opened as the main land bridge into China. But this was consensus warfare, where even this seemingly simple and straightforward stratagem was a compromise, made possible because none of the great powers was prepared to devote major resources to the Burma theatre. The reason was that the three great powers had different objectives. The British were the least uncomplicated; their attention was riveted on Singapore. The Americans focused on China; MacArthur and Nimitz had as their objective the acquisition of a Chinese port. American strategists were convinced of the need to tie down the bulk of the Japanese armies on the Asian mainland, the penultimate step to the invasion of Japan.

Chiang Kai-Shek wanted the Japanese cleared from Burma, if only because he was forced to fight a war on two fronts. The Chinese, however, did not see this being achieved by an invasion from the north unless it was also accompanied by an amphibious operation and landings in the south. The key resource was landing craft. There were simply not enough to service all the needs of the various theatres. The Generalissimo wanted an amphibious operation on the Andaman Islands in the Indian Ocean, a first step to a landing in southern Burma, but there weren't the craft available. Until such an operation could be mounted, the Chinese were not prepared to commit large numbers of troops to the invasion of North Burma. The Kuomintang government were under no illusions that one day, after the Japanese had gone, there would be a final reckoning with Mao Tse-Tung and the Communist forces. The latter were careful to husband their strength and leave all the fighting to the Nationalists, who they hoped would be fatally weakened in defeating Japan.

None of this altered the fact that without a major Chinese effort, the re-conquest of northern Burma was not deemed possible. The fact that Roosevelt rejected all suggestions that the Chinese be required to do anything in return for US aid did not help matters either.

In China Stilwell had enemies. American and Chinese had come within an ace of persuading the Generalissimo to dismiss him, but Mountbatten intervened and persuaded Chiang Kai-Shek to retain 'Vinegar Joe' as his Chief-of-Staff, though no staff existed for him to preside over. Stilwell accepted the compromise, remained deputy to Mountbatten and was also an American theatre commander. But where the Chinese were concerned, Stilwell made it abundantly clear that his mission was over. There was nothing further he could do to enhance the military skills of a mediocre Chinese Army.

After Cairo, Churchill and Roosevelt travelled on to Tehran, where they met Stalin. The Soviet leader insisted that the Allies should launch the Second Front as soon as possible and would sanction no diversification of effort, especially if that meant sending landing craft to other theatres. However, such gloomy dictats were overshadowed when Stalin openly committed the Soviets to enter the war in the Far East once the conflict in Europe was over.

Russia and Japan were not at war, even though Stalin had hinted at such an eventuality on a number of occasions. Such a firm Soviet declaration of intent completely changed the picture. The importance of China began to dwindle, their contribution being no longer so vital to the ultimate defeat of Japan. The Russians could now be counted on to tie down Japanese divisions on the Asian mainland. There was no need for the Americans to take a Chinese port to supply the Nationalists with the wherewithals, war material and troops, to launch an offensive against the Japanese. With the Russians in the Pacific, offensives could be directed straight at Japan and the war over that much sooner.

The American bomber chiefs also had second thoughts. The Navy convinced them that the Marianas offered a much better prospect than China as a launching platform for the new B29 Superfortresses. From these islands, with a secured line of direct access across the Pacific to the United States, the bombers could reach Japan and pound them into submission.

The sooner the war in Europe was over, the better, for that victory would bring the Russians into what the Americans always regarded as the real war – the one against Japan. Roosevelt decreed that no landing craft were to leave European waters until Hitler was defeated. An envoy was sent to Chiang Kai-Shek to inform the Generalissimo that no landing craft would be available for the Andaman Islands until the autumn of 1944. As a palliative, Roosevelt offered the Chinese the option of delaying their own offensive into Burma until that time. When Chiang Kai-Shek accepted without hesitation, the Americans no longer regarded the Chinese as quite the great power they had once thought.

At the end of 1943, when the Chindits had completed their training, the Americans reappraised their priorities with regard to China. For Washington it was now simply too late to bring China's manpower actively into the war, hence strategic sights were adjusted downwards and the region relegated to a tertiary theatre of war. The Ledo Road was to be opened, but only in order to have another option if the Pacific offensives stalled. There was no intention to deploy the B29s to China.

Just as China's importance in the global picture receded, Mountbatten's command was ready to unleash what was to become known as the Third Burma Campaign. This in truth was a very much watered-down affair compared with the plans which had been outlined in Quebec, just four months earlier. Mountbatten backed away from quarrels and confrontations, which probably explains why Wingate was allowed to continue to train his troops for an operation which; for a while at least, nobody intended to mount. Once the Chinese advance had been shelved, there seemed to be no particularly useful role for Wingate to play.

When it came to an offensive, Slim and Wingate were in broad agreement in a number of areas. They were almost alone in advocating that Burma could be taken by advancing from the north southwards. They were equally convinced that the Allied soldiers had the ability to take on the Japanese and defeat them in the jungle. For both, air power was seen as the vitally important ingredient to success. None of this, however, indicated that Bill Slim had been won over to the efficacy of the Chindits. As far as the Army Commander was concerned, Special Force might be useful in certain circumstances, but looking to the immediate future – Burma in 1944 – it was more trouble than it was worth.

Slim's was a brutal but honest judgement, influenced by his conviction that the gap between the fighting quality of Fourteenth Army and the Chindits had narrowed. The former had been revitalized and rebuilt by one of the truly great generals of the Second World War. What began life as two ragged, whipped and morally cowed divisions was beginning to emerge into the finely tuned IVth, Vth and XVth Corps comprised of soldiers who had pride and confidence in their own abilities and the leadership of their commanding general.

They were not so well equipped or pampered as the Chindits, for they were after all the 'Forgotten Army'. But even this seemingly damning epithet had been transformed into a symbol of perverse pride.

Sound training had progressed to offensive patrolling and small-scale actions, all of which had shown that the Japanese soldier was not the superhuman jungle warrior. Slim was ready to return to the offensive, but under conditions where he controlled the battlefield. An advance across the Chindwin, at the end of an ever-extending line of communication and through some of the most difficult terrain in the world, would only be possible if a goodly portion of the enemy forces could first be brought to battle and decisively defeated.

The thinking of Slim and Wingate was strangely similar. Each had the same answer to the Japanese stratagem of outflanking and severing the Allies' lines of communications. When the lines were cut, troops stayed put to form an armoured box or 'stronghold' which would be sustained by air supply. The Japanese strength would be dissipated against such fortifications.

The theory was fine. What Slim needed was for the Japanese to be enticed across the Chindwin and defeated on ground which favoured

Fourteenth Army; but this was not reflected in Mountbatten's strategy.

Mountbatten planned four operations to clear Upper Burma. Stilwell's Sino-American Forces, which later became known as Northern Combat Area Command (NCAC), were to advance from Ledo towards Myitkyina. Second, the main force of Fourteenth Army was to cross the Chindwin and advance south on a broad front towards Indaw. On the coast, XV Corps was to have another stab in the Arakan and advance towards Akyab. Finally, Wingate's Chindits were to launch a deep penetration operation to aid Stilwell's advance. But Mountbatten had to make a personal visit to Stilwell's headquarters to convince the irascible American that the Chindits could assist the Sino-American advance. Stilwell was sceptical about the Chindits.

Although the Allied Armies had improved in quantity and quality, so had the Japanese.

The Burma Area Army under the command of Lieutenant-General Masakazu Kawabe had been reinforced to a strength of eight divisions. The main combat force in central Burma comprised the 15th, 31st and 33rd Infantry Divisions of the Fifteenth Army, led by Lieutenant-General Renya Mutaguchi. Both Japanese commanders were rash men, impetuous enough to accommodate Slim's hopes that they would commit their forces across the Chindwin on to his killing ground.

The Third Burma Campaign opened in the last days of November 1943 as the monsoon came to an end. The Indian Infantry Divisions in XV Corps went over to the attack. Their opponents, the ferocious Japanese 55th Division, fell back in good order against relentless firepower.

At about the same time, two Chinese divisions joined the fray and made very slow, not to say sedate progress against the equally impressive Japanese 18th Infantry Division. Stilwell, 60 years of age and very nearly blind, took personal command in the field. The chain of command in South-East Asia was more akin to a Chinese puzzle, but Stilwell's assumption of a Corps Commander's appointment in addition to his other duties hardly made life any easier.

Wingate remained a law unto himself when it came to a precise or tactical interpretation of Mountbatten's directives, part of the problem being that nobody knew precisely what he had in mind. Like David Stirling in the Western Desert, he kept his ideas not only to himself but in his head. Nothing was ever written down. The difference was that Stirling tried to conform to the wishes of his Army Commander, whereas Wingate refused to confide his intentions to Slim and so the degree of coordination was negligible.

Military power is about intentions and capabilities. In the case of the latter, Wingate had two brigades under training and three ready to take to the field, but air power sufficient only to lift two into battle. Neither did these force levels include the Americans. Merill's Marauders came under Wingate's remit for a few days until Stilwell got his act together. Taking time out from being a Corps Commander, he fired broadsides off in all directions as the conditions demanded – American theatre Commander, Deputy Supreme Commander etc., until the Marauders were secured into his own bailiwick.

Wingate issued his orders. Calvert's 77 Brigade and Lentaigne's 111 Brigade were to be flown into strongholds behind the enemy lines and about 150 miles north of Mandalay. They were to dominate the region around Indaw and the Irrawaddy and block the Japanese lines of communication, thereby isolating those forces fighting against Stilwell and Fourteenth Army.

This objective was no longer to be achieved through guerrillas and harassing attacks, but by means of what Wingate called the stronghold concept. Extensive fortified bases were to be established in territory and in a manner which the enemy could not afford to ignore. The Japanese – so Wingate was convinced – would have no choice other than to divert troops from the front and to slug it out with the Chindits. This would mean that the Chindits became the primary force of decision with the 'ordinary divisions' providing a secondary, if not a mopping-up role.

The date for the airborne operation was set by Fergusson's 16 Brigade, which had drawn the short straw. They had to march into Burma from Assam, and their approach to Indaw would be the signal for the massive airlift involving 9,000 men to get under way.

All the Chindits were assured by no lesser person than Wingate himself that the maximum time they would spend behind enemy lines was three months. Then they would be airlifted out for some well-earned rest and leave while fresh brigades took their place. To place such faith in the omnipotence of air power underlines those aspects of Wingate's strategy which belong to the realm of fantasy. At the time, it simply reinforced the convictions of those amongst the military hierarchy and establishment who considered him mad.

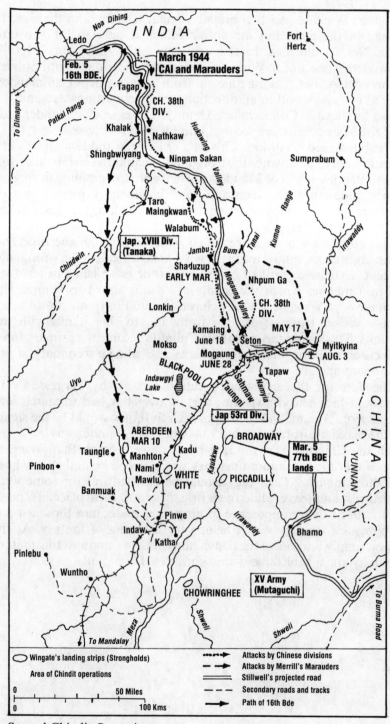

Second Chindit Operation

CHAPTER THIRTY-TWO

The Great Trek of 16 Brigade

Without Wingate the Burma Campaign would undoubtedly have taken a different course, therefore no one can deny that his Special Force did have a very considerable influence on the war.

Looking back on the whole campaign, Tim Biron thought that the most uncomfortable period was the time they spent at Ledo, the rail- and road-head.* He was with 16 Brigade and they travelled up to Assam to complete the final preparations before their long march to Indaw.

The plan was for 16 Brigade to set out from Khalak and march across country to the Chindwin some 60 map miles south. Assault craft would be glidered in to help on the river crossing. They would then continue south, over 100 map miles, through enemy territory to a village called Manhten. The brigade was to secure a stronghold and landing ground code-named *Aberdeen*, where they were to be reinforced by 14 Brigade brought in by air. The two brigades were to attack Indaw, the main Japanese garrison and supply point. It was about 50 miles from *Aberdeen* to Indaw, but easier country to march across.

Security concerns were paramount, so the Brigade's presence in the assembly area was kept secret. The Chindits were hustled up a newly-cut track through the jungle until it petered out in a large stand of

---

*After the war Major Biron wrote of his experiences. *Adventures with a Chindit Battalion* was published in the Shell Company Magazine and I am most grateful to him for allowing me to use the article.

bamboo. Here they were told to make themselves at home. Trampled under so many feet, the rain-sodden ground quickly turned into a sea of mud. There were neither huts nor tents and leeches were everywhere. It was the most miserable place and morale, so finely tuned for battle, quickly plummeted. Left to their own devices by a callous and uncaring rear area staff, the Chindits soon exhausted their supplies of cigarettes and life became even more grim.

The brigade moved out on 5 February, with a month to reach *Aberdeen*. No one was sorry to leave that wretched place, despite the fact that departure signalled the imminence of war. The next part of the journey was by road, the Ledo Road, a marvel of engineering which even had these hard-bitten veterans in open-mouthed wonderment. Biron's column was taken up the road by a mixed Negro/Gurkha Transport Company. The little Gurkhas seemed to drive by peering through the spokes of the steering wheel of their 5-ton Dodge six-by-sixes. There were chains on all six wheels and these were certainly needed; for long stretches the mud was axle-deep. The Chindits hung on for grim death, though they could not fail but be impressed by the skill of the truck drivers as they handled their vehicles in masterly fashion around hairpin bends where the slightest error would have sent men and vehicle plunging hundreds of feet down the mountainside.

Not everybody had the good fortune to ride to the Chindits' base camp. As always, the mules and muleteers had the worst of the journey. They had to march the 80 miles – with mud underfoot, mud splashed over them from passing vehicles in teeming rain (even though the monsoon was supposed to have finished), and there were very poor arrangements at the staging camps for the three overnight stops.

The brigade base camp was only a marginal improvement on the bamboo thickets of the rail-head. Again the men were required to keep out of sight. They found themselves in a camp which could only be reached by way of a river bed and which was inaccessible by anything but men and animals.

The first week they spent as fatigue parties. Officers and men shuttled from road to camp weighed down by supplies and equipment. It was an unpleasant business. Until the sappers were able to span the river with half a dozen crude foot-bridges at critical points, it was impossible to complete the journey without getting soaked up to the thighs.

Wet feet became a permanent feature of life with the Brigade. Army issues socks were poor, and even men who were not too hard on socks had difficulty in making them last. In the early stages of the campaign the supply drops were hopeless, and many Chindits became resigned to marching in bare feet. In Biron's column, dry socks became the major measure of currency. It was not unknown for a day's rations to be bartered for a pair of socks – no mean price to pay early in the campaign when supply drops were few and men permanently hungry.

At last the day came to begin the long march to Indaw. Immediately ahead loomed the Naga Hills, the tops of which seemed permanently blanketed in swirling mist and cloud, so that no one could see how high they were. But to every Chindit they were the first obstacle to be crossed. The maps showed them to be a mass of rugged steep-sided mountains about 5,000–6,000 feet high, but with peaks of often more than 8,000 feet. There were a few bridle tracks maintained by the government, but in most places the tracks linking Naga villages were mere footpaths going straight up and down the hillsides, which were covered in thick jungle.

The track from the Ledo Road took the Chindits straight up the first mountain. Steps had to be cut to enable the mules to get a foothold, and even then there were places where it was too steep for the mules to carry their loads. Men were reduced to scrambling up on all fours to climb some portions of the track.

The Leicesters were to trail-blaze for the brigade, so Biron's column was the second party to leave base camp. By evening of the first day they had covered precisely one mile and climbed 1,500 feet. Some columns in the brigade never even left the base camp.

After the first ridge they did speed up a little, but for the week it took the Chindits to clear the Naga Hills, progress was painfully slow. Marching nose to tail, with all thought of tactical formations long since discarded, the columns climbed out of one valley and along the top of a ridge for a few miles, then dropped down 1,000 feet or more to cross a stream and up the other side. The nights were miserable. It was intensely cold at 5,000 feet and the Chindits, equipped with only one light-weight blanket, had to sleep in clothes still sodden with perspiration from the day's march.

Neither was it uncommon for a column to find itself at the end of the day nowhere near water, and with little likelihood of finding any. Some columns radioed for water to be air dropped, which request created panic among the despatchers at the air base. No one had ever dreamed that water would be a problem in those wet, jungle-clad mountains. Wingate's staff, armed with his special carnet, plundered rear areas for priceless water containers, much to the consternation of the supply depots. Every senior quartermaster knew of Wingate's hot line to the powers that be and dared not challenge the requisition, but the result was that Fourteenth Army were cleared of anything that had a lid and could carry water.

Measured on a map, the brigade covered just fifteen miles in the first week, and the rearmost column was still nearer to base camp than to the point platoon. The columns made better time after they came upon an old government jeep track which was beautifully graded and marked up and down the mountainside. After a few more days the brigade reached a Sino-American outpost and this served to remind them that the war was now very near. Fergusson ordered a two-day halt, time to recover and receive the first properly organized supply drop before pressing on once more.

It was still hard going. The track increasingly followed the river bed, and the Chindits soon ceased to worry about keeping dry. Stretches of up to two miles of watery going were quite common and the medics treated an increasing incidence of skin complaints, something akin to trench foot.

The accuracy of the supply drops was still far from satisfactory. The clearings of deserted villages – nothing more than a few charred poles and overgrown grass – were the only open spaces they could find which were not surrounded by obstacles dangerous to aircraft, on which the Chindits could receive supply drops. They were nearly always far too small and invariably perched on top of a hill. Such tiny drop zones, coupled with the inexperience of many pilots, meant that the Chindits were fortunate to recover 50 per cent of the rations dropped.

It was heartbreaking to watch parachutes being pushed out of aircraft anything up to half a mile away, knowing full well that they were impossible to retrieve. Even if the supplies fell only 200 yards off target, they were liable to land anything up to 500/1,000 feet below.

The Sino-American outpost marked the front line, so as they moved into no-man's land the Chindit columns advanced in battle formation, recce platoon up front and flank guards out. They fully expected to encounter Japanese patrols on the north side of the Chindwin river. Eventually they arrived on the banks of the great river, having seen no sign of the Japanese, and radioed base for the gliders to bring in assault craft to help with the crossing. In the meantime the Leicesters established a small bridgehead on the far bank. Crossing under cover of darkness was a slow business; all they had available was a couple of two-man rubber dinghies. By daybreak Biron's recce platoon was on the far bank, feeling very much alone and exposed. If the Japanese should appear there was no way back and, other than small 2-inch mortars, no fire support either.

There was no word of the gliders, so the Leicesters spent a long and laborious day building log rafts. The work was just about complete when that same evening the gliders arrived, landing on a sandbank which had been prepared and cleared in readiness. All night the crossing went on to the sound of the outboard motors. It was not until noon the next day that the battalion and its mules were across and on the move once more. The rear-guard of the second column waited until the gliders were snatched up and then they too disappeared into the undergrowth.

The total lack of any reaction from the enemy was very disconcerting. Neither Wingate nor his senior officers could decide whether it was a good or bad thing; but he did send a short message to his troops:

'Well done, Leicesters – Hannibal eclipsed.'

It was indeed an incredible physical feat to have surmounted such formidable obstacles and reached the Chindwin on time. But time was now the critical factor. In Assam the other brigades gathered in their assembly areas on the Imphal Plain and the Dakotas waited in the airfields. Twelve thousand men and two thousand animals were assembled to be airlifted into battle. Calvert's 77 Brigade, the original Chindits, were to have the honour of going first, followed by Lentaigne's 111 Brigade, and 14 Brigade, finally selected columns drawn from Rickett's 81st West Africans.

Three landing sites had been selected. Two, given the code-names *Broadway* and *Piccadilly*, were designated as the main landing areas. They were located behind the Gangaw Mountains about 20 miles apart and 25 miles east of the Mandalay-Myitkyina railway, the Japanese principal line of communication of which Indaw was considered to be a vital hub. *Piccadilly* was 40 miles to the north-east of Indaw and *Broadway* 35 miles east-north-east of the town. They were chosen because there was enough flat ground to allow an air-strip to be built and also because there was water in the immediate vicinity.

A third landing ground had been chosen in case one of the other two were compromised. This was code-named *Chowringhee*, after the main street of Calcutta. Inside the great bend of the Shweli river and 60 'map miles' south of *Piccadilly*, it was 35 miles east of Indaw but on the wrong side of the Irrawaddy from the intended area of operations.

Wingate designated 5 March as D-Day for the airborne landings and signalled 16 Brigade to increase its pace. He needed *Aberdeen* operational so that the airborne operations could occur simultaneously.

Fergusson's Brigade pressed on relentlessly, the columns trekking from dawn to dark every day. The only rest they could get was on an occasional supply drop. Biron, marching ahead with his recce platoon, hardly had time to eat any hoarded little luxuries or read his mail before they were on the move again. In one lap of five days' march, they covered 73 miles. But the going was much easier for they used a track which – so their guides told them – had been an important Japanese line of communication used principally by elephants.

Although they had yet to encounter the enemy, it was clear that 16 Brigade was not going to reach *Aberdeen* in time. A signal to this effect was sent to Wingate, where it was received at a particularly sensitive time by the staff. Under the burden of command, their leader was beginning to show signs of strain.

CHAPTER THIRTY-THREE

Into Battle

On the landing grounds at Hailakandi and Tulihal in the Plain of Imphal, the Chindit brigades began to gather in readiness for the airborne operation. Dakotas, Air Commandos and gliders stood in serried ranks waiting for their passengers, men and animals. An elaborate cover operation was implemented to hide the operation from enemy eyes. Diversionary air attacks were launched on Japanese airfields and communications centres to keep enemy planes preoccupied; Allied fighters flew continuous cover above the Imphal Plain, but it was impossible to prevent the occasional solitary, high-flying enemy recce plane from sneaking past their guard. There is no such thing as total security.

General Slim ordered ostentatious air reconnaissance flights over Mandalay in the hope that if the Japanese did have wind of an airborne operation, they would believe that was the target. In contrast Wingate would allow no flights anywhere near to the proposed landing sites before the last 24 hours, when each area was to be the target for a single high-flying photographic reconnaissance mission just to check that all was well.

Wingate established a temporary tactical HQ in a couple of huts on the air-strip at Hailakandi. It was a hive of activity all around. Air Force ground crews, multinational and indistinguishable from the Army in their dusty jungle fatigues, laid out the long nylon elasticated tow-ropes and manhandled gliders into position. Controversy raged, for the considered Royal Air Force view was that the C47 Dakota was incapable of towing two fully-laden gliders. It had never been attempted before. In July 1943, on the occasion of the last big airborne operation over Sicily, the Dakotas had only pulled one glider each, but Cochran was convinced it could be done. This did not take into account the local air conditions, rejoined the old Burma hands, who knew precisely what the monsoon-laden thermals and currents could do to an aircraft, especially when trying to gain altitude to fly over the mountains.

Wingate became very agitated. He overruled establishment advice and backed Cochran's hunch that the Dakotas could pull two gliders. There was a critical shortage of aircraft. Headquarters Fourteenth Army had already turned down his request for more planes and on this occasion Mountbatten, who usually shrank from quarrels and confrontations, supported Slim. This meant that Wingate could not fly 14 Brigade into *Aberdeen* to join Fergusson's columns for the attack on Indaw. In a fit of temper, Wingate mobilized the hot line and cabled his complaints, in the most intemperate language, to the Prime Minister.

Churchill, taken aback at the tone of the message, showed it to General Brooke. 'It looks,' observed the CIGS, 'as if the strain of operations has sent Wingate off his head.'

On the morning of Sunday 5 March, Slim flew into Hailakandi. At dusk that night the first wave of aircraft carrying Calvert's 77 Brigade were to take off for *Broadway*. Slim had made a conscious effort to get along with Wingate, and wanted to be on hand to wish the troops good luck before they left.

In the late afternoon, John Campbell arrived with his platoon at the air-strip. He was due to fly in Glider No. 6 and so was among the first of 77 Brigade to report to the check-point. Calvert, his brigade headquarters, together with an air landing team were in the first flight of five machines. The Waco glider carried 13 fully-armed troops, so Campbell took half the men and the remainder went with his platoon sergeant. Campbell gave his number to a guide waiting at the reception point, shook hands with the sergeant and wished his party well before setting off behind the guide. In single file they trooped between the lines of gliders, stepping over the lengths of nylon rope, men and planes casting conflicting silhouettes against the sun setting on the western horizon.

The Chindits knew the drill, even though this was the first time they had actually set foot inside a real glider. The men sat six to a side on the narrow benches that ran the length of the fuselage; keeping their packs on, they braced their feet against the floor struts on the opposite side. Campbell squatted nervously in the little jump-seat near the door; there were neither straps nor safety harnesses. Nobody spoke, although most could hear the conversations from the two American pilots through the thin bulkhead that separated the cabin from the the cockpit.

Rush to wait – it was typical Army. There was an hour before the first flight was due to take off and soon the atmosphere inside became fetid with sweat. Campbell stepped out to check on the other glider. Men scrambled over one another to the door for a last chance to relieve their bladders and stretch their legs.

Meanwhile, there was high drama across the field at Wingate's Headquarters in this last hour before the operation. An Intelligence officer had driven up with air reconnaissance photographs of the planned landing grounds; the prints were still wet with fluid from the developing tanks. Everything was fine except *Piccadilly*, which was covered in logs. The senior officers, Slim, Wingate, Calvert and Cochran went into a huddle around the jeep. The questions were obvious and plentiful.

* Had the Japanese got word of the operation?

* Had they blocked *Piccadilly* to force Wingate to divert all the flights into *Broadway* where the Japanese were already waiting in concealed ambush?

* Was *Chowringhee* compromised?

* Was it nationwide? Had the Japanese, seeing the preparations in and around Imphal, decided to block every possible landing site to prevent an airborne operation?

It was a crisis and a time for reasoned and careful judgement, but Wingate lost hold of the last vestiges of self-control and became 'very emotional'. In truth he ranted and he raved. Convinced that the Japanese had precise details of the operation, he believed they had been betrayed by Stilwell and the Chinese.

Agitated beyond measure, he demanded that the operation be cancelled.

'It would be murder to proceed,' he exclaimed.

Slim took him by the arm and forcibly propelled him to the nearby shack and away from public gaze. Calvert, whose loyalty to Wingate ('Our Leader', as he called him) had verged on hero-worship, was stunned by the outburst.

Inside the hut Slim worked quietly and patiently and eventually succeeded in getting Wingate to calm down. Once this had been achieved, he called the others inside to continue the conference.

Slim believed there was probably a perfectly innocent explanation for the logs at Piccadilly. It was a calculated risk, but on the evidence he could see no reason to cancel the operation. All of the others agreed except for Wingate, who was still unsure they had not been compromised. Time was pressing, a decision had to be made and all eyes turned to 'Our Leader'. Slim could hardly overrule his subordinate and still leave him in charge of the operation. But Wingate by now was calmer. After thinking for a moment, he looked around the hut.

'It's a great risk if we proceed,' he said.

Slim agreed.

Wingate paused, then looked straight at Slim. 'The responsibility is yours,' he said.

It probably was. Slim was the senior officer present and commanded an army – one which Wingate had fought tooth and nail to remain independent of hitherto. This was hardly an auspicious moment to return to the fold. At the same time, Wingate's abdication of any responsibility speaks volumes for the sort of man he was.

The time had passed for the first aircraft to leave. John Campbell and hundreds of others sat and sweated and wondered at the delay.

There was every reason for the operation to proceed. Slim also knew that a Japanese offensive was about to break in Assam and he hoped that the Chindits would cause confusion and delay, and even persuade the Japanese to divert resources and deal with a threat to their rear.

'The operation will go on,' ordered Slim.

Piccadilly could not be used. Calvert's Brigade would use *Broadway* and *Chowringhee*. Orders were sent to Lentaigne's 111 Brigade, due to fly out on 8 March for *Piccadilly*, to also divert to *Chowringhee*.

A few moments after six, and an hour late, the first Dakotas trundled down the runway. Trailing two gliders and rapidly running out of space, at the last moment it climbed reluctantly into the sky. The moment one was clear an Aldis lamp flashed from the control tower and the next started on its way.

'Brace yourselves!' yelled the co-pilot, but even this timely warning did little to prepare Campbell and his men for the tremendous jerk on take-off. They grabbed hold of one another as the glider wobbled uncertainly into the air. Once airborne there was a slightly eerie sound, but otherwise silence.

At half-minute intervals all 31 Dakotas, pulling 61 gliders successfully took to the air for *Broadway*. It was now the turn of the commanders and their staff to sit and sweat.

Just after four o'clock in the morning, the first signal was received at Wingate's headquarters from *Broadway*. It was sent by Calvert in clear, the single word *Soyalink*. The name of the most disliked article in the K-rations had been chosen as the code for a failure.

The immediate assumption was that *Broadway* had been ambushed. It appeared that Wingate was right and Slim had been wrong. Wingate gave Slim one long look of bitter hatred and without saying a word walked out of the building.

An hour and a half after take-off the Dakota signalled, whereupon the glider pilot pulled a handle in the roof above his head and released the tow-rope.

'Brace yourselves, fellas,' yelled the co-pilot as the nose dipped and the glider headed for the landing site. Campbell clung on to the struts for dear life.

The landing was chaotic. The drill was supposed to be that once the glider had stopped everybody dashed out and helped to push the machine aside so as to allow the next one down. But *Broadway* was pitted with shallow trenches which crossed the landing strip at right angles, and these has not been identified on the aerial photographs. The wheels were torn off and as the tail hit the ground with a spar-shattering crack, there was a bright flash of static electricity which bathed the cabin in a pale blue light. The glider skidded on its belly before crunching to a halt in the undergrowth.

Cameron's was the fifth glider down. Glider No. 5 crashed half a mile from the strip and many others failed even to get that far. Cochran was wrong. The strain had been too great for the Dakotas, as they tried to clear the mountains which lay almost immediately across their path after take-off from the Imphal plain. Tow-ropes broke and aircraft engines overheated. Some Dakotas, close to stalling, were forced to release the tow-ropes or crash. Others struggled on until they had used so much fuel there was not enough to make the flight home so they sent their charges off to fend for themselves. Only 35 gliders reached *Broadway*.

Gliders released prematurely came down all over the place. One crash landed near to a Japanese Divisional HQ and a couple more next to a Regimental HQ, both far from *Broadway*. These landings undoubtedly caused considerable confusion among the enemy.

But at Hailakandi the picture had become much clearer by daylight. More messages were received from Calvert and although there had been casualties,* there had been no ambush. Slim ordered that the remaining airborne operations to *Chowringhee* and *Broadway* should get under way without any further delay, and then prepared to return to Army Headquarters. There more important matters awaited his attention, not the least being an anticipated Japanese offensive across the Chindwin.

Wingate, composed again, walked the Army Commander to his waiting plane. The two men shook hands at the aircraft steps.

---

* Considering the number of gliders which crashed, the casualty rate was remarkably low. Twenty-three men were killed and over a hundred injured.

'You're one of the few senior officers out here who doesn't wish me dead,' said Wingate. Slim made no comment.

On *Broadway*, Campbell's platoon had dug in on the edge of the air-strip ready to repel an enemy attack. There were no Japanese and they spent the night listening to the sound of gliders crashing.

When daylight came the platoon formed part of a rescue and salvage detail; it was only then that the full extent of the disaster became apparent. Amongst the injured were many glider pilots, for there was no protection in the flimsy nose and even less when cargo broke loose on impact.

Later in the day Campbell led his platoon out on patrol. Calvert ordered him to make a wide sweep around the landing site, to look for any signs of the enemy and find the nearest water holes. But they found no sign of the enemy and very little water.

Two nights later, on Wednesday 8 March, Lentaigne's 111 Brigade was airlifted behind enemy lines. On this occasion the gliders were not used; the Brigade travelled in the relative comfort and safety of Dakotas.

The Brigade was to be split three ways. Headquarters and the columns made up from the two Gurkha Battalions flew to *Chowringhee*, while the Cameronians and the King's Own landed at *Broadway*. Two columns, Nos. 49 and 94, were detailed as 'Morris force' for operations in the Sinlumkaba Hill Traits, closer to the Chinese-Hunan border. It took three nights for the airlift to be completed and then the remainder of 111 Brigade set out from their landing site to effect a rendezvous. For those at *Chowringhee* this meant a march of about 130 miles and a crossing of the Irrawaddy. Lentaigne calculated it would take them a fortnight to complete this phase of the operation.

Wingate flew in to *Broadway* in one of the Dakotas that carried some Cameronians. John Campbell was put in charge of his hospitality and reception. With his platoon sergeant, batman Private Kelly and half a dozen others, they manhandled one of the crashed gliders nearer to where Calvert had established 77 Brigade headquarters. They cleared out all the debris and wreckage and rigged up a bed inside, made of parachute silks. Kelly fashioned a bedside table from pieces of plywood on which Campbell placed his torch and a book of poetry, just to give it a homely touch.

Calvert, Wingate and the Borderers' Colonel talked into the night, the main topic being the absence of enemy activity. Campbell and Kelly spent the whole time brewing coffee. A little after three o'clock, Wingate decided to go to bed. Campbell escorted him to his sleeping quarters while Kelly hovered in the background, like all good batmen, to see if his officer needed anything. Wingate never said a word; he looked straight through the young officer and shut the glider's door. Campbell and Kelly headed for the relative comfort of their own foxholes.

When Wingate flew out of *Broadway* early the next morning, Campbell remained in the background as Calvert saw him to his plane. He called Kelly, and together they walked across to the general's sleeping quarters. The inside of the glider was scrupulously clean and the bedside table was bare, the torch and book were gone. It was Kelly's turn to give Campbell a long and withering look.

On March 13, Wingate was able to declare in an order of the day:

> Our first task is fulfilled ... All our columns are inside the enemy's guts ... Let us thank God for the great success he has vouchsafed us and press forward with our sword in the enemy's ribs to expel him from our territory ... This is a moment to live in history. It is an enterprise in which every man who takes part may feel proud one day to say, 'I WAS THERE'.

Undoubtedly, the deployment of more than 9,000 men, their horses and mules, deep inside enemy territory was no mean achievement. But where was the enemy?

After five days behind the lines, the Chindits had sparked very little response from the Japanese. This was all the more surprising since *Broadway* was supposed to be in an area astride the Japanese 53rd Infantry Division's lines of communication and rear area. So it was time to hunt the elusive Japanese out into the open.

Wingate ordered 16 Brigade to leave one battalion at *Aberdeen* and the remainder to march on Indaw. Calvert took the bulk of 77 Brigade some 40 miles south-west to establish a stronghold, code-named *White City*, to block the railway line which ran from Indaw to Mogaung and Myitkyina. Stilwell's forces had reached Shaduzup, at the head of the Mogaung Valley, thanks largely to brilliant outflanking operations against the defending Japanese 18th Infantry Division executed by Merrill's Marauders. In theory, all the Japanese supplies and reinforcements for the battle in the Mogaung Valley had to come by way of the railway from Indaw.

Campbell's column marched off in another direction with the young officer and his recce platoon blazing a trail. Their orders were to head for the Irrawaddy, six inches on the map and 24 miles as the crow flies, but a three-day march nevertheless.

The column was to put a block on the river and deny this vital waterway as part of the line of communication to the Japanese.

CHAPTER THIRTY-FOUR

The Jungle Orphans

Wingate's columns were thrashing around the jungle in vain pursuit of the enemy. By early March the bulk of the Japanese fighting units were already north of the Chindwin. General Renya Mataguchi was a supremely confident commander who believed that the British and Commonwealth divisions which outnumbered him were neither equal in stamina nor able to match the fighting skills of his own troops.

In February Mataguchi launched Operation *Ha-Go* when the Twenty-eighth Army counter-attacked the British XV Corps in the Arakan. Some 5,000 Japanese troops infiltrated the flanks of the forward Indian infantry divisions and blocked their line of communications. It was a very unsubtle and clearly telegraphed version of the 'one-two' strategy. The Japanese intention was to force Slim to send relief and reinforcements from Central Front to the Arakan, following which the main enemy effort would be unleashed against the denuded central sector.

Slim had ample warning of Japanese intentions. In the Arakan the Indian divisions, though cut off, stayed put in the defensive perimeters or 'boxes' and were re-supplied and supported by air power. The defending troops held firm and in the process inflicted a severe reverse on the Japanese, news of which was joyfully received among the foxholes of the Chindwin. Slim could not have provided a greater morale boost to his men before their test.

On 6 March, Mataguchi unleashed Operation *UGO* with the objective of capturing the British base and all its facilities at Imphal, thereby severing the defensive line from Tiddim in the south to the passes over the mountains at Kohima in the north.

As the Japanese 15th and crack 33rd Divisions crossed the Chindwin, Slim concentrated his own superbly trained and now confident 17th and 20th Indian Infantry Divisions at a place of his choosing; it was the killing ground at Imphal.

For the Chindits, the real lesson was becoming apparent: the Japanese were not like the Italians whom Wingate had fought in East Africa. He had never fought a long or sustained battle against the Japanese and failed to appreciate that Mataguchi could not be panicked into withdrawing his troops simply because their enemy had a force ensconced behind them. In any case, the Japanese attacking forces were biased in favour of infantry and light artillery with just a few tanks in support, none of which required sophisticated and vulnerable logistical lines of communication. Indeed, Mataguchi's troops had just three weeks' supplies stockpiled in their own forward areas; he was counting on capturing the British supply bases at Imphal as the only way of replenishing the needs of his own forces.

Mataguchi's decision not to divert forces to deal with the Chindits was only taken after some careful heart-searching. The Chief-of-Staff of the Japanese Fifteenth Army dismissed the threat to their lines of communications for the battles of Imphal. In response to a question from a war correspondent, he exclaimed: 'Good heavens, no! Wingate's men are orphans of the jungle – we'll surround them and starve them out.'

Lieutenant-General Tazoe, Commander of the Vth Air Division – the main Japanese air component in Burma – thought differently. He had been quite bemused by the airlift, and now vastly exaggerated the British capability and pressed for the Imphal campaign to be postponed. On 8 March he saw General Kawabe, the Burma Area Army Commander, whose headquarters were situated in Rangoon University. However, Kawabe backed Mataguchi and refused to be stampeded. Instead he ordered the 15th, 18th and 56th Infantry Divisions to send a battalion each to Indaw; these were to reinforce a Special Force of seven battalions already being formed under command of Major General Mayashi. The forces at Indaw were ordered to be in position by 18 March.

More high-level conferences were called. Lieutenant-General Taketo Kamikasa, Chief-of-Staff to the III Air Army in Singapore, flew in on 12 March for a conference with Kawabe. Mataguchi was there and he responded to the lingering doubts in emphatic terms:

> I can see that these airborne operations are larger than estimated
> ... but I'm glad rather than sorry. The more Wingate brings in
> to Burma, the more they will be caught like rats in a trap. I'd

rather have them where they are than fighting against us at
Imphal.

Everything hinged on Imphal.

There was only one way to defeat the Japanese and that was by a
bruising head-on encounter, or pitched battle in which the Allies –
with their superior weight of firepower – could obliterate the enemy.
This was a battle which the Chindits were neither equipped nor trained
to fight.

At Imphal there was more at stake than the capture of a valuable
piece of real estate with its extensive stores, facilities and supply
dumps, essential as those were to the needs of the enemy. In India,
ferment and civil unrest continued. The Japanese had raised a quisling
force called the India National Army, recruited from Indian Army
POWs taken in Malaya and Singapore. Their titular leader was Subhar
Chandra Bose, an anti-British revolutionary who probably had as
many as 40,000 adherents. The Japanese had armed and equipped
some 7,000 of these to fight alongside their own forces at Imphal. If
Slim failed, the Japanese could easily decide to exploit the political
impact of such a defeat by sending these forces into Assam in the
name of liberation.

The fighting at Imphal was hard, confused and very fluid. In Slim's
own words:

> It swayed back and forth through great stretches of wild country;
> one day its focal point was a hill named in no map, the next a
> miserable, unpronounced village a hundred miles away.
> Columns, brigades, divisions, marched and countermarched, met
> in bloody clashes and reeled apart, weaving a confused pattern
> hard to unravel.*

Imphal sucked in Slim's reserves at an alarming rate, but in the Arakan
the Indian divisions were more than holding their own against a
weakening enemy effort. Slim took a chance and airlifted that front's
reserve, the 5th Indian Division, to Imphal. Between 17 and 31 March,
relays of Dakotas and Air Commandos shuttled into Imphal lifting
the entire division, its equipment, weapons and animals. Their arrival
was most timely, for as the battle reached its critical peak another
threat appeared at Kohima. The Japanese 31st Infantry Division of
15,000 men hacked their way through 40 miles of near-impenetrable
jungle to cut the sole road running from the Imphal plain into India.
A scratch garrison of 1,500 troops – 4th Battalion Queens Own Royal
West Kents and the 20th Mountain Regiment Indian Artillery –

*William Slim, *Defeat into Victory* (Cassell, London, 1956).

with 1,000 base area troops and non-combatants held the enemy at Kohima. They slugged it out at close quarters for 15 days. The carnage was terrible. When relief forces from the 2nd British Infantry Division eventually broke through the last of the Japanese road-blocks to effect a rescue, the survivors – some 800 men – were reduced to a single defensive box just 350 yards square.

The Chindits, through no fault of their own, remained no more than an appendage to the main events. But there was one exception. Calvert established *White City*, a blocking position very close to the main railway line leading to Indaw. This came under incessant attack and had to be heavily fortified and reinforced. Artillery and barbed wire were airlifted in, sandbagged emplacements dug and the perimeter mined. The 3rd West African Brigade was flown in to provide the garrison in the hope that this would relieve Calvert's men to take the fight to the enemy, but it was not to be. More often than not, Calvert's columns were needed to help defend their fortress. But *White City* was successful in that it did put a stranglehold on Japanese supplies intended for the battle against Stilwell.

In contrast, John Campbell's column spent a month with an elaborate blocking ambush on the Irrawaddy. On this supposed vital supply artery, they intercepted two Burmese-crewed barges loaded with cane sugar; there was no other river traffic.

There were other setbacks. On 17 March the Japanese air force attacked *Broadway* in strength and, catching the defences by surprise, destroyed the half-dozen Spitfires which were then operating from the air-strip. From then on the only air cover was that which could be spared from the distant fields at Imphal, where they were already fully stretched providing air support for their own battle.

Neither did all of the columns in Lentaigne's brigade make their rendezvous. The problem was the swift-flowing Irrawaddy, which proved too strong for the horses and mules. Two columns, Nos. 30 and 40, together with Brigade HQ, had set out from Chowringhee. On 10 March they arrived, hot-foot and breathless, on the southern bank of the Irrawaddy. Gliders arrived that night with assault boats and outboard motors, and they prepared to make the crossing the following night.

A flight of three P-51 Mustang fighters pulverized the far bank and the first platoons from the 4/9th Gurkhas crossed over to establish a bridgehead and probe inland. There were no signs of the enemy even as far as Thagnya and Hlebo, two small river settlements upstream from the crossing site.

Throughout the remainder of the night the Gurkhas of 30 Column crossed six at a time in the four assault boats which they had operating. Mules had always refused to swim at night when they practised this manoeuvre on the rivers of Central India. At daylight they attempted to tow the swimming mules across, but the depth of water and swift-flowing current proved too much. Try as they might, the Chindits could not coax more than twenty of the stubborn beasts to make the crossing. Even those pulled singly, or with a strong swimmer alongside, turned for the shore once they found themselves in deep water.

It was chaos. All along the east bank there were mules and saddles, broken harnesses, dumps of equipment and sodden, exhausted Gurkhas. Noise apart, the operation was in full view of the river bank up to five miles in both directions. The Japanese, Lentaigne reasoned, must by then know of their presence and have forces en route to attack the columns. Strung out on both sides of the river, the brigade could not have been more vulnerable.

Lentaigne ordered the remainder of 30 Column and Brigade HQ to cross and to redistribute their loads and equipment on the few mules they had on the far shore. It just meant that every Gurkha would have to carry even more than was already weighing him down. He instructed all of the remaining animals and 40 Column to join Morris force, already some two days march east of *Chowringhee*. They would have a hard task to catch up with them.

In the late afternoon the crossing was completed as arranged. They sank the assault boats with their outboard motors, and headed inland to bivouac for the night a couple of miles from the river. Thereafter the trek continued for another 14 days, taking two supply drops en route and no contact with the enemy. On 24 March, within the bend of the Ngabe Chaung, the columns of 111 Brigade reached their rendezvous. They were now in their intended area of operations and Lentaigne immediately issued instructions to his column commanders. Demolition of the railway, ambush sites and assaults against known and supposed enemy bases were planned. First, however, a massive supply drop was arranged so that the Chindits could begin fully supplied with all their needs.

Air supply was still proving a haphazard business for many of the columns, now dispersed over hundreds of square miles of Burma.

Tim Biron's column of Leicesters headed south from *Aberdeen*. They were trail-blazing a route for a two-battalion attack which Wingate had ordered to take place against Indaw on 26 March.

They moved through country where villages were more common and their surrounding paddy-fields larger. They had no great difficulty thereafter in selecting suitable areas for supply drops. Even so, a good area did not guarantee a good drop and it was not uncommon to find parachutes half a mile away. All kinds of things happened at drops, which nearly always occurred at night. Planes would arrive sometimes too late, sometimes too early, sometimes too high, rarely too low. Aircraft would often fly too fast, causing the 'chutes to break away from the canisters. Many a Chindit has involuntarily leapt out of his bed space at the sound of something crashing through the trees above him just in time to see a canister land on his ground-sheet.

Now that 16 Brigade was in its operational area, there were supply dropping activities almost every night for some column or other. One night Biron sat waiting for their planes when a plane flew over and the pilot came through on the radio with a Yankee twang:

'Say, fellas, are you 23 column?'

'No.'

'Are you wanting rations?'

'Yes.'

'Well, if I can't find any of my guys, I'll come back and drop this lot on you.'

Sure enough, he came back in 90 minutes and let the column have his load, including enough picks and shovels to dig the Maginot Line.

Their sister column was also having a drop a few miles away. They not only received all the luxuries due for Biron's column in the way of fresh bread and tinned fruit, but into the bargain had a complete load of anti-tank mines, armour-piercing ammunition and coils of Dannert wire. The latter were dropped free and they were fortunate to escape without serious casualties.

When they started out on the campaign, the Chindits anticipated that they would be heavily engaged in battle more often than they were, and for that reason never expected to be able to write letters home, let alone have them flown out. The Light Plane Force – squadrons of L5 spotter planes flown by Cochran's Air Commando supporting the Chindits – performed miracles of flying. Nothing was ever too difficult for them to attempt. When the Chindits were unable to build a strip for them, they would swoop down and snatch up the mail. They dropped messages and urgent supplies; they would search for stragglers who got lost and drop rations to them. Sick and wounded were flown out by these indomitable pilots from air-strips which were little bigger than a pocket-handkerchief and fraught with hazards. The effect of these small planes on Chindit morale was truly amazing.

Even though the enemy had proved elusive, the strain was beginning to tell on Fergusson's Brigade. They had been on the march for fifty days and the long and arduous journey, coupled with the strain of living behind enemy lines and the imminence of attack, was beginning to tell. Chindits were becoming very prone to internal disorders and malaria was rife. If the patient was capable of marching he marched, and his pack was carried on a mule. If he was incapable of walking, he was strapped into special panniers on a horse or mule. It was incredible how some men managed to drag their feet along for mile after mile without falling out completely.

On 20 March Wingate flew in to meet Fergusson in person. The Brigade Commander asked for a couple of days' rest for his column before they deployed for the attack on Indaw, but Wingate was convinced that the element of surprise was still in their favour and so ordered the attack as planned. He promised, however, to have Brodie's 14 Infantry Brigade flown in to *Aberdeen* to support the attack on Indaw.

With the crisis at Imphal and the massive airlift still under way bringing 5th Indian Division up from Arakan, there were no additional planes available to carry another Chindit brigade into battle. Brodie could only lift his brigade into *Aberdeen* as and when space became available, but even so the bulk of them were behind the lines by 25 March.

Wingate ordered Brodie to cut enemy communications between Wuntho and the Chindwin, but no mention was made of Indaw. Neither did Wingate inform Fergusson of his change in plans.

CHAPTER THIRTY-FIVE

Epitaph: The Death of Wingate

At 5pm on the afternoon of Friday 24 March, Wingate left Imphal to visit Cochran who had his HQ at Lalaghat. With him were some members of his staff, three USAAF sergeants thumbing a lift back to their outfit and a couple of war correspondents. They flew in a Mitchell B-25 bomber which Cochran had placed at Wingate's disposal.

At about the same time a second aircraft, a Lockheed Ventura carrying the Commander of the Third Tactical Air Force, Air Marshal Sir John Baldwin, took off from the same air-strip. Baldwin saw Wingate's plane flying smoothly over the Bisheapur hills before he turned west for Chittagong.

The Mitchell became overdue and the control tower at Lalaghat called up the plane, but there was no response. Cochran was told, but at first nobody was unduly alarmed. Radio reception was notoriously unreliable and in any case Wingate might have diverted to another strip. As time passed concern began to mount and eventually, when the Mitchell's fuel reserves would have been exhausted, Mountbatten's Headquarters and Slim at Fourteenth Army were informed. The word spread like wildfire that Wingate was missing. Military censors put a news blackout on the story, for there was still a chance that the aircraft might have crash-landed or come down on one of the strips which honeycombed the region, many of which had no regular means of radio communication.

Slim wrote of that time:*

---

*William Slim, *Defeat into Victory* (Cassell, London, 1956).

257

> As the hours passed and no news of any sort arrived, gloom descended upon us. The immediate sense of loss that struck, like a blow, even those who had differed most from him – and I was not one of these – was a measure of the impact he made.
>
> There could be no question of the seriousness of our loss. Without his presence to animate it, Special Force would no longer be the same to others or to itself. He had created, inspired, defended it and given it confidence; it was the offspring of his vivid imagination and ruthless energy. It had no other parent.

On Saturday 25 March, Wingate and everyone else on the aircraft was posted as missing and the Army wheels of bureaucracy cranked into motion.

Three days later, a search party sent out from Bisheapur came upon a wreckage which was scattered over half a mile along the Western slopes of a mountain-side. No doubt if it happened today, accident investigators with all their forensic skills would be able to isolate and identify the cause. In March 1944, in the middle of a desperate campaign, those who found the wreckage could only report that the plane must have hit the mountain-side with tremendous force, and that all on board died instantly. Near to one of the blackened lumps of metal that had once been an engine, the rescue party found the only item to be recovered intact – Wingate's solar topee, upright, undamaged and unmarked.

Confirmation of Wingate's death evoked a flood of effusive obituaries. Mountbatten, who had become thoroughly disenchanted with this 41-year old protégé of their patron, wrote to Lady Edwina, but with his biographer in mind:

> I cannot tell you how much I am going to miss Wingate.... Not only had we become close personal friends, but he was such a fire-eater, and it was such a help to me having a man with a burning drive to fight. He was a pain in the neck to the generals over him, but I loved his wild enthusiasm and it will be very difficult for me to try and inculcate it from above.*

News of Wingate's death was radioed in code to the columns in the field. Late at night on 27 March, John Masters was woken by 111 Brigade's Intelligence Officer who came with a message.

Masters read the note by the light of his torch. 'General Wingate killed in an air crash. Lentaigne to fly out immediately to assume command of Force.'

There had been some argument at Mountbatten's Headquarters

---

*Philip Ziegler, *Mountbatten*, p. 276 (Guild Publishing, London, 1985).

before it was decided to make this appointment. Senior members of staff had taken the opportunity to press their case for the immediate disbandment of the Special Force and the return of valued fighting men to the 'real' war. But there were wider international political implications at stake, not least the commitment made to Stilwell. Lentaigne was the senior brigadier in Special Force and his would be a safe appointment; he had never formed part of Wingate's inner sanctum, that close coterie which included Fergusson, Calvert, Cochran, some of the staff and a few column commanders. All of 111 Brigade's battalion commanders were with their columns so John Masters, though only a major, assumed command.

Lentaigne's first instruction was to Masters. He was to move the brigade 45 miles north-west to Pinlebu and much nearer to what they believed to be the Japanese lines of communication. Many – veterans and historians alike – have castigated Lentaigne for betraying Wingate; but when Lentaigne assumed the mantle of Special Force it had already become apparent to any dispassionate observer that Wingate's concept of long range penetration as a form of guerrilla warfare had not proved a success. It was also clear that Wingate's over-elaborate yet rather ill-conceived tactical plan was becoming disjointed.

Once Major-General Mayashi had gathered his forces, he responded aggressively to the Chindit presence. *Broadway* came under heavy attack and all flights were stopped for three days during the heaviest fighting before the enemy were repulsed. Calvert's *White City* stronghold was far too provocative in its position and came under continued, near incessant attack. So the strongholds, intended as sanctuaries where Chindits could rest between offensive guerrilla-type operations, required all of the garrison's strength to defend them. Far from resting the Chindits found themselves under siege in conditions which soon bore a greater resemblance to the Western Front of 1917 than guerrilla warfare. Artillery pieces, 25-pounder howitzers and heavy mortars were lifted in along with their gunner crews, and all thought of long range penetration disappeared.

A major reverse also greeted Lentaigne upon appointment. Fergusson had been heavily repulsed at Indaw. This attack, which Wingate himself had ordered, broke his own basic rule of long range penetration – namely, that it was folly to attack a heavily-defended base. Fergusson's Brigade proved the wisdom of those words. The Japanese defenders had used their time wisely, digging fortifications, siting machine-gun nests, laying barbed wire and sowing mines.

Fergusson had only infantry. Wingate had assured his columns that they would never want for artillery; they had their own private air force. But with the battle at Imphal reaching a dangerous crescendo,

Cochran had no superior to appeal to when he found some of his resources being sucked into the main event. There was nothing left for 16 Brigade at Indaw when the needs of *Broadway* and *White City* had priority. If those bases fell, then the Chindits would be in severe difficulty.

Radio communications had failed. Fergusson was out of touch with his rear base at *Aberdeen* and so unaware that 14 Brigade was not part of the attacking force at Indaw. On 30 March, Fergusson took it upon himself to stop any further assaults against enemy defences which had shown not the slightest sign of weakening. The columns fell back in orderly withdrawal to *Aberdeen*.

On 3 April, Lentaigne flew into *Aberdeen* and there met his brigadiers. They needed to agree a new plan of campaign, since the Chindits were exerting no great influence on either Imphal or Stilwell's advance. Two issues were particularly important. First, Fergusson's brigade was by now in a very weakened state and had to be relieved. Second, it was important to withdraw from the Indaw area before the onset of the monsoon. Not only would air support become more problematic, but a lengthy route march across country and in monsoon conditions would be out of the question, Lentaigne believed, for tired and heavily laden soldiers.

It was decided to abandon *White City*, *Aberdeen* and *Broadway*. The four remaining brigades – namely 77th, 14th, 11th and 3rd West African – would concentrate and launch a coordinated attack on Mogaung from the south, while Stilwell's forces attacked from the north. A new stronghold close to Mogaung and code-named *Blackpool* was to be established as their rear base and air-strip.

Lentaigne abandoned any further pretence of long range penetration. As far as he was concerned, this group's only utility lay as fighting men in the big conventional battles which were then being waged. It is also interesting to note that if Fergusson or Calvert objected to this betrayal of the leader's concepts they chose not to voice their views, let alone refuse to serve under Lentaigne's command. The tactical realities were plain enough, and nobody was about to tilt at windmills.

In a very real sense the assumption of command by Lentaigne on the death of Wingate marks the transition of the Chindits back into the fold of the conventional Army. The remainder of the story is a postscript, though none the less bloody. On 6/7 April the Japanese launched a new and even more frenzied assault at *White City*; the stronghold held, but the fighting – much of it hand to hand – proved very costly.

Lentaigne met with Mountbatten and Slim on 9 April and they approved the plan. Much as they might have wished, there was no way the Chindits could be brought into play to help at Imphal or Kohima. The air effort to lift 5th Indian Division from the Arakan had absorbed all the capacity available, so the Chindits might just as well be of use to Stilwell.

Stilwell did not agree; he wanted the Chindits to remain in the area of Indaw. His own forces had now entered the Mogaung Valley, largely thanks to his brutal use of Merrill's Marauders who had played the Japanese at their own game of outflanking by shallow penetration. Stilwell believed the sycophants who passed for a staff when they told him he was on the threshold of the glory which had eluded him. This foul-mouthed and cantankerous general, of mediocre talent, had no wish to share his cabbage patch or ease the pressure off the Japanese at Indaw. Once *Blackpool* was opened, he argued, then in his capacity as Deputy Supreme Commander, he would allow Special Force to concentrate against Mogaung.

In the meantime, the Japanese assault against *White City* had reached a new intensity. Lentaigne saw his opportunity while the Japanese were so preoccupied and led his three brigades (16th, 111th and 14th) in a concerted attack on Indaw. On 18 April Indaw was captured, and the Chindits lost no time in ensuring its destruction as an enemy base. Before they withdrew 21 dumps of supplies, petrol, food and ammunition were put to the torch.

Indaw could just as easily have been bombed.

On 27 April, the 16th Brigade occupied the West Indaw airfield which the Japanese had abandoned. This was the brigade's swan-song as Chindits. Lentaigne ordered their evacuation by air from West Indaw.

There were not too many aircraft to spare, and since the men and their mules had to be evacuated it took the Dakotas three nights to airlift the brigade out to Imphal. Tim Biron had survived the vicious battle for Indaw and was on one of the last aircraft out of there. The irony of that flight was not lost on him – that it took them just an hour to reach Imphal over country which it had taken fifty days to cross on foot. Biron was pleased about one thing, however. The boots he had had specially made in India had survived all those miles of marching intact. They had been a wise investment. Others had gone through three and even four pairs of Army issue boots.

The Leicesters were not kept in Imphal where the battle, though still raging, had passed its peak. Within a couple of days they continued their journey to Chittagong, thence on once more to Calcutta.

John Campbell was less fortunate. On 17 May Special Force came under the overall command of Stilwell, who deployed them in battle with his usual cynical disregard for the finer points of command. *White City* had been abandoned on the nights of 10 and 11 May, while

Blackpool was established and garrisoned by Masters and 111 Brigade. Under no illusions about what lay ahead, since *Blackpool* was situated very close to Mogaung, Masters had artillery, mines and barbed wire flown in once the air-strip was operational.

The weather by this time had broken and in the most appalling monsoon conditions the Chindit brigades force-marched across country for the battle of Mogaung. For many the real ordeal had yet to begin. Despite the fact that they were nothing more than infantry, they were required by their American commander to fight conventionally as if they had the full complement of logistical back-up and fire support.

Stilwell had at his command five Chinese divisions, Merrill's by now exhausted Marauders and the four thin Chindit brigades. On the same day that the latter came under his command, the airfield at Myitkyina – about 70 miles north of Mogaung – was captured by the Marauders in a truly brilliant operation. After its capture the Marauders were a spent force, their fighting strength down to a few hundred diseased and exhausted men. But when the Marauders failed to capture the town of Myitkyina, Stilwell was furious, for he had prematurely announced its fall to his own press corps.

In pique, if not revenge, Stilwell continued to treat the Marauders like dirt. It is hard to imagine how any American commander could have behaved so badly and yet not be called to account for his misdeeds. He had run the Marauders into the ground and broken every promise he had ever made to them. Merrill, their Commander, had suffered a heart attack, while his men's morale had faded with their last physical reserves of strength. The new Commander was Colonel Hunter, who declared the unit unfit for action and formally handed Stilwell a document which detailed charges of incompetence and dereliction of duty against both the general and his staff.

Stilwell pulled the Marauders out of the line and sent Hunter back to the United States by sea, by special order. This allowed his own envoy time to fly ahead and prepare the whitewash in the Pentagon.

The Japanese launched a series of fierce assaults on *Blackpool*. At the end of May, despite a most desperate and heroic defence by the Chindits, their position had become untenable and Masters was forced to abandon the stronghold.

By this time there were fewer than 2,000 men, including the additional gunners, remaining in 111 Brigade, for they had suffered over 800 casualties since the start of the campaign. Masters successfully evacuated the bulk of his garrison and was with the rearguard when a young Medical Officer from the Medical Dressing Station (MDS) approached him:

'Can you spare a moment please, sir?'

Masters walked down a track into a bamboo thicket where the MDS was located. On stretchers lay nineteen men, all with the most terrible wounds; one had no face, another's body ended at his waist, hips and legs were all gone. All were comatose with morphine and obviously close to death.

'None of these men have any chance at all, sir,' cried the doctor. 'I give you my word of honour, two hours at the outside, and I have no more morphia.'

'Very well,' said Masters. 'But I don't want them to see any Japanese.'

The young doctor, tears streaming down his face, nodded speechlessly. As Masters headed back along the track to deal with the living, behind him – one by one – single carbine shots echoed through the bamboo.

Once clear of *Blackpool*, 111 Brigade were used by Stilwell as a blocking force to hold back the Japanese as they tried to relieve their own garrison at Mogaung. The actual assault on Mogaung was meant to be a joint effort between the Chinese 38th Division and Calvert's 77th Brigade, itself down to less than 600 men.

The Chinese did little and it was Calvert's troops who captured Mogaung. When the town fell on 26 June Calvert had 400 men left in the brigade. In the communiqué which Stilwell issued announcing the surrender, no mention was made of 77th Brigade. All credit went to the Chinese.

The irrepressible Calvert signalled Lentaigne: 'Chinese take Mogaung, 77th Brigade take umbrage.'

Lentaigne knew the truth but there was little he could do since his own relationship with Stilwell had soured to the point where they barely communicated.

By the end of June, the condition of those men who had survived without being battle casualties was giving cause for concern among every senior officer except Stilwell. Masters demanded a medical examination of his brigade, and so persistent had become the complaints that Mountbatten felt obliged to fly to Stilwell's HQ and intervene personally. At first Stilwell would not accept the evacuation of the Chindits until the town of Myitkyina had fallen, despite the fact that the medical evidence was overwhelming. In Calvert's and Master's brigades, there were few men who had suffered less than three attacks of malaria, while some had suffered six or even more. Average weight loss was in excess of two stone and the incidence of death from cerebral malaria and typhus was rising alarmingly.

Stilwell refused to listen to reason until Mountbatten pointed out the possible legal consequences of keeping in battle men who were not capable of defending themselves. The American then agreed to a medical for the two brigades. Calvert's brigade were declared unfit to a man and evacuated. After the doctors had finished Masters had enough men to man a guard company of 70 soldiers; the remainder were flown out to India.

John Campbell was evacuated sick with malaria about a week before the rest of the column were sent back to India. His platoon sergeant came up just before he was taken on a litter to an aircraft. 'Can I have your American hammock, please?'

It was the only decent bit of kit Campbell had left – a proper US Army issue field hammock complete with an awning. He had acquired it from an unsuspecting glider pilot at *Broadway* early in the campaign, but it was no use to him now. The sergeant said his goodbyes and left clutching his new possession.

The last Chindits to remain in battle and under Stilwell's command were the luckless 14 Brigade, who stayed until Myitkyina fell in August and Stilwell had proved his point.

A fifth of all the Chindits – some 3,628 men – were casualties, sick, wounded, missing or killed.

Special Force was disbanded.

Conclusion

It is very easy to punctuate military history with 'if onlys' or 'what ifs' and this is especially true of the Chindits. Had Wingate lived it is quite possible that he would have been promoted to a Corps command and I for one cannot escape the conclusion that it would have been disastrous for those men he then led into battle.

I belong to that generation of military historians who, even though middle aged, have never experienced war, and this makes me vulnerable to criticism from those who have. I find the accounts of the Chindits breath-taking in their bravery and feel humbled by their endurance and determination. I am left simply with the question of whether a modern generation is capable of withstanding such an experience.

The Chindits were raised because of the fanatical conviction of one man that he had the answer to defeating the Japanese in the jungle. Despite their subsequent sacrifice it is difficult to escape the conclusion that the Chindits contributed little strategically to the conflict. The British and their Allies recaptured Burma because of General Bill Slim's equally determined conviction that the opponent had to be defeated in a single decisive clash of arms. At Imphal and Kohima, maybe more by luck than judgement, the Japanese were enticed onto a killing ground and destroyed in a titanic battle in which men of the calibre of the Chindits were sorely missed.

All of the special forces raised, with the single exception of the Royal Marine Commandos, no matter their pedigree or record, were disbanded with almost indecent haste the moment war was over. No thought was given to future needs and those specialist skills so painfully acquired were promptly discarded. It is interesting to note that Britain alone among the Allies indulged in this act of military vandalism.

Even though the Royal Marines still existed, the ways and means of mounting large scale amphibious operations were not sustained. The price of such muddled thinking was paid a decade later at Suez.

Can we have confidence today that the politicians and military strategists have got it right? While it is comforting to believe fifty years on that the circumstances of the Second World War could not be repeated, such thoughts are naive. Mikhail Gorbachev loudly proclaims 'Glasnost' and smiles broadly for the benefit of the Western press, but there is no evidence that the Soviet forces massed in central Europe are any less of a threat. He proudly proclaims his objectives of making Russia strong and powerful, but for what purpose? Indeed the Soviet military have never possessed such a capability as that which they dispose today, and the shaky political foundations of their empire makes for an even more uncertain future.

Among the impressive military resources deployed by the Kremlin are literally thousands of highly trained Spetsnaz. These are specialist troops who are intended to fulfil a single objective – the paralysis of Western leadership, political and military, at the moment of war. In the meantime this elite experiences valuable training on the job, in Afghanistan, Angola and elsewhere among the world's trouble spots.

The Western powers deploy their own special forces. The received wisdom of the experts is that the Europeans are better than the Americans. More than thirty years ago the British government set the ball rolling when it was forced to admit the error of its ways and recall to the colours the SAS to fight communists in Malaya. By that time the French were wishing that they hadn't so slavishly subjected Wingate's philosophy of the 'stronghold' on their own elite; les Paras and the Foreign Legion were decimated at Dien Bien Phu.

Have we learned from the lessons of our military past? Today the SAS is still with us as an elite fighting unit. Though under-funded and under-resourced it remains the envy of everybody else's special forces including no doubt the Soviets. Royal Marine Commandos continue the tradition as amphibious shock troops, an elite force of specialists in all types of warfare in unusual terrains. Their need is unquestioned but in a cost conscious age their future is by no means certain.
means certain.

In the Falklands the yawning gap that existed between the conventional battalion and elite units, the special forces, such as the Parachute Regiment and Marines, was there for all to see. Yet there are still those in the military hierarchy who would question the validity or relevance of such expensive formations on the nuclear battlefield of Western Europe. But recent developments have resulted in the reduction of nuclear weapons and the prospect that such a battlefield will be increasingly conventional in character. In circumstances such as these the need for special forces is perhaps greater than ever.

Index